PETER BERRESFORD ELLIS is one of the foremost living author-
ities on the Celts and the author of many books in the field
including *The Celtic Empire* (1990), *Celt and Saxon* (1993),
*Celt and Greek* (1997), *Celt and Roman* (1998) and *The
Ancient World of the Celts* (1998). Under the pseudonym
Peter Tremayne he is the author of the bestselling Sister
Fidelma murder mysteries set in Ireland in the 7th Century.

Other titles in this series

*A Brief History of The Boxer Rebellion*
Diana Preston

*A Brief History of British Kings & Queens*
Mike Ripley

*A Brief History of British Sea Power*
David Howarth

*A Brief History of Christianity*
Bamber Gascoigne

*A Brief History of The Circumnavigators*
Derek Wilson

*A Brief History of The Druids*
Peter Berresford Ellis

*A Brief History of The Dynasties of China*
Bamber Gascoigne

*A Brief History of Fighting Ships*
David Davies

*A Brief History of The Great Moghuls*
Bamber Gascoigne

*A Brief History of The Hundred Years War*
Desmond Seward

*A Brief History of Infinity*
Brian Clegg

*A Brief History of The Royal Flying Corps in World War I*
Ralph Barker

*A Brief History of Science*
Thomas Crump

*A Brief History of The Tudor Age*
Jasper Ridley

# A BRIEF HISTORY OF
# THE
# CELTS

## PETER BERRESFORD ELLIS

**ROBINSON**
London

ROBINSON

First published in hardback in Great Britain in 1998 as *The Ancient World of the Celts*
by Constable, an imprint of Constable & Robinson Ltd

This revised paperback edition published in 2003 by Robinson

A CIP catalogue record for this book
is available from the British Library.

ISBN: 978-1-84119-790-6 (paperback)
ISBN: 978-1-47210-794-7 (ebook)

Printed and bound in Great Britain by CPI Group (UK) Ltd, Croydon CR0 4YY

Papers used by Robinson are from well-managed forests
and other responsible sources

MIX
Paper from
responsible sources
FSC® C104740

Robinson
is an imprint of
Little, Brown Book Group
Carmelite House
50 Victoria Embankment
London EC4Y 0DZ

An Hachette UK Company
www.hachette.co.uk

www.littlebrown.co.uk

# CONTENTS

| | | |
|---|---|---:|
| | *List of Illustrations* | vi |
| | *Map* | viii |
| | *Preface* | xi |
| 1 | The Origins of the Celts | 1 |
| 2 | An Illiterate Society? | 17 |
| 3 | Celtic Kings and Chieftains | 27 |
| 4 | The Druids | 47 |
| 5 | Celtic Warriors | 61 |
| 6 | Celtic Women | 81 |
| 7 | Celtic Farmers | 97 |
| 8 | Celtic Physicians | 105 |
| 9 | Celtic Cosmology | 115 |
| 10 | Celtic Road Builders | 125 |
| 11 | Celtic Artists and Craftsmen | 137 |
| 12 | Celtic Architecture | 149 |
| 13 | Celtic Religion | 159 |
| 14 | Celtic Myth and Legend | 179 |
| 15 | Early Celtic History | 197 |
| | *Suggestions for Further Reading* | 223 |
| | *Index* | 227 |

# LIST OF ILLUSTRATIONS

*Between pp. 76 and 77*

2nd century BC silver horse harness found at the Villa Vecchia Manerbio
Cernunnos, the horned god, panel from the Gundestrup cauldron in the
National Museum, Copenhagen (Werner Forman Archive, London)
Celtic inscription from Gaul, 2nd/1st century BC (G. Dagli Orti,
Paris)
Stylized head from the Hallstatt period, in the Keltenmuseum Hallein
(AKG/ London, photo Erich Lessing)
Realistic head from the Le Tène period from the 3rd century BC, in the
Musée Granet Art (G. Dagli Orti, Paris)
A visualization of Caesar's 'wicker man' from Aylett Sammes' *Britannia
Antiqua Illustrata*, 1676 (E.T. Archive, London)
Celtic afterlife depicted on the Gundestrup cauldron in the National
Museum, Copenhagen (AKG/London, photo Erich Lessing)
Illustraion of a Druid from *Costumes of the British Isles* (1821),
Meyrick and Smith (E.T. Archive, London)
Bronze shield dating from the 1st century BC, British Museum, London
(E.T. Archive, London)
Celtic war helmet dating from the 1st century BC, British Museum,
London (Werner Forman Archive, London)
A female figure of the early Celtic period in the Museum in Este,
(G. Dagli Orti, Paris)

Bucket found at Aylesford, Kent dated to the 1st century BC, British Museum, London (Werner Forman Archive, London)

Reconstruction of a typical Celtic farm building of the 1st century BC (Mick Sharp Photography)

Horned helmeted figure holding a spoked wheel depicted on the Gundestrup cauldron, National Museum, Copenhagen (AKG/ London, photo Erich Lessing)

The Corlea Road, a causeway across a bog in Co. Longford, dated to 148 BC (Top, The Heritage Service, Dublin/Professor Barry Rafferty, University College, Dublin)

Celtic coin dated to the 1st century BC, Musée de Rennes, Brittany (Werner Forman Archive, London)

*Between pp. 140 and 141*

The Desborough Mirror (British Museum, London)

The Snettisham Torc (British Museum, London)

Flagon, one of a pair from Basse-Yutz in the Moselle, dated to the 5th century (British Museum, London)

The broch of Carloway on the Isle of Lewis, Scotland (Ancient Art and Architecture Collection, London)

Reconstruction of a 'crannog', Graggaunowen, Co. Clare ( Bord Fáilte, Dublin)

Cernunnos, from the Gundestrup cauldron, National Museum, Copenhagen (E.T. Archive, London)

Section of the Gundestrup cauldron depicting Danu, National Museum, Copenhagen (Werner Forman Archive, London)

7th century BC bronze wheeled cauldron, Landesmuseum, Graz (AKG/London, photo Erich Lessing)

Model ship from the 1st century, the National Museum of Ireland, Dublin (Werner Forman Archive, London)

The Cerne Abbas Giant, Dorset (Fortean Picture Library, photo Janet Bord)

The Uffington White Horse (Images Picture Library, Charles Walker Collection)

Plate from the Gundestrup cauldron, National Museum, Copenhagen (G. Dagli Orti, Paris)

Lindow Man (British Museum, London)

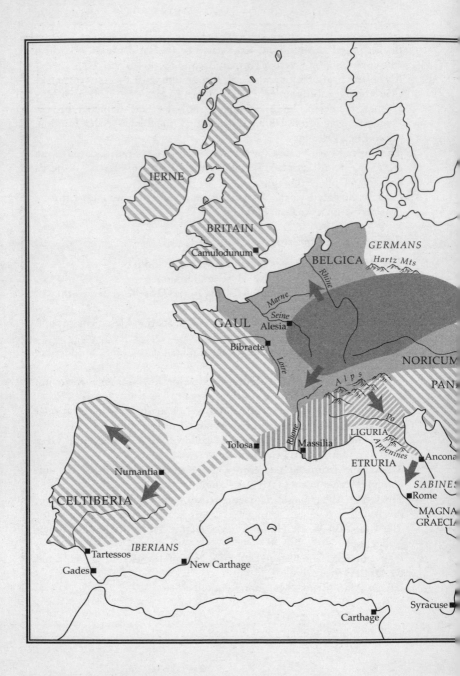

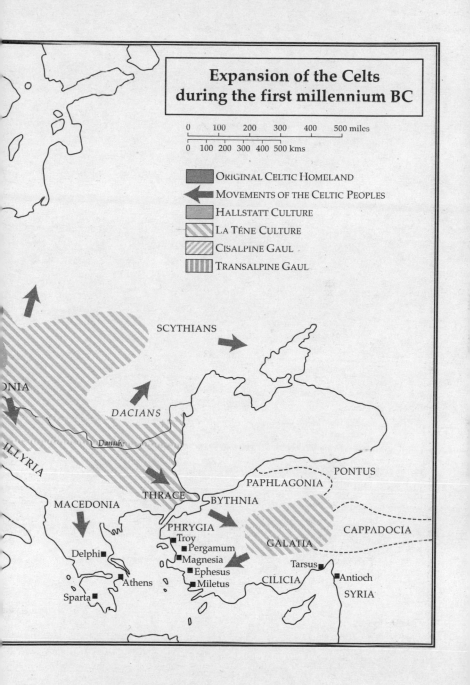

# Expansion of the Celts during the first millennium BC

| 0 | 100 | 200 | 300 | 400 | 500 miles |

| 0 | 100 | 200 | 300 | 400 | 500 kms |

ORIGINAL CELTIC HOMELAND
MOVEMENTS OF THE CELTIC PEOPLES
HALLSTATT CULTURE
LA TÉNE CULTURE
CISALPINE GAUL
TRANSALPINE GAUL

SCYTHIANS

DACIANS

ONIA

ILLYRIA

Danube

THRACE

MACEDONIA

BYTHNIA

PAPHLAGONIA

PONTUS

Delphi

PHRYGIA
Troy
Pergamum
Magnesia
Ephesus
Miletus

Athens

Sparta

GALATIA

CAPPADOCIA

Tarsus

CILICIA

Antioch

SYRIA

# PREFACE

At the start of the first millennium BC, a civilisation which had developed from its Indo-European roots around the headwaters of the Rhine, the Rhône and the Danube suddenly erupted in all directions through Europe. Their advanced use of metalwork, particularly their iron weapons, made them a powerful and irresistible force. Greek merchants, first encountering them in the sixth century BC, called them Keltoi and Galatai. Later, the Romans would echo these names in Celtae, Galatae and Galli. Today we generally identify them as Celts.

The ancient Celts have been described as 'the first Europeans', the first Transalpine civilisation to emerge into recorded history. At the height of their greatest expansion, by the third century BC, they were spread from Ireland in the west across Europe to the central plain of what is now Turkey in the east; they were settled from Belgium in the north as far south as Cadiz in Spain and across the Alps into the Po valley. They not only spread along the Danube valley but Celtic settlements have been found in southern Poland, in Russia and the

Ukraine. Recent evidence has caused some academics to argue
that the Celts were also the ancestors of the Tocharian people,
an Indo-European group who settled in the Xinjiang province
of China, north of Tibet. Tocharian written texts survive from
the eighth to ninth centuries AD.

That the Celts left a powerful military impression on the
Greeks and Romans there is little doubt. In 475 BC they
defeated the armies of the Etruscan empire at Ticino and took
control throughout the Po valley; in 390 BC they defeated the
Romans and occupied the city for seven months – it took
Rome fifty years to recover from that devastating disaster; in
279 BC they invaded the Greek peninsula, defeating every
Greek army which was sent against them before sacking the
Greek holy sanctuary of Delphi and then returning back to the
north. Some of them crossed into Asia Minor and established
a Celtic kingdom on what is now the central plain of Turkey.
So respectful of the Celts' fighting ability were the Greeks that
they recruited Celtic units into their armies, from Epiros and
Syria to the Ptolemy pharaohs of Egypt. Even the fabulous
Queen Cleopatra had an élite bodyguard of 300 Celtic warri-
ors which, on her defeat and death, served the equally famous
Herod the Great and attended his funeral obsequies in 4 BC.
Hannibal used Celtic warriors as the mainstay of his army
and, finally, after the conquest of their 'heartland' Gaul, the
Celts even served the armies of their arch-enemy, Rome.

Yet warfare was not their only profession. They were basically farmers, engaging in very advanced agricultural techniques whose methods impressed Roman observers. Their
medical knowledge was highly sophisticated, particularly in
the practice of surgery. As road builders they were also tal-
ented and it was the Celts who cut the first roads through the
previously impenetrable forests of Europe. Most of the words
connected with roads and transport in Latin were, significantly, borrowed from the Celts. As for their art and craftsmanship, in jewellery and design, they have left a breathtaking

legacy for Europe. They were undoubtedly the most exuberant of the ancient European visual artists, whose genius is still valued and copied today; their masterpieces in metalwork, monumental stone carvings, glassware and jewellery still provoke countless well-attended exhibitions throughout the world.

Their philosophers and men of learning were highly regarded by the Greeks; many of the Greek Alexandrian school accepted that early Greeks had borrowed from the Celtic philosophers. Even some Romans, who could never forgive the Celts for initially defeating them and occupying Rome, begrudgingly acknowledged their learning. Their advanced calendrical computations, their astronomy and 'speculation from the stars', also impressed the classical world.

The early Celts were prohibited by their religious precepts from committing their learning to written form in their own language. In spite of this, there remain some 500 textual inscriptions of varying lengths in Celtic languages dating from between the fifth and first centuries BC. The Celts used the alphabets of the Etruscans, Greeks, Phoenicians and Romans to make these records. Moreover, many Celts adopted Greek and Latin as languages in which to achieve literary fame; Caecilius Status, for example, the chief Roman comic dramatist of the second century BC, was an Insubrean Celtic warrior, taken prisoner and brought to Rome as a slave.

The Celts produced historians, poets, playwrights and philosophers, all writing in Latin. It was not until the Christian period that the Celts felt free enough to write extensively in their own languages and then left an amazing literary wealth with Irish taking its place as the third literary language of Europe, after Greek and Latin. Irish, according to Professor Calvert Watkins of Harvard, contains the oldest vernacular literature of Europe for, he points out, those writing in Latin and Greek were usually writing in a language which was not a *lingua materna*, a mother tongue, but a *lingua franca*, a common means of communication.

Thanks to the texts written by the Celts of Ireland and Wales, in particular, we know the vibrant wealth of Celtic myth and legend, the stories of the ancient gods and goddesses; by comparing these texts to the commentaries of the classical writers we can even discover something of early Celtic philosophy.

It is humbling to know that this civilisation, with at least 3000 years of cultural continuum, has not yet perished from Europe. There are still some two-and-a-half millions who speak a Celtic language as a mother tongue. The Celtic peoples survive in the north-west of Europe, confined now to the Irish, Manx and Scots (Goidelic Celts) and the Welsh, Cornish and Bretons (Brythonic Celts).

It is, however, the early Celtic world that this book is concerned with, the period before the birth of Christ. In the following pages, the story of the origins and ancient history of one of the greatest ancient peoples of Europe is revealed; with the use of fresh materials which have been recently uncovered, a new examination and understanding of a civilisation which has touched most of Europe and, indeed, parts of the Middle East and North Africa, is presented. This is a thematic survey of the visual wealth left to us by the Celts, as well as an introduction to their colourful early history and fascinating culture.

*        *        *

Within a few months of the first publication of this book something of a mini-storm broke out in which I, as the author, was involved. A group of archaeologists claimed that 'the ancient Celts did not exist!' The claim was dumbfounding to the world of Celtic scholarship. It had the same impact as if someone entered a university Classics department and declared that the Ancient Greeks had never existed.

The general public became aware of the furore when archaeologist Dr Simon James published *The Atlantic Celts: Ancient
People or Modern Invention?* (1999). He argued that there was
no evidence of Celtic peoples in Britain or Ireland during the
Iron Age and that the idea of an insular Celtic identity was but
a product of the rise of nationalism in the eighteenth century.
Dr James, however, was not the first to propound this view. It
was a time when, significantly, political devolution to Wales
and Scotland was high on the Government's agenda and a
resurgence of interest in matters Celtic was underway.

Dr John Collis, then at Sheffield, had already expressed
himself 'dissatisfied' with using the term 'Celtic' to describe
the Iron Age period in these islands. When, in March 1997, the
renowned Celtic art specialists, Ruth and Vincent Megaw,
published an academic paper in the journal *Antiquity* entitled
'Ancient Celts and modern ethnicity' Collis replied that their
definition of a Celtic society was 'both false and dangerous'.
A few months later in the summer issue of the *British Museum
Magazine*, Dr James entered the argument in support of Dr
Collis in what looked like a complete turnaround from his previous position. Up until then, Dr James appeared to have had
no reservations about referring to the existence of 'Iron Age'
Celts (see his *Exploring the World of the Celts*, 1993, and
*Britain and the Celtic Iron Age*, with Valery Rigby, 1997). His
'new' approach again appeared in a *British Museum
Magazine* article – quoted in the London *Financial Times*
weekend section (14/15 June 1997) with a gleeful announce-
ment to the world: 'The Celts – it was all just a myth!'. This
he followed with a fresh attack on Ruth and Vincent Megaw
in the March 1998 edition of *Antiquity*.

At first, like many Celticists, I was of the opinion that if we
ignored the absurdity of the statement it would go away. It did
not. *The Independent* (London) asked me to write a brief
rebuttal in its 5 January 1999 issue. But then came Dr James'
new book *The Atlantic Celts: Ancient People or Modern*

*Invention?*, after which *The Scotsman* invited Dr James and myself to exchange a series of written arguments, subsequently published as a full page feature, 'The Saturday Debate: The Celts: ancient culture or modern fabrication' (27 March 1999). In the same year, a BBC radio programme invited us to 'slug it out' on the airwaves, and the *Irish Democrat* asked me to write a piece – 'Did the ancient Celts exist?'

The reader will undoubtedly ask the question – how can so many books have been written over the last century or two about a people who had not existed? Had the world of scholarship had some mass hallucination?

Dr James' main argument was that the term 'Celtic' should be abandoned when referring to the 'Iron Age' in Britain and Ireland, for the reason that 'no one in Britain or Ireland called themselves "a Celt" before 1700'. Dr James also maintained that there were no migrations to, or invasions of, the British Isles by historically attested Celts from the continent.

In response, we can say equally that no one called themselves Anglo-Saxons in the time when everyone accepts Anglo-Saxons existed. Furthermore, though the 'invasion' theory – an explanation provided by archaeologists for bringing the Celtic languages and cultures (such as Hallstatt and La Tène) to Britain – may not have been proved, it remains true that something did bring Celtic languages and cultures to the British Isles, and a movement of a few or many people would explain how this could have happened in the days before mass communication. A convincing example of movement implanting language was provided by Eusebius Hieronymus (St Jerome, *c*.AD 342-420) when he identified that the people of Galatia (central Turkey) were speaking the same Celtic dialect as he had heard among the Treveri, at Trier, in what is now Germany. Settlers had transplanted the Celtic language there in the third century BC. It is also clearly the case that from the sixteenth century AD onwards, the English language arrived in many lands across the globe by population movements both large and small. Yet another example is provided by the archaeological, linguistic and literary evidence of Belgic Celtic movements between Gaul and Britain for some centuries prior to the arrival of the Romans. The main point is that, although we cannot say for sure how such languages reached the British Isles, what remains certain is that *these languages were Celtic*. And from the inception of Celtic scholarship, the definition of 'Celt' is a people who speak, or were known to have spoken within modern historical times, one of the languages classified as the Celtic branch of Indo-European.

When the British Isles emerged into recorded history, becoming known to the Mediterranean world in the sixth and fifth centuries BC, we have evidence that its inhabitants spoke one or another form of a Celtic language – the insular Celtic forms today represented by their modern descendants, Irish, Manx and Scottish Gaelic and Welsh, Cornish and Breton. The evidence comes in the form of names and words recorded in early references in the classical world and personal names recorded on British coins issued in Britain long before Romans invaded the island – facts that Dr James appears to dismiss. It is a telling truth that no place name survives prior to the Celtic place names in the British Islands. Professor Kenneth Jackson's *Language and History in Early Britain* (Edinburgh University Press, 1953) is the seminal guide to this topic and has been an inspiration to a generation of Celtic scholars. This 752-page book sets out the linguistic evidence for the existence of a Celtic language in 'Iron Age' Britain.

Another obvious piece of evidence comes directly from the writing of Julius Caesar: *'Qui ipsorum lingua Celtae, nostra Galli appellantur'* ('In their own language they are called Celts, in our tongue Gauls'). Clearly this contradicts the idea propounded by Dr James that these people did not call themselves Celts until the eighteenth century.

Writing on this point, Dr James states that while there were

Celtic-speaking peoples here in the Iron Age *they were not necessarily Celts* [my italics] but people who had somehow been absorbed into a Celtic-speaking cultural ethos. My response to this is the reminder that Celtic is, and always has been, a linguistic term and not a biological one. To talk of biological attributes and to try and separate and identify individual 'racial' groups who, at this stage, shared a common language and culture is dangerous.

If the logic of Dr James' view were followed, it would be equally wrong to talk of any ancient group of people by linguistic definition. Thus there would be no Anglo-Saxons, no Slavs, no Latins and certainly no Greeks. In Iron Age Britain we would have to become linguistically cumbersome in the extreme if we went down such a path. We could not even speak of Ancient Britons, because no one called himself or herself an 'Ancient Briton'. We would have to be specific and speak of the Cantii, Coritani, Cornovii and Trinovantes – conveniently forgetting, by the way, that these are all Celtic names.

Dr James wrote to me: 'I am being deliberately polemical . . . It is intended to draw attention to the real discrepancies between the ideas of your field and mine. My long-term hope is that this will help to precipitate genuine co-operative work to seek synthesis.'

As it stands, that is a laudable aim. But Professor Barry Raftery, of University College, Dublin, Ireland's foremost archaeological authority on the Iron Age, and Professor Barry Cunliffe, the leading archaeological expert on Britain's Iron Age, both in the same 'field' as Dr James, have dismissed the idea that the ancient Celts did not exist and see the claim as simply 'anti-Celtic revisionism'. The people living in both islands during the Iron Age not only spoke Celtic languages but also shared a common religious system, a mythology and cultural expression – even a comparable law system. They were, by the only meaningful scholastic definition, Celts.

In a strong attack on my arguments in the subsequent issue

of the *Irish Democrat*, Dr James, I believe, clearly demonstrated that he was indeed more concerned with modern politics than the ancient Celtic civilisation. One of the best
studies on the background to the modern resurgence of the
'Celtic idea' had just been published: Norman Davies' *The
Isle: A History* (Macmillan, 1999). Dr Davies had succinctly
discussed why, in an effort to rubbish the rise of modern Celtic
nationalism, some people might like to remove the Celts as an
entity from history.

As regards the Continental Celts, it took a little longer for
the French to join the revolt, but in 2002 Professor Christian
Goudineau, a Professor at the College de France, chairman of
Antiquités Nationales and president of the Scientific Council
of Mont Beuvray, who had previously courted controversy as
an archaeologist, decided that the Gaulish Celts had not
existed either. Julius Caesar had it all wrong when he wrote
his book *Commentarii de bello Gallico* (*Commentaries on the
Gaulish War*). Professor Goudineau's views in his book *Par
Toutatis! Que reste-t-il de la Gaule?* were immediately seized
on by *The Times* (appropriately on 1 April) and *The
Independent* (4 May), and several other publications, who
seemed more concerned to attack René Goscinny's famous
cartoon character 'Asterix the Gaul' than to contribute to any
serious historical discussion.

Certainly, archaeologists, especially in television documen-
taries, in recent years have resorted more and more to talking
about the 'Iron Age People' in Britain, Ireland and France. In
April 2003 when the University of Leicester announced the
discovery of the hoard of Celtic coins minted by the
Corieltauvi long before the arrival of the Romans they decided
to announce that 'in excess of 3,000 silver and gold coins have
been found, mostly made by the local Iron Age tribe – the
Corieltauvi'. That is sad for it does not inform people who this
'Iron Age tribe' was, nor explain what language they spoke or
what culture they followed. 'Do You Speak Iron Age?' is a joke

now often heard among Celtic Studies students in modern universities.

That the Celts will weather this mini-storm, I have no doubt, as they have weathered similar attempts to eradicate them from the historical map.

I am delighted that *The Ancient World of the Celts* is appearing in a new, easily accessible edition in the Brief History Series. Such a general introduction appears to be needed more than ever following their confused helter-skelter descent into Iron Age People.

Peter Berresford Ellis, April 2003

# 1

# THE ORIGINS OF THE CELTS

When the merchant-explorers of Greece first started to encounter the people they came to refer to as Keltoi, at the start of the sixth century BC, the Celtic peoples were already widely spread through Europe and still rapidly expanding. It was Herodotus of Halicarnassus (c. 490–c. 425 BC) who says that a merchant named Colaeus, from Samos, trading along the African coast about the year 630 BC, was driven off course in his ship by tides and winds and eventually made landfall at the Tartessus, the modern River Guadalquivir in southern Spain. In the valley of the Guadalquivir are the modern cities of Cordoba and Seville. At Tartessus, Colaeus found a tribe of the Keltoi exploiting the rich silver mines of the area.

About 600 BC merchants from Phocis, in central Greece, made a treaty with these same Keltoi to trade goods for their silver. The king of these Keltoi was named Arganthonios, which seems to derive from the Celtic word for silver, *arganto*. Herodotus tells us that his name became a byword for longevity among the Greeks for he reportedly died as late as 564 BC.

From where did the Greeks derive the name Keltoi? Julius Caesar gives the answer at the beginning of his *De Bello Gallico* (*Gallic War*). He refers to the Gauls as those 'who are called Celts in their own language'. So, it appears, and logically so, that Celt was a name that the Celts called themselves. If this is so, what does the name mean?

Numerous doubtful etymologies have been put forward. One suggests an Indo-European root *quel*, denoting 'raised' or 'elevated'. This survives in the Latin *celsus* and the Lithuanian *kéltas*, comparable to the old Irish word *cléthe*. Thus it would be argued that the Celts described themselves as 'exalted', 'elevated' or 'noble'. Another suggestion is the Indo-European root *kel-*, to strike, surviving in the Latin *-cello* and the Lithuanian *kalti*. This seems just as unlikely as the first suggestion. Henri Hubert suggested that it might be cognate with the Sanskrit *cárati*, to surround, found in the old Irish *imm-e-chella*.

Of all the suggestions, perhaps the most acceptable so far has been that the word derived from the Indo-European root *kel-* meaning 'hidden'. This survived in both old Irish as *celim* (I hide) and old Welsh, *celaf*. The Celts were 'the hidden people', perhaps a reference to their religious proscription against setting down their vast store of knowledge in written form in their own language. As Caesar observed in his *Gallic War*: 'The Druids believe that their religion forbids them to commit their teachings to writing, although for most other purposes, such as public and private accounts, the Celts use the Greek alphabet.' In old, and even in modern Irish, the word *celt* still exists for an act of 'concealment'. The word *celt* is also used for a form of dress or mantle, designed to 'conceal' or 'hide' the genitalia, which is now known in English as a kilt.

The various ancient names incorporating the word *celt* are probably names identifying the person's ethnic background although Professor Ellis Evans argues they are more likely to be from the root *kel-*, to exalt. The father of Vercingetorix,

Celtillus, who held suzerainty over all the Gaulish tribes, might well have been known as 'exalted' but in Irish mythology, the Ulster hero Celtchair's name is clearly shown to mean 'mantle' or 'concealment'.

However, the fact that there were personal names incorporating the synonymous terms 'Celt' and 'Gaul', in whatever form the Greeks and Romans chose to present them, did lead to some confusion when the classical writers tried to link the Celts into their own cultural concepts and creation myths. Appian (Appianos of Alexandria who flourished *c.* AD 160) tried to explain the origin and names of the Celts by writing about two kings called Keltos and Galas who he said were the sons of the Cyclops, Polyphemus, and his wife Galatea. Of course, the character of Galatea, whose name meant 'milk white' (from *galakt*, the Greek word for milk), was used by Theocritus, Virgil and Ovid as the eponymous ancestor of the Galatae. It is argued that she actually took her place in Greek and Roman literature following the impression the Celts made on the Greeks during their invasion and sack of Delphi. Greek writers frequently remarked on the 'milk white' skin of the Celts.

Dionysius of Halicarnassus (*fl. c.* first century BC) records a story of Keltos being the son of Heracles (Hercules) and Asterope, daughter of Atlas. Yet another Greek, Diodorus Siculus (*c.* 60–*c.* 30 BC) made the Celts originate with Galates, whose parents were Heracles and the daughter of a local king of Gaul.

I find that it is not stretching the imagination to suggest that when the Greek merchants first started to encounter the Celtic peoples and asked them who they were, the Celts simply replied, 'the hidden people' – that is, to Greek ears, Keltoi.

As there is no documentary evidence about the Celts prior to these early Greek writings, some scholars argue that it is not justifiable to speak of 'Celts' before the sixth century BC. Others argue that we can build a reasonable picture of Celtic life during the first millennium BC by the use of comparative Indo-European linguistics and archaeological evidence.

So, who were the Celts and where did they come from?

The first European people north of the Alps to emerge into recorded history, the Celtic peoples were distinguished from their fellow Europeans by virtue of the languages which they spoke and which we now identify by the term 'Celtic'. (The use of this term to identify this group of languages was only adopted with the development of Celtic studies.) The Scot, George Buchanan (1506–1582), was one of the first to recognise the relationship between the surviving Celtic languages. By the time the Celtic peoples first appeared in written records, they had already diversified into speaking differing dialects, so we may usefully speak of the existence of several Celtic languages even though their speakers retained common links in terms of social structure, religion and material culture.

These Celtic languages constituted an independent branch of the Indo-European family of languages. The Indo-European family encompasses most of the languages spoken in Europe, with a few notable exceptions such as Basque, Finnish, Estonian and Hungarian, and also includes the languages of Iran and northern India. At some point in remote antiquity, there was a single parent language which we call 'Indo-European' for want of a better designation. This parent language, as its speakers began to migrate from where it was originally spoken, diversified into dialects. These dialects then became the ancestors of the present major European and North Indian language groups: Hellenic (Greek), Italic (Latin or now the Romance languages), Celtic, Germanic, Slavonic, Baltic, Indo-Iranian, Indo-Aryan (including Sanskrit), Armenian, Anatolian, Tocharian, Hittite and so forth.

Even now there remain common forms of construction and vocabulary among all the Indo-European languages which are not found in other languages. For example, the word 'name' incorporates a very profound and ancient concept, and it survives with hardly any change in the Indo-European languages. 'Name' in English comes from the Anglo-Saxon *nama*; this is *namn* in Gothic; *name* in German; *noma* in Frisian; *nomen* in Latin; *namn* in Norse; *naam* in Dutch; *onoma* in Greek; *namman* in Sanskrit; *aimn* in Irish; *anu* in old Welsh but *enw* in modern and so forth.

Other features common to the Indo-European group include a clear, formal distinction of noun and verb, a basically inflective structure and decimal numeration. An interesting example of the relationship between the Indo-European languages can be seen in the cardinal numbers, one to ten. 'One, two, three' sounds very similar to the Irish *aon, dó, tri*, the Welsh *un, dau, tri*, the Greek *énas, duo, treis*, the Latin *unus, duo, tres* and the Russian *odin, dva, tri*. But they bear no relation to the Basque *bat, bi, hirur* or the Finnish *yksi, kaksi, kolme*, because those are not Indo-European languages.

The earliest Indo-European literatures are Hittite and classical Sanskrit. Hittite writing emerged from 1900 BC and vanished around 1400 BC, surviving on tablets written in cuneiform syllabics which were not deciphered until 1916. The classical Sanskrit of the Vedas is of later origin, usually dated around 1000–500 BC.

Where was this parent language originally spoken and when did it begin to break up? It is probable, but only probable, that the speakers of the parent tongue originated somewhere between the Baltic and the Black Sea. It also seems probable that the parent tongue was already breaking into dialects before the waves of migrants carried it westward into Europe and eastward into Asia. Although it is still a matter of argument among academics as to when this parent language might have existed, most speculation puts the date at around the fourth millennium BC.

Professor Myles Dillon was one of several Celtic scholars who argued that the Celtic dialect, the ancestor of the Celtic languages, began to emerge from the Indo-European parent about the start of the second millennium BC. What is extraordinary are the close similarities that have survived between Irish and Vedic Sanskrit, two cultures which developed thousands of miles apart over thousands of years. When scholars seriously began to examine the Indo-European connections in the nineteenth century they were amazed at how old Irish and Sanskrit had apparently maintained close links with their Indo-European parent. This applies not only in the field of linguistics but in law and social custom, in mythology, in folk custom and in traditional musical form.

The following examples demonstrate the similarity of the language of the Vedic Laws of Manu and that of the Irish legal texts, the Laws of the Fénechus, more popularly known as the Brehon Laws:

| Sanskrit | Old Irish |
|---|---|
| *arya* (freeman) | *aire* (noble) |
| *naib* (good) | *noeib* (holy) |
| *badhira* (deaf) | *bodhar* (deaf) |
| *minda* (physical defect) | *menda* (a stammerer) |
| *names* (respect) | *nemed* (respect/privilege) |
| *raja* (king) | *rí* (king) |
| *vid* (knowledge) | *uid* (knowledge) |

*Arya* gives us the much misunderstood term Aryan; the old Irish *noeib* becomes the modern Irish *naomh*, a saint; and the Irish *bodhar* (deaf) was borrowed into eighteenth-century English as 'bother'. To be 'bothered' is, literally, to be deafened. Finally, the word *vid*, used not only for knowledge but for understanding, is the root of *Veda*; the Vedas constitute the four most sacred books of Hinduism – the *Rig Veda, Yajur Veda, Sama Veda, Atharva Veda*. The same root can be seen in the name of the Celtic intellectual caste, the Druids – i.e. *dru-vid* which some have argued meant 'thorough knowledge'.

Unfortunately, no complete 'creation' myth of the Celts has survived. When these myths came to be written down, in the insular Celtic languages of Irish and Welsh, Christianity had taken a hold and the scribes bowdlerised the stories of the gods and goddesses, thus obscuring their symbolism and significance. That the Celts did have a vibrant and rich pre-Christian mythology, including a creation myth, is seen not only in the Christianised stories but in the few allusions in the classical writers. However, most of the classical writers tend, like the Christians after them, to incorporate the Celtic myths and gods into their own cultural ethos.

The fact is that many of the surviving Irish myths, and some of the Welsh ones, show remarkable resemblances to the themes, stories and even names in the sagas of the Indian Vedas. Once again, this demonstrates the amazing conservatism of cultural tradition. By comparing these themes we find that Danu, sometimes Anu in old Irish and Dôn in Welsh and also surviving in the epigraphy of the Continental Celts, was the mother goddess. She was the 'divine waters' which gushed to the earth in the time of primal chaos and nurtured Bíle the sacred oak, from whom the gods and goddesses sprang. Her waters formed the course of the Danuvius (Danube).

The story associated with the Danuvius, which is arguably the first great Celtic sacred river, has similarities with myths about the Boyne, from the goddess Boann, and the Shannon, from the goddess Sionan, in Ireland. More important, it bears a close resemblance to the story of the Hindu goddess Ganga, deity of the Ganges. Both Celts and Hindus worshipped in the sacred rivers and made votive offerings there. In the Vedic myth of Danu, for she exists as a deity in Hindu mythology as well, the goddess appears in the famous Deluge story called 'The Churning of the Ocean'.

Echoes of the Celtic creation myths survive in the *Leabhar Gabhála* which tells how Bith, with his wife Birren, their daughter Cesara and her husband Fintan, and their son Lara and his wife Balma, arrived in Ireland at the time of the Deluge. But there are traces of other Deluge myths, including the Welsh story of the overflowing of Llyon-Llion, the Lake of the Waves, from which Dwyvan and Dwybach alone escaped by building Nefyed Nav Nevion, the Welsh Ark. The Deluge was created by Addanc, a monster who dwelt in the lake.

What is important about the creation or origin myths of the Celts is the fact that, in the words of Caesar, 'the Celts claim all to be descended from Dis-Pater, declaring that this is the tradition preserved by the Druids'. Certainly, later Celtic kings in Ireland claimed divine ancestry. However, Caesar uses the term applied to the Roman god of wealth and of the under-world. This has caused confusion as scholars attempt to search the Celtic pantheon for an equivalent.

In the Vedas, the sky god was called Dyaus and is recorded as the one who stretched, or reached, forth a long hand to protect his people. This is cognate with Deus in Latin, Dia in Irish and Devos in Slavonic. It means, significantly, 'bright one' and presumably denotes a sun deity. In the Vedas we find Dyaus was called Dyaus-Pitir, Father Dyaus; in Greek this became Zeus, also a father god; in Latin Dia became the word for 'god' while in the same word, altered into Jove, we find Jovis-Pater, Father Jove. When Caesar talks of the Celtic Dis-Pater he is not talking about the god of wealth and the underworld at all but the equivalent to Jove. The Celtic Dis-Pater emerges in Irish references to Ollathair, the All-Father god. He is the sky god; Lugh is often given this role in Irish while Lleu is also found in Welsh. Significantly, the name again means 'bright one' as it does in Sanskrit. More importantly, the Irish god is Lugh Lamhfhada (Lugh of the Long Hand) while his Welsh counter-part is Lleu Llaw Gyffes (Llew of the Skilful Hand).

So, if we accept the classical writers, the ancient Celts believed that they were physically descended from the sky god who himself was descended from Danu, the 'divine waters'.

But now we must come back to a more temporal point of origin for the Celtic peoples.

Archaeology combines with documentary and linguistic evidence to show that the Celtic peoples began to appear as a distinctive culture in the area of the headwaters of the Danube, the Rhine and the Rhône, that is Switzerland and south-west Germany.

The documentary evidence begins with Hecataeus of Miletus (*c.* 500–476 BC) and with Herodotus of Halicarnassus, whom we have already mentioned. Many later commentators, including Romanised Celts themselves, confirmed this. Herodotus mentioned that 'the Danube traverses the whole of Europe, rising among the Celts . . .' But he incurred the ridicule of modern scholars by adding that the Celts 'dwell beyond the Pillars of Hercules, being neighbours of the Cynesii, who are the westernmost of all nations inhabiting Europe'. Perhaps he, or his copyists, left out the magic word 'also', for the Celts, when he was writing, dwelt not only at the headwaters of the Danube but at the Tartessus in southern Spain.

Place-names in Switzerland and southern Germany provide linguistic evidence; even today, rivers, mountains, woodland and some of the towns still retain their original Celtic names, including the three great rivers themselves. The Danube or Danuvius was named after the Celtic mother goddess, Danu. The Rhône, first recorded as Rhodanus, also incorporates the name of the goddess prefixed by the Celtic *ro*, great (there is also a Rodanus which is an affluence of the Moselle). And the Rhine was originally recorded as Rhenus, a Celtic word for a sea way found in the old Irish *rian*.

Dr Henri Hubert, in the 1930s, argued that the survival of so many Celtic place-names for so long after Celtic-speaking peoples had ceased to live in the area pointed to the names being of indigenous form and of long usage.

There is strong reason for believing that the names are abo-
riginal, or, at least, very ancient, since there are so many
names of rivers and mountains among them. We know that
such names are almost rare in Gaul. Many names of French
rivers and mountains come from the Ligurians, if not from
still further back. Now the names given to the land and its
natural features are the most enduring of place-names. The
first occupants of a country always pass them on to their
successor.

Support for Dr Hubert's argument comes easily to the
English reader. Although the English started to settle in south-
eastern Britain, that area which became England, from the
fifth century AD, driving out the Celtic population, they
adopted many of the original Celtic place-names: names of
rivers and streams such as Aire, Avon, Axe, Dee, Darwent,
Dart, Derwent, Don, Esk, Exe, Ouse, Severn, Stour, Tees,
Thames, Trent, Wye; names of hills and forests such as Barr,
Brent, Cannock, Chevin, Creech, Crich, Crick, Lydeard,
Malvern, Mellor, Penn, Pennard; names even of towns such as
London, Carlisle, Dover, Dunwich, Lympne, Penkridge,
Reculver, York, and of areas such as Kent, Thanet, Wight,
Craven, Elmet, Leeds.

The large number of Celtic place-names still surviving in
Switzerland and south-west Germany are therefore an indication that when the Celtic peoples appear in historical record
they were already well settled in this area.

The third source of evidence for the origin of the Celts is
archaeological. In terms of artefacts, patterns of settlement
and land use and so forth, archaeologists have identified two
distinct periods of Celtic culture emerging in this region; one
is called Hallstatt and the other La Tène.

According to archaeological evidence, the Celtic peoples
descend from a mixture of the Bronze Age Tumulus culture (*c.*
1550–1250 BC) and the Urnfield culture (*c.* 1200 BC). Drs

Jacquetta and Christopher Hawkes, in the 1940s, first described these cultures as 'proto-Celtic'. Dr John X.W.P. Corcoran, in his essay 'The Origin of the Celts', agreed that the Urnfield culture may, indeed, be identified with the early Celts as there was little to distinguish these people from their descendants of the Hallstatt culture, other than the latter's use of iron.

Archaeologists now date the Hallstatt culture from 1200 BC to 475 BC. Previously, they dated it from 750 BC but new finds have made them revise their dating. The fully developed Celtic culture was identified as an iron-using economy and named after one of the first sites to be distinguished at Lake Hallstatt in the Salzkammergut in Upper Austria. The culture was identified by a mainly geometric-based art which evolved from its Urnfield antecedents. Examples were found in a series of graves of 'princes', who were laid out on four-wheeled wagons with splendidly decorated yokes and harnesses. The graves were in spacious chambers beneath a mound or barrow. The wagons and chariots demonstrated the use of an advanced technology, which implied an equally sophisticated knowledge of road construction.

These people knew about iron-smelting and the use of other metal. Iron tools and weapons rendered the Celts superior to their neighbours and were doubtless the basis of their sudden eruption throughout Europe at the beginning of the first millennium BC. The archaeological evidence also shows that the Celtic peoples from this area were developing a trade with the Mediterranean world; artefacts from Greece, Etruria and Carthage have been found in these tombs. Roman civilisation had not begun when many of these 'princes' were laid to rest in their splendid tombs.

The Hallstatt period eventually ended in the emergence of a new culture, which archaeologists call La Tène after discoveries made in the shallows at the north-eastern end of Lake Neuchâtel in Switzerland. This appears to have been a place of Celtic worship where countless artefacts were cast into the water as votive offerings. The La Tène period, from the fifth century to the first century BC, saw the emergence of new decorative art forms, and of fast two-wheeled chariots and other transport innovations. Living standards now seemed exceptionally high throughout the Celtic world. The Celts were first and foremost skilled farmers, both agricultural and pastoral, whose economy was based on their produce and livestock. The development of irrigation systems along the Po valley, where they had settled, demonstrated considerable engineering ability. This is also seen in their road-building and transport systems. They mined salt, a highly important product. They expanded to exploiting the natural resources of their land, including gold, silver, tin, lead and iron. Their craftsmen were second to none, manufacturing high quality tools and weapons, household goods and ornaments for personal adornment. They built their structures mainly in wood, which has not lasted – although where they chose to build in stone, mainly in Ireland and Britain, there is evidence that they were no inferior craftsmen.

They were also open to trade, their goods providing them with strong purchasing power for those luxury goods that the Mediterranean climate of Greece and Italy produced more easily than the harsher climates of the north. Celtic society was more wealthy and stable than the classical writers would allow.

The Celts were divided into tribes ruled by kings; over-kings had power over several tribes. To speak of 'tribes' can give a wrong picture to our modern minds. These Celtic tribes could be as small as 20,000 strong or as large as 250,000. Caesar records that the Helvetii on their migration into Gaul numbered 263,000. Often these tribes formed great coalitions, like the Belgae and the Brigantes.

Celtic tribal rulers introduced the idea of coinage slightly in advance of Rome, albeit based on their contacts with Greece, at the end of the fourth century BC. The coins were cast in gold, silver or bronze in moulds of clay which had been prepared to give pieces of exactly equal weight. These pieces were then hammered between two stamps with amazing designs that were probably of mythological or religious significance.

The La Tène period was one in which the Celtic peoples achieved their greatest expansion. From their original homeland, speakers of Celtic languages moved across the Alps into the Po valley by the seventh century BC, defeating the armies of the Etruscan empire and pushing them back south of the Apennines. Later, the Celtic Senones, a tribe whose name seems to mean 'the veterans', would cross the Apennines and defeat the Roman legions, occupying Rome for seven months before settling on the eastern seaboard of Italy then called Picenum.

Celtic-speaking peoples were already in the Iberian peninsula (Spain and Portugal), settling there from about the ninth century BC. They had reached Ireland and Britain soon after, if not before. They were settled from what is now modern Belgium (still bearing the name of the Belgae) south through modern France which was known as the land of the Galli (Gaul). About the seventh or sixth centuries BC, Celtic-speaking tribes moved relentlessly eastwards along the Danube valley establishing themselves in what are now the Czech and Slovak states – Bohemia was named after the Celtic tribe the Boii; they settled in Illyria (through the Balkans) and reached as far as the Black Sea. For some time they were the ruling class of Thrace. They moved into the Greek states but did not stop, carrying on eastwards into Asia Minor. The state they established on the central plain of what is now Turkey, Galatia, provided the ancient world with clear evidence of how a Celtic state was governed. Individual bands of Celtic mercenaries and their families went to serve the rulers of, and to settle in, Syria of the Selucid kings, Israel of Herod the Great, Egypt of the Ptolemy pharaohs and Carthage until its defeat by Rome.

They had covered a vast territory. Ephoros of Cyme (*c.* 405–330 BC) described the Celts as occupying an area the size of the Indian sub-continent – a fact which his fellow Greek Strabo (64 BC–after AD 24), from Amasia, in Pontus, questioned. However, Professor David Rankin has pointed out that Ephoros was not far wrong.

The second and first centuries BC saw the start of the inexorable recession of their borders in the face of the growth of the Roman empire and the Germanic and Slavic migrations. Inevitably, the conquerors then wrote the history books and, lacking balance from a strong native literature prior to the Christian era, the Celts have been painted as warlike, flamboyant, given to an excess in alcohol and food and hardly more than high-spirited children needing the more civilising hand of Rome and the Germanic heirs of the Roman imperial ethic. As is always the way of conquerors, the peoples they seek to conquer are denigrated and painted in the worst possible light.

Of the classical writers, whose words many seem to accept without question, only the Greeks, with the exception of those Greeks in Roman employment, tended to be unbiased commentators on the Celtic world. The Romans and their allies usually had their own agenda. Julius Caesar, for example, whose work is often quoted as a great authority to be accepted without argument, was, after all, a Roman soldier with political ambition; a general who had set out to bring the entire Celtic world crushed under the heel of the Roman empire for his own political aggrandisement.

Many scholars seem to regard Caesar as if he was an expert who had spent his life studying the language and sociology of the peoples he was fighting against. Those same scholars would probably be the first to quibble at the suggestion that Lieutenant General Frederick, Lord Chelmsford be deemed an expert on Zulu culture because he campaigned against them in 1879. Yet time apparently alters all things. Caesar, with his prejudices, his attempts at justification and his downright inaccuracies, becomes an inviolable authority. Virgil says in his *Eclogues* that 'time bears away all things, even the mind'. Certainly there seems an unwillingness to question the words of classical commentators on the Celts, simply because they were written 2000 years ago and more. Time has borne the mind away so far as open-minded discussion of source and bias is concerned.

Since Rome's conquest of the Celtic world, the picture that has been conjured is that of wandering hordes of Celtic warriors, brightly clothed or without any clothes at all, raiding the 'civilised' centres of Rome and Greece without provocation, drunken, ruthless, bloodthirsty, searching for plunder. It is an image that is no longer acceptable, as the following pages will demonstrate.

# 2

# AN ILLITERATE SOCIETY?

In 1970 a reviewer for *The Times* of London, writing about an exhibition of early Celtic art at the Royal Scottish Museum and subsequently at London's Hayward Gallery, commented: 'Little definite is known about the Celtic peoples because they left no written records.' It was the one occasion where the current author wrote an indignant letter to *The Times* correcting the statement. Even if the reviewer had been speaking merely of the ancient Celts, he would have been in error. One of the great 'myths' about the Celtic peoples is that they were an 'illiterate' society.

In support of this idea that the Celts were illiterate, a passage from Julius Caesar is usually cited. What the Roman general actually wrote was:

The Druids believe that their religion forbids them to commit their teachings to writing, although for most other purposes, such as public and private accounts, the Gauls use the Greek alphabet. But I imagine that this rule was originally established for other reasons – because they did not want their doctrine to become public property, and in order to prevent their pupils from relying on the written word and neglecting to train their memories; for it is usually found that when people have the help of texts, they are less diligent in learning by heart, and let their memories rust.

When this text is read carefully, one can see that what Caesar is saying is that while the Celts did not write native books of philosophy, history and such, the Celts were literate, with the Gauls, in particular, using the Greek alphabet. Archaeology has demonstrated that the Celts also used other alphabets to write their various dialects in. They used Phoenician (Iberian), Etruscan, Greek and Latin letters and sometimes combinations of all, depending on the area the texts came from. In fact, to date, we have some 500 Celtic inscriptions and pieces of textual evidence from a period dating between the sixth and first centuries BC. New Celtic textual discoveries have become frequent in recent years.

The earliest Celtic inscriptions occur in the Etruscan alphabet. The Etruscans had learnt the art of writing by the mid-seventh century BC and there are about 10,000 examples of Etruscan writing which survive. None of the Etruscan inscriptions or texts have so far been interpreted because it is not an identifiable Indo-European language nor can a cognate language be found which might present a clue to interpretation. However, using the Etruscan alphabet, the oldest inscriptive monuments fashioned by the Celts are dated to around the end of the sixth century BC.

Some thirty-three early inscriptions were found between the Rivers Ticino and Adda, tributaries of the Po. After Sir John Rhys' work on these inscriptions, some Celtic scholars became dubious about their authenticity until it was realised that Celtic was not one homogeneous language but that there were dialect differences between these inscriptions and other written Celtic remains. There are a further two inscriptions found engraved on war helmets discovered in 1912 at Negau, Lower Styria, not far from Marburg on the Drave, which are proper Celtic names engraved in Etruscan letters. These are also dated to the sixth century BC.

As Latin influences began to penetrate the area there was a change from Etruscan lettering to Latin characters. Graffiti on pottery, manufacturers' names and marks, and funereal inscriptions show that the Celts were far from illiterate. One funereal inscription at Todi was actually bilingual in Celtic and Latin.

There are around sixty inscriptions from southern Gaul, some dated to the third century BC. Inscriptions using Greek characters seem to have been more popular here at this period before Rome had penetrated into the area. Over twenty more inscriptions using the Latin alphabet, including potters' records, as well as texts, have been found north of Narbonensis, notably the Coligny Calendar and the graffiti from La Graufesneque in the Cévennes. The La Graufesneque graffiti were found in 1901 and date back to the first century AD. The words are carved into fragments of burnt clay in a cursive Latin script.

Perhaps one of the most fascinating is a text found in 1887 at Rom (Deux-Sèvres) on a thin lead plate in Latin script dated to around the end of the first century BC, which is a poetic dedication to the Celtic horse goddess, Epona. Dr Garrett Olmsted, who has made the most recent translation of the inscription, comments that the closest example to the Rom inscription is a Vedic hymn to Indra, demonstrating yet again the common Indo-European root of the Celtic and Sanskrit traditions.

The text, as Dr Olmsted gives it in translation, reads:

It was set up for you, Sacred Mother. It was set out for you, Atanta.

This sacrificial animal was purchased for you, horse goddess, Eponina.

So that it might satisfy, horse goddess Potia; we pay you, Atanta, so that you are satisfied; we dedicate it to you.

By this sacrificial animal, swift Ipona, with a filly, goddess Epotia, for a propitious lustration they bind you, Catona of battle, with a filly, for the cleansing of riding horses which they cleanse for you, Dibonia.

This swift mare, this cauldron, this smith-work, beside fat and this cauldron, mind you, moreover with a filly, Epotia, noble and good Vovesia.

The poet here is using various synonyms for Epona in his invocation of her.

The other corpus of textual evidence comes from the Iberian Celts, notably from northern Spain in the area between Saragossa and Burgos, and includes some of our lengthiest texts in Celtic languages. Notable among them was a text found in 1908 at Peñalba de Villastar, in the Spanish province of Tereul, where an inscription was found carved in Latin letters dated to the first century BC; it seemed to be a Celtiberian votive offering to the god Lugus. A similar inscription was found at Luzaga (Guadalajara).

My argument that the Celts were not an illiterate society – if we take illiteracy to signify merely ignorance of letters or litera- ture, for one must not forget that they had a very sophisticated oral tradition as most ancient societies had – has been endorsed several times since 1970. An excavation at Botorrita, 20 kilo- metres south of Saragossa, the ancient site of Contrebia Belaisca, revealed a bronze tablet some 40 centimetres by 10 centimetres, inscribed in Celtiberian, using a variant Iberian script. This dated from the second century BC. The 200-word text gave instructions relating to a Celtic ritual, and is now in the Archaeological Museum in Saragossa. In the early 1990s another long text in Celtiberian was discovered at the same site at Botorrita.

Through 1968–1971 at Chamalières, south-west of Clermont-Ferrand, a Gallo-Roman sanctuary was excavated. The sanctuary was the source of two natural springs where several thousand wooden votive gifts were found. In January 1971, a lead tablet was discovered there inscribed in Gaulish and dated to the second half of the first century BC, or early first century AD. It was an appeal to the god Maponus for protection and consisted of 336 letters, one of the longest Gaulish Celtic texts. Maponus was the 'Divine Son' whose cult is also found in Britain and who may be equated with Mabon in the tale of Culhwch and Olwen.

In August 1983, at l'Hospitalet-du-Larzac, 14 kilometres south of La Graufesneque, another lead tablet was found inscribed with a text amounting to 160 words which seemed to be another invocation to the deities.

The exact number of texts found in Eastern Europe and Galatia has not been calculated – nor have they yet been evaluated from a linguistic point of view – although we are speaking of perhaps one hundred or more. Celtic coins also supply a rich field of personal names from which we may learn word roots and sound values. Then there is the insular Celtic textual evidence.

To put the earliest Celtic inscriptional remains in context we should point out that the earliest Latin inscriptional remains are almost contemporary, dating from the beginning of the sixth century BC. There is an inscription in stone, the Lapis Niger, from the Forum and an inscription on a fibula giving a manufacturer's name. However, it is difficult to find many Latin inscriptions prior to the third century BC. For the Romans, Greek was the language of learning until the third century BC when a Latin literature began to take shape with the works of poets such as Gnaeus Naevius (c. 270–190 BC) and Quintus Ennius (239–169 BC), both of whom were from the Greek areas of southern Italy. But soon a 'Celtic school' of writers emerged, usually Celts from Cisalpine Gaul, northern

Italy, who adopted Latin as a *lingua franca* to write in rather than writing in their mother tongue. Caecilius Statius, a young Insubrean warrior captured at the battle of Telamon in 225 BC and taken as a slave to Rome, earned his freedom and became Rome's leading comic dramatist. The titles of forty-two of his works are known.

Many of the writers we now think of as 'Roman' were in fact Celts using the imperial language instead of their mother tongue. H.W. Garrod, in his introduction to the *Oxford Book of Latin Verse* (1912), was one of the first to point out that Cisalpine Gaul had become the home of a vigorous school of poets with a common quality which could be identified as Celtic.

This school of Celtic writers was not confined to the Celts from the Po valley, the first to be conquered by the Roman empire and 'Latinised'. Throughout the Celtic world, by virtue of the spread of the Roman empire in its military form and then in its Christian form, Celts adopted Latin as their *lingua franca*. Their work included not only poetry but also history, biography and philosophy.

However, the bulk of Celtic learning, story-telling and history was to remain an oral tradition until the start of the Christian era, which is when Irish took its place as Europe's third-oldest literary language after Greek and Latin. The written language emerged in two phases. The first was the development of a native Irish alphabet – Ogam. This was named after Ogma, the god of eloquence and literacy, who was also known to the British and the Continental Celts as Ogmios.

Ogam is frequently mentioned in the myths and sagas. It is an alphabet of short lines drawn to meet or cross a base line, originally using twenty characters. The language it represents is archaic; most of the surviving inscriptions date from the fourth to sixth centuries AD and are on stone. There are some 370 inscriptions, the bulk surviving in Ireland but with a few in Wales, Scotland, the Isle of Man and Cornwall. Some of them are bilingual with Latin. Of these inscriptions, the greater number are concentrated in south-west Munster, particularly Co. Kerry, and have been argued to be a creation of the Munster poets.

From later Irish texts in Latin script we hear that in earlier times Ogam was used to write ancient stories and sagas; it was incised on bark or wands of hazel and aspen. These 'rods of the Filí' (poets) were kept in libraries or Tech Screptra. We have evidence of this from Aethicus of Istria, who wrote a *Cosmography*, used by Orosius Paulus in his *History Against the Pagans*, composed in seven books in AD 417. Aethicus reports that he sailed to Ireland and spent time there examining their books which he calls *ideomchos*, implying that they were particular to Ireland and strange to him. Aethicus could well have been examining these Ogam-incised 'wands', which was how the Chinese originally recorded their literature. However, while we have numerous references to their existence, it is only the Ogam-inscribed stones that have survived.

A clue to what happened to these early Irish books can be found in the *Leabhar Buidhe Lecain (Yellow Book of Lecan)* compiled about 1400 by Giolla Iosa Mór Mac Firbis, a work containing copies of many early texts, even one dating from the fifth century BC. This text, written by Benignus, mentions that Patrick, in his missionary zeal, burnt 180 books of the Druids. The Irish Christian sources are all fairly clear that books existed in Ireland before the coming of Christianity.

However, Irish literature began to emerge from the sixth century AD. The flowering of Irish literature demonstrated that it was the result of a lengthy period of a sophisticated oral tradition. While the literary language was flourishing from this period, the oldest surviving complete manuscript books which provide sources for Irish mythology, history and many other matters only begin to date from the twelfth century AD, though there are many fragmentary texts from earlier periods.

One of the earliest is *Leabhar na hUidre* (*Book of the Dun Cow*) compiled in AD 1106. *Leabhar Laignech* (*Book of Leinster*) was compiled around AD 1150 at the same time as another book known simply as Rawlinson Manuscript B 502 (see Chapter 14).

The wealth of Irish literary material is tremendous, reaching a great outpouring in late medieval times before the start of the English conquest and the systematic destruction of the language and libraries. The great Celtic illuminated Gospel books, produced during the seventh to tenth centuries AD, have been acknowledged to comprise one of the peaks of European artistic creation. Around thirty are known to have survived. Judging by these, what was destroyed must have been an awesome treasure.

To put the Irish survivals in context, it is worth pointing out that the earliest surviving copies of Julius Caesar's famous *De Bello Gallico* date only from the ninth century AD.

Literature in Welsh followed the Irish, with manuscripts surviving from the ninth century AD, although material written as early as the sixth century AD is copied. Welsh was certainly flourishing as a literary language by the eighth century AD but, apart from the fragmentary remains, the oldest book entirely in Welsh is the *Llfyr Du Caerfyrddin* (*Black Book of Carmarthen*) dated to the twelfth century.

Survivals in the other insular Celtic languages, Scottish Gaelic, Manx, Cornish and Breton, are of a much later period.

The literatures of Irish and Welsh also contain two complete Celtic law systems, which enable us to make many conjectures about the early social systems of the Celts. The Laws of the Fénechus (free land tillers) of Ireland are more popularly called the Brehon Laws, from *breaitheamh*, a judge. They are obviously the result of many centuries of oral transmission. The earliest complete copy of these laws is found in the *Book of the Dun Cow*, and several fragmentary texts have survived. The first known codification was made in AD 438 when

King Laoghaire of Tara established a nine-man commission to examine the laws, revise them and set them down in writing. St Patrick was one of three clerics who served on this commission with three judges and three kings. Tradition has it that the laws were first given to the Irish by King Ollamh Fodhla in the eighth century BC.

Many of the early Norman and English settlers found the Brehon Laws more equitable than those of England and adopted them. It was not until the seventeenth century that the law system was finally smashed by the colonial administration.

The Brehon Laws show fascinating parallels with the Vedic Laws of Manu in India, which are echoed in the Welsh law system, the Laws of Hywel Dda. Hywel Dda (Hywel the Good) was Hywel ap Cadell who ruled Wales about AD 910–950. He decreed that the laws of Wales be gathered and examined by an assembly presided over by Blegwywrd, archdeacon of Llandaff. The revised laws were then set down in writing. The laws survive in some seventy manuscripts of which only half predate the sixteenth century.

Another fascinating aspect of the Irish literary treasures is the fact that although the oldest surviving medical books in the language date from the early fourteenth century, they constituted the largest collection of medical manuscript literature, prior to 1800, surviving in any one language. This confirms the reputation of the Irish medical schools, which were famous during the Dark Ages, and also underlines the classical writers' references to the advances of Celtic medicine and the archaeological finds which support this.

Early Irish texts on cosmology are now coming to light in many European repositories, forgotten for centuries. These confirm that the Irish shared many perceptions of the world and cosmology with the Vedic writers. The Coligny Calendar had long demonstrated that this was so among the Continental Celts.

One other set of literary remains from Ireland deserves brief attention. From the seventh century there survive the genealogies of the Irish kings and chieftains stretching back to the mists of time. The main bulk of the surviving early genealogies dates from the twelfth century, although quoting from the earlier texts, and includes one of the most unusual works in early European literature – the *Banshenchas*, a work of the lore of women's genealogies. These pedigrees trace the lines of the Irish kings back to 1015 BC.

We can see, then, that, whatever other accusation might be levelled against the ancient Celts, they were certainly not an illiterate society. Bards, story-tellers, historians, poets, genealogists and law-givers had a special place in the ancient Celtic world. This fact is commented on by the classical writers, and is confirmed in the Brehon Laws of Ireland where, under the etiquette of the Gaelic court, the Ollamhs, or professors, took precedence immediately after the princes of the blood royal and before chieftains and territorial lords. The Ollamhs were allowed to wear six colours at court whereas chieftains were restricted to five. The Chief Ollamh, or Druid, was even allowed to speak at the assembly before the High King. The ancient Celts clearly accorded learning special respect and reverence. The popular Roman view of the ancient Celts as 'savage' and 'barbarian' failed to recognise the reality of their society. It is fitting that we end our survey on Celtic literacy with a comment of Joseph Cooper Walker from his *Historical Memoirs of the Irish Bards* (1768): 'Can that nation be deemed barbarous in which learning shared the next honours to royalty?'

# 3

# CELTIC KINGS AND CHIEFTAINS

By the time the first identifiable Celtic culture emerged, the Hallstatt period, the Celts were ruled by kings who were immensely rich; they lived in magnificent fortresses and were buried in great tombs, timber-lined and often of oak wood, under large barrows, with splendid grave goods to assist them in the Otherworld. The rulers of this society were buried with their chariots, wagons, personal ornaments and jewellery, and utensils containing food and drink. The poorer classes continued to be buried in simple cremation graves as they had been during the Urnfield period.

Like most early Indo-European peoples, early Celtic society was based on a caste system. At the bottom end there were the menials and producers equivalent to the *sudra* and the *vaishya* in Hindu society. Next came the warrior caste, equivalent to the Hindu *kshatriya*. Then came the intellectual caste, which included all the 'professional' functions – judges, lawyers, doctors, historians, bards and priests of religion, the Druids. These were equivalent to the Hindu Brahmin. Similar caste divisions are found in Greek and Roman society.

When we get our first glimpse of Irish society, the Celtic structure had not greatly changed. There was a menial caste which was divided into several sub-classes ranging from prisoners to herdsmen and house servants. The *ceile* was the producer, the basis of the entire society. Above them came the warriors and nobles, the *flaith*, often coming under the title of *aire* (noble), which is cognate with the Sanskrit word *arya*, freeman. Then came the professional class, originally the Druids.

At the top of society, among both the ancient Celts on the Continent and the later insular Celts, there came the kings and queens; indeed, there was a whole range of kings from minor kings who paid allegiance to more powerful kings, to over-kings or high kings.

The word for a king in the Celtic group of languages was *rix*, in Gaulish, cognate with the word for king in other Indo-European languages: *rajan* in Sanskrit (hence Hindi, *raj*), *rex* in Latin and so forth. Now this concept of kingship in Indo-European meant one who stretched or reached out his hand to protect his people. The very word for king also meant an act of stretching or reaching. In old Irish, for example, *rige* was not simply kingship but was the act of reaching. In modern Irish *righ* still means 'to stretch'. The same idea can be seen, albeit a little in disguise, in Latin – *porrigo*, to stretch or reach. It is a compound of *pro* and *rego*, to guide, direct, govern or rule. In modern English the very word 'reach' is of the same root. Indeed, the word 'rich' in English, and in most of the Germanic languages as well as French from the Germanic Frankish, also comes from the root word for 'exalted, noble and kingly'.

Gods with 'long hands', such as Lugh Lamhfhada in Ireland and Dyaus in Vedic literature, are symbolic of the concept of royalty. In the old Irish king lists we find that Oenghus Olmuchada of the Long Hand is recorded as ruling in Ireland in 800 BC. Indeed, one of the most notable modern symbols in recent years has been the 'Red Hand' of Ulster. Today it is viewed as the rather threatening symbol of the Ulster 'Loyalist' planter tradition. In fact it goes back long before their adoption of it for it was the heraldic badge of the Uí Néill dynasty, the symbol of the Celtic Kings of Ulster. It appears on the seal of Aedh O Néill, King of Ulster in 1334–1364. The Uí Néill dynasty would rush on their foes with the war-cry: '*Leamh Dearg Abu!*' (The Red Hand forever!) In medieval times their armoured warriors wore a Red Hand badge, and examples have been found from the fourteenth and fifteenth centuries. However, the symbolism goes even further back, to the tradition of the Milesian invasion. Eremon, son of Golamh, or Míle Espain, the progenitor of the Gaels, had taken an oath that, out of his siblings, he would be the first to land on the shores of Éireann. When he saw that his ship was not going to be first, he cut off his hand and threw it on shore. In this legend, we find an echo of the symbolism of the reaching out of the hand. Eremon, in spite of his brother Eber's claims, became, according to the Druid Amairgen, the first high king of Ireland.

*Rí* and *rigan* remain in the Goidelic languages as words for king and queen, but in Welsh the word for king has changed to *brennin*. It is argued that this derives from Brigantinos – i.e. 'spouse of Briganti', the goddess known as the 'elevated one' (cognate of Brigit) – and thus reflects the ritual mating of a king with a goddess of sovereignty. An example of this union is when the three goddesses (Children of Danu) Éire, Banba and Fótla met the Milesians and Eremon became king of the northern half of the country while his brother Eber became king of the southern half. Éire sealed her union by handing her royal husband a golden goblet of red liquor. Nine kings of Ireland are said to have cohabited with Medb for she would not allow any king to sit at Tara unless she was joined with him. While Medb appears as queen in Connacht and Medb Lethderg appears as queen in Leinster, it is possible that the traditions are confused for Medb is clearly a goddess representing sovereignty.

Kings were regarded as divine. They descended from the gods and usually had to ritually mate with a goddess, a recurring theme in Irish mythology. The traditions of Hindu and Celtic kingship, as seen in early Irish sources, are particularly close and the fortunes of the king were seen as being fundamentally bound to the fortunes of the land. Ritual marriage took place between the king and the land in various symbolic forms. Rituals and tests were practised in choosing a king. There were sacred inauguration stones, such as the Lia Fáil (Stone of Destiny), which was known as the Stone of Scone and on which Scottish kings were inaugurated. This was looted from Scotland by Edward I and remained in Westminster Abbey until 1997 when it was returned to Scotland. The teaching was that the inauguration stones for kings and chieftains gave a loud cry if they recognised the foot of a rightful king.

Certain rituals particularly delineate Celtic society as Indo-European. In the bull festival, or *tarbhfheis*, a bull was slain and a Druid feasted on the flesh and drank of a broth made from the cooked animal. He then went into a meditative trance, while four others chanted over him, and he was thought to receive a vision of the next true king. Bulls, revered for strength and ferocity and virility, were venerated by all the Celtic peoples. The esteem in which they were held can be judged from numerous figurines and statuettes and other artwork dating from the seventh century BC. Bull sacrifice is found on the famous Gundestrup Cauldron, where there is an image of a slain bull, and its importance is all-pervasive in the Celtic world. Queen Medb invaded Ulster to steal the Brown Bull of Cuailgne when its owner, Daire mac Fiachniu, refused to part with it.

Another ritual is described by Gerald of Wales (Giraldus Cambrensis) in his *Expurgatio Hibernica*. He describes the inauguration ceremony of an Irish king where a mare was ritually slaughtered and the king-elect ate of the flesh of the beast then drank and bathed in a broth made from the carcass. It was a ritual in which the king sought fertility for himself and his people. This may have symbolised a ritual mating with the horse goddess Epona (*epos*, a horse) who came to be adopted even by the Romans. Horse sacrifice also appears in another Indo-European culture, in the Hindu ritual of *asvamedha*.

Caesar suggests that some tribes of the Belgae were familiar with a dual monarchy – two kings sharing the throne. He mentions in particular the tribe of the Eburones. Certainly dual monarchy occurs several times in more recent Irish king lists where brothers often shared the throne, for example Fergus and Domnall, sons of Muirchertaig, who ruled in AD 566, or Cellach and Conall Cáel, sons of Máele Cobo, who ruled in AD 654, or Diarmait and Blathmac, sons of Aedo Sláine, who ruled in AD 665. We also find two Celtic rulers leading a combined Celtic army to threaten Rome in 223/222 BC – Aneroestes and Concolitanus.

Caesar mentions that some Celtic kings exercised authority on both sides of what is now the English Channel. We learn that Commius, the king of the Atrebates in Gaul (discounting the boast that Caesar had made him a king – he had probably merely recognised him as such), also exercised sovereignty over the Atrebates of southern Britain. Caesar also refers to the Suessiones: 'They had been ruled within living memory by Diviciacus, the most powerful king in Gaul, who controlled not only a large part of the Belgic country, but Britain as well.' Diviciacus appears to have ruled about 100 BC.

We find that King Marcus Cunomorus of Cornwall in the sixth century AD also ruled Carhaix in Cornouaille in Brittany. There are other references to Celtic kings exercising authority both in Britain and on the Continent.

However, Caesar suggests that kingship was falling out of fashion among the Celts of southern and central Gaul and was being replaced by a magisterial rule. He believed that, among the Aedui, kings had been replaced by elected magistrates drawn from the aristocrats. As this was the form of government that Rome had adopted in 510 BC, following the expulsion of their kings, perhaps Caesar misread the situation, especially if these tribes were practising dual kingship and the Celtic electoral form, instead of the autocratic kingship with which Rome was more familiar. He might well have seen in the two kings, whose powers were delineated by law and limited by the rights of their nobles and peoples, the two consuls who governed Rome. In the case of the single Aedui 'magistrate' elected from the aristocracy, Caesar might have misunderstood the system of kingship which emerges in the ancient Irish Brehon Laws, whereby a king was elected by members of certain aristocratic families; the eldest son did not automatically succeed to his father's throne, as we shall see.

It is interesting to note that the Germanic branch of Indo-European adopted a different linguistic concept for kingship. The words 'king', '*könig*' and '*koning*' are derived from the Indo-European root *gen*, a people, a nation, or descent. The word is found in Greek and Latin, as well as old Irish. We come near to understanding why the word developed into a term for the office of king when we find in old Irish the phrase that a king was appointed *do thaobh a ghlun ngeineamha* – by virtue of his ancestry.

This ancestry was all-important for the appointment of kings. The Celtic form of kingship seems to be a descendant of the Indo-European form, and it survived into the Irish Laws of the Fénechus. It was not until the seventeenth century AD that this law system was eradicated from use in Ireland by English colonial law. We can see from comparisons with other known Celtic systems, such as the form of government in Galatia, that the Fénechus or Brehon system was representative of the wider Celtic system.

Kings did not succeed by primogeniture; that is, the eldest

son did not necessarily become the successor of his father. It was necessary for the survival of the people to have a strong man on the throne, strong in mind as well as strength, one who could defend his people against any threat from without or within. So the man who showed a fitness for the post could be a younger son of the previous king just as well as an elder son; indeed, he could be a brother of the king, an uncle even, or a cousin or grandson. The choice was usually made within three generations and it was those three generations who usually approved of the choice. Often, and this emerges in the Brehon Laws, the successor to the king was appointed during the king's lifetime to prevent dispute. In Ireland, this form was called *tanistry* and the heir-apparent was the *tanist* or 'second'.

We find traces of matrilineal descent among certain Celtic groups. The Venerable Bede believed that the Picts, a Brythonic Celtic population in Scotland which became absorbed into a Goidelic-speaking homogeneous society, had a matrilineal kingship. However, this is not proven although we find a late Irish tradition that the Picts acquired womenfolk from the Irish on condition that their kingship should pass through the female line.

If kingship among the Celts was usually patrilineal, how can we account for the appearance of female rulers such as Onomaris, Cartimandua and Boudicca, and for the obviously prominent positions of the 'Vix princess', the 'Rheinheim princess' and other women who apparently ruled in their own right? We shall be dealing with the remarkable position of women in Celtic life later. It is clear both from grave finds and from reports among the classical writers that women could and did occupy high social positions, even ruling a tribe or, like Cartimandua, a confederation of tribes. The Roman historian Tacitus puts these significant words into the mouth of Boudicca: 'This is not the first time that the Britons have been led to battle by a woman.'

Certainly in Irish literature we find Queen Medb as the real leader of Connacht and her husband Ailill deferring to her dominant personality. The genealogies of Ireland and historical accounts mention one female high king, Macha Mong Ruadh (Macha of the Red Hair), recorded as the seventy-sixth monarch and daughter of Aedh Ruadh who founded the palace of Emain Macha (Navan) near Ard Macha (Armagh). The date of her death is recorded as 377 BC and she is listed as the only female ruler in the period before Christ.

The Brehon Laws have only one reference to female rulers. This occurs in the *Bretha Cróilge* which contains a list of categories of women who are prominent in society, including a 'woman who turns back the streams of war' and is 'the ruler of hostages' (those taken in battle). There also survives the twelfth-century AD collection of genealogical lore about Irish women, which we have previously referred to, the *Banshenchas*.

However, most references to the office of kingship do demonstrate a patrilineal model. One possible explanation for the existence of female rulers lies in the fact that, according to the Brehon Laws, the *banchomarbae* or female heir could inherit full property rights if there were no male heirs. Perhaps, therefore, the woman could also become ruler if there were no male heirs? According to Dr Sophie Bryant: 'Although the rule of female succession existed under the Brehon Law, it may generally be regarded as a proof of late date in the author who asserts it as a rule; and it must be rejected from any statement of the ancient law of succession.' Dr Bryant places the date for the establishment of female succession as the late sixth century AD. Yet how does she explain the earlier existence of female rulers?

The Hallstatt period is divided into four phases by archaeologists. A and B correspond to the period 1200–800 BC or the Bronze Age. From 800 BC we find the start of the Iron Age or Hallstatt C, ending in 600 BC. This third period is the time of the rise of the wealthy kings and their rich burial mounds.

This was also the time of the building of great fortified settlements. Around the major burial chambers of the kings have been discovered warrior graves, less wealthy than those of the kings and more numerous, thus demonstrating the rise of a powerful aristocracy to support the kings.

In the Hallstatt D period, 600–475 BC, the rich graves of these Celtic kings tended to have shifted to the west, to south-western Germany and along the westward Rhône, west to the Loire and north to the headwaters of the Seine. These graves show trading links with the Mediterranean, especially with Greece and Etruria. The reason is simple. The kings had moved their seats of power to be on the river-trading routes opened up by the establishment of the Greek trading colony at Massilia (Marseilles) near the mouth of the Rhône. One of the features of the Hallstatt princely graves is that there were no weapons of war, swords and shields, placed within them. In graves of the later La Tène period, swords, helmets, shields and other weapons become common. Can we deduce anything from this change? Does it imply that the early Celtic kings were not so much warriors as civil leaders, but that their descendants were more war-oriented?

Some of the best-surviving graves of the Hallstatt Celtic rulers have been excavated only in recent decades. One of the most unusual was found at Vix, near Châtillon-sur-Seine in the Côte-d'Or. This stands at the headwaters of the Seine whose name derives from the Celtic Sequana, a river goddess whose worship is attested by a wealth of votive offerings found near the source of the river. The 'princely grave', as it was designated, was excavated in 1953 and dated to the end of the sixth century BC. What distinguished it from the majority of kingly graves was that it contained the skeleton of a thirty-five-year-old woman. She lay on the chassis of a four-wheeled wagon or chariot which obviously served as a bier. The wheels had been removed and placed against the inner wall of the timber chamber.

That she was a noble of importance could be seen by her golden torc made from 480 grams of gold. The other items included a bronze krater with a capacity of 1100 litres, the biggest surviving vessel of its kind from this period. The finds from this spectacular grave are in the municipal museum of Châtillon-sur-Seine.

Not far away, 5 kilometres south of the hill of Mont Lassois, a further four princely graves were discovered, also dating from between the sixth and fifth centuries BC. These finds, archaeologists argue, indicate that this was the centre of a powerful Celtic kingdom.

The krater demonstrates that the Hallstatt kings were trading with the Mediterranean: it is of fine Greek workmanship and contained wine – grapes were not grown at this period north of the Alps. Archaeologists have found many wine jars (*amphorae*) in the area dating from the sixth century BC.

Although the 'princess of Vix', as she is known, was unusual, there are further examples of the graves of prominent noble women. The later grave of the fourth century BC found at Waldalgesheim, 5 kilometres west of Bingen, in North Rhine, Westphalia, showed a noble woman with the remains of a two-wheeled wagon, a golden torc, two gold arm-rings, and a bronze jug. These are to be seen in the Rheinisches Landesmuseum. Another noble woman was found in a chariot burial grave at Wetwang Slack in Yorkshire, in the territory of the Parisii. A further grave from the fourth century BC, known as that of the 'Rheinheim princess', produced some 200 pieces of jewellery and personal effects, including a gold torc, armlets, a mirror and gilt-bronze wine flagon. This was discovered in 1954 during sandpit excavations. The burial chamber was originally part of a group, and the body of the 'princess' was found in an oak-lined chamber.

Almost due south of Vix is Camp de Château, a hilly area

in the Furieuse valley in the French Jura. Archaeological finds here, including some wagon burials, dated to around the late sixth century BC, would indicate that this was the site of another rich 'princely seat'.

Excavations in 1978–79 uncovered one of the richest of the kingly graves. This was found under a low mound in a field at Hochdorf, in the Baden Würtemberg region. It was estimated that the original mound would have been 6 metres high and 60 metres in diameter. The burial chamber, entirely lined with wood and hung with drapes and tapestries, was in excellent condition.

The Celtic king had lain in his tomb undisturbed for 2500 years. He lay on a great bronze couch, some 3 metres long, the couch being supported by eight female figurines mounted on wheels. In punch dot carving, the bronze couch was decorated with images of warriors, dancers and wagons. Traces of fabric, probably of clothes and hangings and upholstery, were found, some of them embroidered. Fabrics hanging from the walls and decorations of flowers and boughs of symbolic trees adorned the interior.

The king himself was a man of forty years old, standing 1.87 metres (6 foot 2 inches), obviously tall and strong in life. He wore a gold belt plate, a decorated dagger encased in gold. There was the traditional gold tore at his neck, and gold bracelet on his arm. Amber beads and gold and bronze brooches were probably laid on his chest for they had fallen nearby. He appeared to have been wearing ankle-length boots with curled or pointed toes. They had gold embossed fittings with holes for laces. An iron razor, a wooden comb and a conical bark hat had been placed near his head. Fish hooks and a quiver of iron-tipped arrows were nearby. He lay, significantly, on the western side of the tomb – the west being the direction of the Otherworld. The phrase 'to go west' was used as a euphemism for death until this century in English. To the east stood a four-wheeled wagon or chariot with iron and bronze plates. Bronze

decorative horse harnesses were nearby together with other
items such as an iron axe, spear and a fine set of bronze dishes.
Hanging on hooks on the south wall were nine large drinking
horns, nine being a significant number in Celtic myth.

Nine was always the number of the immediate bodyguard
of kings in Irish myth. Queen Medb travelled with nine chariots, two of them before her, two behind, two at her side and
her son in the middle. King Loeghaire, setting out to arrest St
Patrick, ordered nine chariots 'according to the tradition of
the gods', while Bricriu was guarded by eight swordsmen, and
Fionn Mac Cumhail had eight companions. The number nine
occurs in other forms and it has been argued that the ancient
Celtic week consisted of nine nights followed by nine days.

The fact that this king, while a man of wealth and power,
was not buried with weapons, such as are found in warriors'
graves, but with items depicting feasting and hunting and
fishing, might mean that he was not perceived as a man of war.

At Grafenbühl, in the eastern part of the town of Asperg in
the Ludwigsburg area, archaeologists unearthed the skeleton
of a man in his thirties in a central grave chamber, clearly
another wealthy Celtic king. While there were the remains of
a chariot, several pieces of furniture and a drinking vessel, the
grave had been plundered and more valuable items taken. It
has now been built over.

Two royal graves of the Hallstatt period were excavated at
the nearby village of Hirschlanden. The most significant find
was two life-sized statues (stele). The first, discovered in 1964,
was thought to be of a 'warrior', but when the second one was
found in 1997 it was correctly claimed as a Celtic 'prince'. The
figures were thought to have stood on top of the graves.

In the same area in 1879 another royal grave was excavated
in Kleinaspergle but the central chamber proved to have been
plundered. The original grave had a height of 6 metres and
diameter of 60 metres. Indications were that this was a tomb
of someone of great significance. In a neighbouring chamber

the grave robbers had missed a richly endowed tomb with jewellery and drinking vessels, including two Attic dishes from
Greece and some imported pottery dating from *c*. 450 BC;
these were decorated by Celtic craftsmen with layers of gold
foil. All the finds from the area are now in the Würtem-
bergisches Landesmuseum in Stuttgart.

One of the best-known ancient Celtic royal centres is at
Heuneburg, on the west bank of the Danube, in the
Sigmaringen district. It was occupied from the Bronze Age
down to the Middle Ages, but reached a peak of importance
in the sixth and fifth centuries BC when the royal centre covered
an area of 3 hectares enclosed by fortified walls, some standing nearly 4 metres high. Nearby were several royal grave
mounds including that of Hohmichele, one of the biggest
Celtic grave mounds in Central Europe.

Hohmichele lies 1.5 kilometres west of Heuneburg. The
mound was 14 metres high and 80 metres in diameter. During
1937–38 archaeologists found a central grave chamber, lined
with wooden boards, but sadly its contents had almost vanished through grave robbers. Around it were lesser graves
among which was the intact grave of a man and a woman
found with a four-wheeled wagon and harness and many utensils and items of jewellery. However, many of the most prominent graves have fallen victim to grave robbers over the
centuries.

Some graves have not yet been excavated, such as that at
Hohenasperg, a hill west of Ludwigsburg, regarded as the site
of one of the most important early Celtic kingdoms and near
many princely graves of the late Hallstatt and early La Tène
periods. The reason why no archaeological excavation has
taken place is because the site has been extensively built over.

Some of the best princely graves of the La Tène period are
at Rodenbach, dating to the fifth century BC. Here, the royal
corpse had golden rings on his arms and fingers, and weapons
and utensils were also discovered. These are now in the

Historisches Museum der Pfalz. Schwarzenbach, excavated in 1849, produced two princely graves containing golden jewellery, dishes, weapons, gold masks and other riches. Most of the finds have mysteriously disappeared, probably looted from Berlin in 1945. Two more graves found at Wesikirkchen, in Merzig-wadern in the Saar, and dated to the fifth/fourth centuries BC, also revealed some rich material which is now in the Rheinisches Landesmuseum in Bonn and the Rheinisches Landesmuseum in Trier.

Royal graves have not been discovered in such profusion in Britain but this might well be due to prolonged ravaging of sites, grave robbing and building. One of the most exciting finds was made at Deal, in Kent, where the grave of an adult male, buried *c.* 200–100 BC, was recently excavated. He had been buried with a shield, too fragmentary to restore, although bronze decorations and ornamentations revealed a characteristic Celtic shape. He also had a sword. What was more exciting was that he wore a crown, also of bronze. Archaeologists have, so far, been nervous of identifying him as a king, in spite of the crown, wondering whether he might be simply a warrior priest. It would be doubtful if a person other than a king wore such headgear.

We can see from just these few examples of royal graves of the early Celtic period the power of the ancient Celtic kings. There is one Celtic area which, hitherto, has failed to yield discoveries matching the magnificent Hallstatt and La Tène princely burials on the Continent, and that is Ireland. There seems no trace of chariot burials at all. However, Irish records show that in pre-Christian times there were 'royal cemeteries' in various parts of the country for the interment of kings and their families. In the remarkable *Senchus na Relec* (*History of Cemeteries*), contained in *Leabhar na hUidri*, compiled *c.* AD 1100, we are told that Croghan was called *Relig na Ríg* (Burial Place of the Kings). It was situated near Tulsk, Co. Roscommon, the seat of the kings of Connacht.

The old records also state that kings and chieftains were buried in varied ways, some lying flat, others sitting, but often in a standing posture, arrayed in full battle gear with shield and weapons and with their face turned towards the territories of their enemies.

When can we begin to put names to the early Celtic kings? Unfortunately, not until the start of the sixth century BC, if we ignore the Irish king lists and genealogies. We shall come to these in a moment. On the Continent, however, the Greeks give us the name of Arganthonios, the Celtic king who made a trade agreement with the Greek merchants of Phocis. His people exploited the silver mines in southern Iberia and his name has the Celtic root for 'silver' in it. Later Roman historians speak of Ambicatus, the sixth-century BC king of the Bituriges, who they claimed dominated the Celtic tribal kingdoms north of the Alps. Ambicatus' name translates as 'He who gives battle all round'. We also know of his nephews, whom he sent to seek new lands to settle – Bellovesus (He who can kill) and Segovesus (He who can conquer). Then we come to Brennus, the leader of the Senones, the conqueror of Rome during 390 BC. But does his name imply 'king' (from *brennin*) or is it a form of Bran meaning 'raven'? Brennus had exactly the same name as the main leader of the Celtic invading army which sacked Delphi in 279 BC.

We know the names of Aneroestes and Concolitanus who commanded the Celts in the events which led to their greatest defeat on the Italian peninsula in 222 BC at Telamon. We know of Viridomarus who perished in single combat with the consul Marcus Claudius Marcellus and whose name derives from *viro* (man) and *marus* (great). He called himself a 'son of Rhenus', which made scholars leap to the conclusion that he was a mercenary from the Rhine. They overlook the fact that the Celtic name Rhenus was also given to a river in the Po valley – the Reno. Judging from the accounts, Viridomarus appeared to be the ruler of the Insubres of the Milan area. He must not be confused with another Viridomarus who was an Aeduan leader and rival to Eporedorix (King of horsemen) in Julius Caesar's time.

We know the names of Iberian Celtic kings as well, such as Avaros whose capital was Numantia and who valiantly held out against the Roman siege in 153 BC. His successor was Rhetogenes, a name which seems to imply that he was of the 'ancestry of the wheel', perhaps a reference to divine ancestry of the wheel, or solar, god. And there is Virithos of the Lusitani whose name seems to imply a 'reborn man' (*viri*, man, *athios*, reborn, recognisable in the old Irish *athgainiur*, I am reborn).

There was a powerful 'over king' of southern Britain called Cassivellaunus; either he took his name from his tribe or vice versa. The name means 'Lover of Belenus', the god. His power is clear from the fact that he was given command by all the petty kings of southern Britain to meet Julius Caesar's second attempt at invasion and conquest in 54 BC.

But now other names are emerging and ones we can put more flesh on. There is Vercingetorix, son of Celtillus (Great King of Heroes), who was acknowledged king of an alliance of the Gaulish peoples in their struggle against Caesar. After his initial success, forcing Caesar to retreat for the first time in his military career, Vercingetorix' forces were trapped in Alesia and he surrendered. Taken to Rome, he was kept for years in an underground prison before being ritually slaughtered to celebrate Caesar's triumph over the Gauls. It may also be remembered that Cingetorix (King of Heroes) was one of four British Celtic kings, of the Cantii, who came to Caesar's camp in southern Britain. The other kings of the Cantii who met Caesar were Carvilius, Taximagulus and Segovax.

It is from Caesar, of course, that we know the names of many of the Gaulish kings including Diviciacus, pro-Roman king of the Aedui who addressed the Roman Senate in 61 BC. The name appears to mean 'Avenger'. (He is not to be confused with another Diviciacus, a powerful king of the

Suessiones ruling about 100 BC and minting his own coins.) Diviciacus' anti-Roman brother, Dumnorix (King of the World), was held hostage by Caesar and cut down by his soldiers while trying to escape.

Deiotaros I of Galatia proved to be one of the most politically adept of Celtic kings. 'The Divine Bull' ruled the three united tribes of Celtic Galatia from his fortress at Blucium, where he once entertained Julius Caesar; he survived many of the internal squabbles of the Roman republic to keep his kingdom fairly independent before he died *c*. 41 BC aged about eighty.

The 'Belenus' name continues with the famous Cunobelinus, the Hound of Belenus made even more famous by Shakespeare as Cymbeline. Cunobelinus succeeded Tasciovanos *c*. AD 10; under his rule London grew to prominence as a trading port and Britain became a leading commercial centre. Cunobelinus never sought Roman friendship but there is no record of his doing anything to excite Roman enmity. He was powerful, issuing his own coinage, like his predecessors, and it was only on his death in about AD 40 that Rome decided to seize its chance and attempt a conquest. Many of the petty British kings had argued againt Cunobelinus' son Caractacus being his successor, including Caractacus' own brothers, Togodumnus and Adminius. They were joined by another king called Bericus (perhaps Verica on British coins) who went to Rome to persuade the emperor to set them up in his place. Such traitors were the diplomatic excuse Rome needed for the invasion of Britain.

Caractacus (Caradog), acknowledged as over-king of southern Britain during the Claudian invasion of the country, is one of the more romantic Celtic kings, holding out for nine years against the might of the invading Roman legions before being betrayed by a Celtic queen named Cartimandua and taken, with his family, in chains to Rome. His eloquence saved their lives and he was sentenced to live in exile in the city.

Cartimandua (Sleek Pony) was another fascinating Celtic ruler. She was queen of the Briganti (Exalted Ones) who occupied the land stretching across what is now northern England from the Irish Sea to the North Sea. This was a tribal confederation. She had allied it to Rome following the conquest of the southern British tribes. She divorced her husband Venutius, and married his charioteer. The Romans had to send armies several times to help her fight against Venutius and his allies. Eventually the power of the Briganti was smashed. Unfortunately, we do not know the fate of Cartimandua.

Perhaps one of the most famous early Celtic rulers was Boudicca, whose name is translated as 'Victory' and Latinised as Boadicea, the queen of the Iceni in what is now East Anglia. In AD 60, having been provoked by the arrogance of a Roman official who had had her flogged and her two daughters raped, Boudicca led a mass uprising against the Romans. Her initial victories were devastating. She annihilated the IX Hispania Legion and sacked and destroyed the Roman colonial capital at what is now Colchester and their trading centres at London and St Albans. However, the Romans regrouped and won a devastating victory over the British Celts. Although Boudicca was never captured, reports had it that she and her two daughters took poison.

When Agricola attempted to conquer northern Britain, or Caledonia, he encountered a king named Calgacos (Swordsman). The historian Tacitus puts a speech into Calgacos' mouth before the battle of Mons Graupius which is often quoted for the line, 'they made a desert and called it peace'.

In the north-west fringes of Europe, Celtic kingdoms survived until the late medieval period, although their conquerors tried to disguise the fact by giving the kings a variety of titles from duke to prince to earl. The last king of Cornwall seems to have been a Howell who surrendered to Athelstan in AD 931. James VI of Scotland, on the death of Elizabeth I in

1603, agreed with alacrity to become James I of England. Llywellyn, the penultimate ruler of Wales, was killed by English troops at Cilmeri in 1282. His brother Dafydd ruled for only a few months before being captured and beheaded and, by the Statute of Rhuddlan, in 1284, Wales was annexed to the English crown. Francis II of Brittany had to surrender to the French King Charles VIII at St Aubin-du-Cormier; while his daughter Anne reasserted Breton independence for a while, she was inevitably faced with a marriage to Charles and the union of the crowns of Brittany and France.

In 1541 Henry VIII made himself king of Ireland and forced the Irish royal families to surrender their titles in a policy called 'surrender and regrant'. The kings (the office of high king had already vanished) had to surrender their title and lands and were then granted the title of 'earl' together with some of their land back as a fiefdom from Henry as feudal king. In July 1543, for example, Murrough O'Brien, 57th King of Thomond, and direct descendant of the famous high king Brian Boru, surrendered to Henry at Greenwich. In return he was created Earl of Thomond and Baron Inchiquin. Conor O'Brien, 18th Baron Inchiquin, still lives on the family estates.

Other Irish kings were less fortunate. Donal IX The MacCarthy Mór, last regnant King of Desmond and titular King of the two Munsters, fought on, as did his family. They never surrendered and so did not enjoy titles and estates. Similarly, the O'Neills of Ulster, finally defeated, had to flee abroad where their descendants still live in Spain and Portugal.

It is worth noting that the indigenous Celtic aristocracy of Ireland, whose genealogies mostly date from twelfth-century records, is one of the most ancient in Europe. Today's surviving heads of the Irish royal dynasties have a traceable lineage, accepted by genealogists and heralds, going back nearly 2000 years, perhaps longer if we may put some trust in the genealogies of the earlier periods.

For example, the pedigree of the Uí Néill kings of Ulster starts with a descent from Eremon, the first Milesian monarch, who is said to have ruled the northern half of Ireland in the year of the world (i.e. 1015 BC), coming down forty-one generations to Lugaid Riab nDerg who ruled in AD 65–73. From there every generation is listed down to Niall of the Nine Hostages, who ruled in AD 379–405. Today, the two houses of the Uí Néill dynasty, as represented by Don Hugo O'Neill, Prince of Clanaboy, in Portugal, and Don Marcos O'Neill, 11th Marques del Granja of Seville in Spain, can trace their unbroken lines back to Niall. Therefore, technically, they have unbroken genealogies of 3000 years. The same may be said for the current MacCarthy Mór, Prince of Desmond, whose line descends from Eber Fionn, brother of Eremon, who ruled the southern half of Ireland in 1015 BC. The MacCarthys constituted the Eóghanacht dynasty in Ireland which ruled Munster in the south and later Desmond (south Munster) until the late sixteenth century.

However, while the genealogists and heralds accept the genealogies back to the first century AD, they prefer to leave aside the genealogies stretching BC as 'unproved', although not going so far as some sceptical scholars who dismiss them as 'pseudo-genealogies' and the surrounding texts as 'pseudo-histories'.

# 4

# THE DRUIDS

There is no class of Celtic society that so intrigued the classical world as the Druids. The writings of the Greeks and Romans concerning Druids, with all their misinterpretations and misconceptions, have become the basis for a veritable 'Druid industry' which was created from the seventeenth century and has lasted into modern times.

We saw in Chapter 3 that Celtic society was based on a caste system and that the second level was the intellectual class. This class encompassed all the professional occupations – judges, doctors, historians and genealogists, philosophers, storytellers, astronomers and astrologers, as well as the priestly orders who mediated with the deities. After them, in rank, came the warrior-nobles; the producers; the menials; and lastly those who had no position in society, hostages, prisoners and those who had lost their 'civil rights' through crime.

As with most things Celtic, it is the Greek writers who first record the name Druidae and then not until the second century BC. Diogenes Laertius, a Greek living in the third century AD, quoted the works of more ancient writers, such

as Soton of Alexandria (*fl. c.* 200–170 BC), which discussed
the Druids. The name is clearly one of Celtic origin
although linguists still battle over its exact meaning. There
is popular support for the claims of Strabo and Pliny the
Elder that the word was cognate with the Greek word *drus*,
an oak. The Indo-European root is also found in Irish and
Welsh as *dair* and *dar*. Hence it is thought the word might
be *dru-uid*, oak knowledge. This last *uid/wid/vid* root is the
same as the Sanskrit *vid*, to know or to see, and is seen in the
Hindu Vedas, which means 'knowledge', the most ancient
religious texts surviving in an Indo-European language.
Therefore the idea is that Druid means 'those whose knowledge is great'.

The classical texts referred to Druids only in Gaul and
Britain. Druids are not mentioned as existing among the
Cisalpine Celts, the Iberian Celts, the eastern Celts or the
Galatian Celts. Neither are the Druids mentioned in connec-
tion with Ireland, although, of course, we know that they
existed there from subsequent native literature.

Does this mean that the Druids were confined to the
Gaulish and British Celts? Some scholars tend to be very
literal, and where there is a source, even though written by a
hostile witness, it is often accepted without question on the
basis of its antiquity.

The answer to the question, of course, depends on what
your interpretation of the function of a Druid is. If one
accepts that the Druids were an intellectual caste or class, as
Caesar lets slip and Dion Chrysostom later spells out, comparing them rightly with the Brahmins of Hindu society, then
we may argue that Druids or their class equivalent appeared
throughout Celtic society. That the Druids encompassed
several intellectual fields may certainly be accepted from the
evidence.

We also find that the Celts did have specific names for their
priests, such as *gutuatri* meaning 'speakers (to the gods)', a

Gaulish cognate to the Irish *guth*, voice. The *gutuatri* are known from inscriptions and a reference to a *gutuatros* put to death by Caesar, mentioned in Aulus Hirtius' addition to the *Gallic War*. Hirtius was one of Caesar's lieutenants in Gaul.

Other words are also used to describe the priestly functions, such as *antistites*, *sacerdotes* and *semnotheoi*. The term *semnotheoi* is preserved by Laertius from Soton and is used as a synonym for a Druid, but perhaps only describing a particular Druidic priestly function.

Several Greek and Latin writers speak of Dryades or Druidesses and the existence of such female Druids is certainly confirmed by native Celtic sources, although the classical sources seem to place more emphasis on male Druids.

The earliest sources on the Druids, written by Greeks, are known only in quotation from the later Alexandrian school; significantly, these sources are respectful of the Druids and, indeed, the Celts in general. We will deal with these shortly but first we must examine those sources by which the Druids have, sadly, become more popularly known: the anti-Celtic writings of the Romans and Romanophiles.

It would appear that the work of Poseidonios (*c.* 135–*c.* 50 BC) of Apamea, Syria, was used as the major source material on the Celts of Gaul by all our main pro-Roman writers on the Druids. Therefore, our knowledge of the Druids, in this respect, rests with only one writer. Poseidonios' work is used by the Alexandrian Greek, Timagenes, *c.* mid-first century BC; the Roman general, Gaius Julius Caesar (100–44 BC); the Sicilian Greek, Diodorus Siculus (*c.* 60–*c.* 21 BC); and the Greek geographer from Pontus, Strabo (64 BC–AD 24). The scholar Alfred Klotz believed that Poseidonios' work had already been lost by the first century BC and that Timagenes was the intermediary who passed it on by quoting large sections of it. Those quotations are substantially the passages used by all other writers.

Strabo, in his *Geographia*, says:

. . . the Druids, in addition to the science of nature, study
also moral philosophy. They are believed to be the most just
of men, and are therefore entrusted with the decision of
cases affecting either individuals or the public; indeed in
former times they arbitrated in war and brought to a stand-
still the opponents when about to draw up in line of battle;
and murder cases have been mostly entrusted to their decision . . . These men, as well as other authorities, have pro-
nounced that men's souls and the universe are
indestructible, although at times fire or water may (tem-
porarily) prevail.

Diodorus makes a similar statement and quotes Timagenes
as the authority on the Druids. Both Strabo and Diodorus
divide the Gaulish intellectual class into Bards, Vates and
Druids. 'The Bards are singers and poets; the Vates interpret-
ers of sacrifice and natural philosophers . . .' We find some
confirmation of this when the insular Celtic records cite the
same classes of intellectuals in Ireland – *Drui*, *Bard* and *Fili*.
We can only quote Timagenes from the quotations of other
writers. In disfavour with the emperor, he burnt his works
before he left Rome. However, Ammianus Marcellinus (*c*. AD
330–395), a Greek from Antioch, quotes him extensively and
mentions that the Druids had an organisation, a corporate life
(*sodalicis adstricti consortis*). Caesar also says that they were
a highly organised fraternity.

All the Druids are under one leader, whom they hold in the
highest respect. On his death, if any one of the rest is of outstanding merit, he succeeds to the vacant place; if several
have equal claims, the Druids usually decide the election by
voting, though sometimes they actually fight it out. On a
fixed date in each year they hold a session in a consecrated

spot in the country of the Carnutes, which is supposed to be the centre of Gaul.

The Carnutes were the Celtic tribe in the region between the Seine and the Loire. The chief town of the tribe was Cennabum which is present-day Orléans.

Diodorus gives a much more comprehensive description of the Celts of Gaul than do his contemporaries, and he dwells on their belief in the immortality of the soul. There can be little doubt however that Strabo and Diodorus are ultimately deriving their information from a common source for they appear to be following a similar text. But Strabo's work was a pointed attack on the Celts which was written as a justification for the conquest of Gaul and subsequent attempts to suppress the Celtic intelligentsia and their centres of learning.

Caesar, at least, is quite clear on who the Druids are. He calls them 'an intellectual class'.

The Druids officiate at the worship of the gods, regulate public and private sacrifices [rituals], and give rulings on all religious questions. Large numbers of young men flock to them for instruction, and they are held in great honour by the people. They act as judges in practically all disputes, whether between tribes or between individuals; when any crime is committed or a murder takes place, or a dispute arises about an inheritance or a boundary, it is they who adjudicate the matter and appoint the compensation to be paid and received by the parties concerned. Any individual or tribe failing to accept their award is banned from taking part in sacrifice [religious service] – the heaviest punishment that can be inflicted upon a Gaul. Those who are under such a ban are regarded as impious criminals. Everyone shuns them and avoids going near or speaking to them, for fear of taking some harm by contact with what is unclean; if they appear as plaintiffs, justice is denied them and they are excluded from a share in any honour.

Because of the special position of the Druids in society, Caesar informs us:

> The Druids are exempt from military service and do not pay taxes like other citizens. These important privileges are naturally attractive; many present themselves of their own accord to become students of Druidism, and others are sent by their parents and relatives. It is said that these people have to memorise a great number of verses – so many that some spend twenty years at their studies.

What is interesting is that Caesar adds:

> The Druidic doctrine is believed to have been found existing in Britain and thence imported into Gaul; even today those who want to make a profound study of it generally go to Britain for the purpose.

This seems to imply that there were colleges and schools in Britain and, indeed, in Ireland.

Caesar's description of the Druids dwells mostly on their religious aspect and so, to the undiscerning reader, they appear simply as a priesthood. We have already discussed in Chapter 2 his comments on the fact that the Druids were forbidden to commit their teachings to writing. Another of his observations, echoed by the other writers, is:

> A lesson which they take particular pains to inculcate is that the soul does not perish, but after death passes from one body to another; they think that this is the best incentive to bravery, because it teaches men to disregard the terrors of death.

Caesar points out:

> They also hold long discussions about the heavenly bodies
> and their movements, the size of the universe and of the
> earth, the physical constitutions of the world, and
> the powers and properties of the gods; and they instruct the
> young men in all these subjects.

We will deal with the cosmological ideas and beliefs of the
Celts in Chapter 9.

Marcus Tullius Cicero (106–43 BC), who was acquainted
with the *princeps* of the Aedui, Diviciacus, says he was also a
Druid.

> The system of divination is not even neglected among bar-
> baric peoples, since in fact there are Druids in Gaul; I myself
> knew one of them, Diviciacus, of the Aedui, your guest and
> eulogist, who declared that he was acquainted with the
> system of nature which the Greeks call natural philosophy
> and he used it to predict the future by augury and inference.

Pliny the Elder was of a family of Roman colonists who
settled among the Celts of the Po valley after their conquest.
His *Naturalis Historia* is his chief and only surviving work, in
which he gives one of the most complete accounts of the
Druids as natural scientists, doctors of medicine and magicians. As Pliny was himself fascinated by magic, it is under-
standable that he should dwell on this aspect. Pliny was the
first writer to bring the oak grove into our popular picture of
Druids, as well as mistletoe.

> The Druids – for so they [the Celts] call their *magi* – hold
> nothing more sacred than the mistletoe and the tree on
> which it grows provided that it is an oak. They choose the
> oak to form groves, and they do not perform any religious

rites without its foliage, so that it can be seen that the
Druids are so called from the Greek word.

Pliny thereby opened the floodgates for writers to conjure
images of Druids and oaks and mistletoe. Lucan in his
*Pharsalia* has the Druids parading around eerie enchanted
woods in secret groves. Lactantius Placidus, in his com-
mentary on the *Thebais* of Publius Statius, talks of the Druids
as 'those who delight in oaks' and speaks of such groves as
'dense and ancient, untouched by human hand and impervi-
ous to the beams of the sun. There the pale and uncertain light
serves only to increase the awe and ominous silence.'
Pliny becomes lyrical on the Druids and oaks.

Anything growing on those trees they regard as sent from
heaven and a sign that this tree has been chosen by the gods
themselves. Mistletoe is, however, very rarely found, and
when found, it is gathered with great ceremony and especially on the sixth day of the moon . . . they prepare a ritual
sacrifice and feast under the tree, and lead up two white
bulls whose horns are bound for the first time on this occasion. A priest attired in a white vestment ascends the tree
and with a golden pruning hook cuts the mistletoe which is
caught in a white cloth. Then next they sacrifice the victims
praying that the gods will make their gifts propitious to
those to whom they have given it. They believe that if given
in drink the mistletoe will give fecundity to any barren
animal, and that it is predominant against all poisons.

One cannot help but agree with the Celtic scholar Nora
Chadwick when she describes this as a 'picturesque fantasia'
ranking with stories of King Alfred and the burning of the
cakes or Cnut and the waves or Bruce and the spider. It has
become a classic of universal popular knowledge but without
substance.

Cornelius Tacitus gives us invaluable information on Druids as historians when, in his *Histories*, he speaks of attempts to stir up insurrection in Gaul in AD 69.

The Gauls began to breathe new life and vigour, persuaded that the Roman armies, wherever stationed, were broken and dispirited. A rumour was current among them, and universally believed, that the Ratians and Sarmatians had laid siege to the encampments in Maesia and Pannonia. Affairs in Britain were supposed to be in no better situation. Above all, the destruction of the Capitol announced the approaching fate of the Roman empire. The Druids, in their wild enthusiasm, sang their oracular songs, in which they taught that, when Rome was formerly sacked by the Celts, the mansion of Jupiter being left entire, the commonwealth survived that dreadful shock; but the calamity of fire, which had lately happened, was a denunciation from heaven in consequence of which, power and dominion were to circulate round the world, and the nations on their side of the Alps were in their turn to become masters of the world.

The fact that in AD 69 the Druid historians of Gaul retained a knowledge of the defeat and occupation of Rome in *c.* 390 BC is fascinating and shows clearly how well the oral traditions were kept by the Celts. This should persuade us to pay more attention to the histories of Ireland dealing with ancient times but not committed to writing until the Christian period. Oral tradition must have been just as reliable as written tradition.

The early surviving sources about the Druids are written in support of Rome and its conquest of the Celts and suppression of the Druids. In AD 54 the Roman emperor Claudius officially prohibited the Druids by law. It was an obvious move for Rome to make: in order to conquer any people and absorb them, you first have to get rid of their intellectuals and destroy their cultural knowledge. It is only later that there emerged a group of Greek scholars, mainly in the school of Alexandria, who began to examine older Greek sources and develop a less bellicose and more appreciative view of the role of the Druids. This group was mainly concerned with gathering sources and traditions and meticulously citing their authorities, creating encyclopedias rather than producing first-hand empirical observations.

Professor Stuart Piggott tended to be dismissive of 'all second-hand library work, with no empirical observations' or 'field work among the Celts'. As opposed to the Roman-orientated accounts which sought to denigrate the Celts and Druids, he believed that the Alexandrian texts idealised the Druids. Certainly we could go so far as to say that the Alexandrian school was not concerned with propaganda in support of the Roman empire.

It is thanks to the Alexandrian school that we have references to earlier writers who had studied the Celts and the Druids but whose work no longer survived in its entirety. Timaeus (c. 356–260 BC) was used extensively as an authority by Diogenes Laertius and Clement of Alexandria. Soton of Alexandria (fl. 200–170 BC) was another major source quoted. Greek writers from Herodotus (c. 490–425 BC) to Alexander Cornelius Polyhistor (b. c. 105 BC) are quoted, although they did not use the specific term 'Druid' to describe Celtic intellectuals.

Dion Chrysostom (first century AD) was the first figure of importance in the new school and he had indeed conducted 'field work', having come from Bithynia next to Galatia and travelled widely there among the Celts. He is highly respectful of the Druids whom he compares, accurately, with the Brahmins of Hindu society. He mentions their intellectual attainments, crediting them with advances in branches of ancient wisdom, and describes their political influence.

The Celts appointed Druids, who likewise were versed in the art of seers and other forms of wisdom, without whom the kings were not permitted to adopt or plan any course, so that in fact it was these who ruled and the kings became their subordinates and instruments of their judgement, while themselves seated on golden thrones, and dwelling in great houses and being sumptuously feasted.

It is from the Alexandrian school that we first hear of the similarities between Druidical teaching and Pythagorean teaching, although opinion differed as to the direction in which this knowledge had travelled. Hippolytus (c. AD 170–c. 236) claimed that the Druids adopted Pythagorean ideas through the agency of Pythagoras' slave Zalmoxis, a Thracian who, according to Hippolytus, took the teaching to the Celts. Clement of Alexandria (c. AD 150–211/216), on the other hand, argued that Pythagoras picked up his ideas from the Celts, specifically the Druids.

In fact, the reincarnation philosophy of Pythagoras and his followers is only superficially the same as the teaching of the Celts. We will discuss this matter in more detail in Chapter 13.

It was Diogenes Laertius who wrote that the Druids taught in triads and that the basis of their philosophy was 'to honour the gods, to do no evil, and to practise bravery'. Laertius quotes from a writer called Aristotle who wrote a work called *Magicus*. However, this Aristotle is not to be confused with the famous Aristotle (384–322 BC), the pupil of Plato. The Aristotle who wrote *Magicus* was writing in the second century BC, and his is one of the earliest works to mention the Druids and deal with Celtic philosophy.

By the time the Celts started to commit their knowledge to writing in their own tongue, not only had their world become very much reduced in size but they had become Christian. This very act of becoming Christian was the means whereby the Druidic proscription on committing their knowledge to writing was lifted. Yet, at the same time, the general Christian attitude was to depict their pagan forefathers, especially the Druids, in as biased a manner as the pro-Roman writers had, but for different reasons.

In the emerging Christian world, the Druids were generally portrayed as opponents to Christianity, upholders of the ancient religion, and thereby were relegated to the role of shamans, magicians and 'witch doctors' although the degree of prejudice varied from writer to writer. There existed a sufficient number of writers, particularly among the early Irish scribes, who were still respectful of the Druids as an intellectual class and, indeed, held the view that the early Celtic saints were Druids, members of that class.

The references in the Irish texts and in the law texts agree that the Druids were regarded as the intellectual class in Ireland as well as in Gaul and Britain, and that their number included all the learned professions. The scholar P.W. Joyce listed eight points of similarity between the Irish and the Gaulish Druids, according to textual evidence.

As Christianity began to absorb the Celtic peoples, the Druids, both male and female, as the intellectuals, were the first to encompass the new learning. The fact that many of the early Celtic saints, male and female, were Druids or the children of Druids is significant. Christianity did not fight a battle with the Druids; the Druids absorbed the new religion and were the first to start promulgating its beliefs, thus giving rise to the phenomenon we now call the Celtic Church.

The term 'Celtic Church' is not strictly an accurate one because the early Christian churches among the Celtic peoples were in most essentials based on the Roman Christian ethos. Neither was there an identifiable organisation with a central leadership. Nevertheless, the Celtic population had developed their own form of Christianity and its ideas and customs were firmly based on their own cultural expression. It produced several fascinating early Church philosophers, such as Hilary of

Poitier and the famous Pelagius. It was Pelagius who was accused of trying to 'revive Druidic natural philosophy' and was eventually excommunicated by Rome after a conflict with Augustine of Hippo (AD 354–430).

For some centuries afterwards, Rome continued to accuse the Celts of following the teachings of Pelagius. In fact, all they were doing was following their own centuries-old philosophical outlook. This is amplified in Chapter 13.

Unfortunately, during the seventeenth century, in Germany, France and England, romantics began to reinvent the Druids having, in the wake of the Renaissance, discovered references to them in works such as Caesar's. Today there are countless 'Druidic movements' throughout the world, none of which has anything to do with the Druids of reality; with the Druids who were the intellectual class of Celtic society in the ancient world.

# 5

# CELTIC WARRIORS

The ancient Celts have been painted by classical writers as savage and making war for no reason at all except the 'fun' of it. They were, according to these writers, merely simple, barbaric children. As Strabo says: 'The whole race . . . is madly fond of war, and they are high-spirited and quick for battle, but otherwise simple . . .' Pausanias says that 'they rushed on their enemies with the unreasoning fury and passion of wild beasts. They had no kind of reasoning at all. They slashed with axe or sword and blind fury never left them until they were killed.' Livy, Florus and many others speak of Celtic warriors 'fighting like wild beasts'.

This is the image of the Celts that has been passed down even to the present day. Is it a just view? After all, the very people producing these descriptions of the Celts were also the same people who were conducting a systematic war against them. The conquerors always write the history books and we see the conquered through their prejudiced eyes.

Discerning historians have begun to read the ancient texts more carefully. For example, it is generally accepted that a

Celtic horde, for no reason at all, swept down on Rome in July 390 BC and attacked it. In fact, the story of Rome's conquest was not that simple.

We learn that one tribe, the Senones, had crossed the Apennines in search of new land to settle and had encamped outside the Etruscan city of Clusium. Brennus, their leader, asked the city fathers to grant them lands on which to settle in peace. The city elders viewed the newcomers as a threat and appealed to Rome, which had just exerted its military authority over the old Etruscan empire. Rome sent three ambassadors, the Fabii brothers, to negotiate between the Celts and Clusium. The Fabii brothers were young and arrogant.

Due to their arrogance, negotiations quickly broke down. An Etruscan army marched out of Clusium to face the Senones. Even Livy says that the Roman ambassadors then made a fatal step: 'they broke the law of nations and took up arms'. During the battle, the Fabii joined the ranks of the Etruscans and Quintus Fabius killed a Celtic chieftain. When the Celts realised that the supposedly 'neutral' Roman ambassadors were actually fighting for the Etruscans, they broke off the battle and withdrew to discuss this breach of international law.

The Celts were strict believers in law and the role of ambassador was a sacred trust. Indeed, the Romans later incorporated into Latin the Celtic word *ambactus*, which became 'ambassador' in many modern European languages. The Celts were horrified by the Romans' behaviour. They held a council meeting and decided to send their own ambassadors to Rome to lodge a complaint with the Roman Senate.

We are told that the Roman Senate, having listened to the Celtic ambassadors, found that the Celtic demand for an apology was reasonable; however, according to Livy and Plutarch, the Fabii were so powerful as patricians that the Senate felt obliged not to take action. They referred the matter to the people of Rome who not only approved of their actions but, to add insult to injury, elected the Fabii as military tribunes with consular powers for the following year. Livy admits: 'The Celtic envoys were naturally – and rightly – indignant!'

Plutarch even says that the *fetiales*, the college of Roman priests, selected for life among the patrician class and specialists in international law and negotiations, denounced the actions of the Fabii. However, Rome had made its decision. The Celtic ambassadors warned Rome of the consequence. The Senones, and we are speaking of one Celtic tribe here, then marched on Rome to exact retribution. It was a distance of 130 kilometres from Clusium. They did not harm anyone on their march to the city.

Contrary to all expectation the Celts did them [the people of the countryside] no harm, nor took aught from their fields, but even as they passed close by their cities, shouted out that they were marching on Rome and had declared war only on the Romans, but the rest of the people they regarded as friends.

This scarcely accords with the general view of the mindless barbaric horde which swept down on Rome. The Senones defeated the Roman army at the Allia, 18 kilometres north of the city, in a classic battle and moved on to Rome itself. They occupied the city for seven months before extracting an apology and a ransom in gold. They then withdrew. They did not want to form any empire over the Romans, simply to punish them for a transgression of accepted international behaviour.

So the image of the Celts as making war for the sake of making war is one we can dispense with. However, classical writers, particularly Roman writers or Greeks in Roman employ or patronage, loved to talk about Celtic savagery, the qualities of being fierce and uncivilised. By Rome's own bloodthirsty standards, any Celtic cruelty seems to have been quite mild.

Like all the Indo-European societies, the Celts did have a warrior caste – the equivalent of the Sanskrit *kshatriya*, the Roman *equites* and the Greek *hippeis*, which we generally tend to translate as 'knights'. The Celts were no different from other Indo-Europeans in that they had gods of war; their aristocracy or warrior caste had ostentatious weapons and armaments and took pride in individual heroism.

We also learn that they had special élite warrior bands which we will discuss shortly.

It is lucky that archaeology often acts as an antidote to the prejudices of the Roman writers. As Dr P.F. Stary pointed out: 'When the Romans described the Celts in terms of war, they did their best to disparage and degrade not only their abilities as fighting men but even their weapons.' Ironically, the Etruscans and then the Romans learned a great deal from the advanced weaponry of the Celts. Their own weapons, war helmets and shields, and even their tactics, owed much to Celtic innovations. Dr Stary emphasises that the Celtic weapons were 'a major influence on the Etruscan and Roman military systems'.

He also says: 'Fortunately, many Celtic weapons are known from graves, mainly in eastern and northern Italy, which give a good picture of the Celtic warrior's equipment and point to a longer occupation in the regions. Further, several Etruscan representations of Celtic warriors are known and form the basis for a better understanding of the Celtic influences on the "superior" Etruscan and Roman military systems.'

When the Celts first emerged into the Mediterranean world, iron helmets had generally ousted the weaker bronze war helmets. From graves we find these iron helmets appearing in the fourth century BC. Some are exquisitely rich, such as the mid-fourth-century BC helmet from Amfreville, France, with repoussé gold and inlaid with red glass, or the Agris helmet decorated with gold and coral inlay. Many of these helmets had fabulous decorations, often with extraordinary crests, hinged cheek pieces, internal neck guards and other embellishments. According to Diodorus Siculus:

> On their heads they wear bronze helmets which possess large projecting figures of enormous stature to the wearer. In some cases, horns form one part with the helmet, while in other cases, it is relief figures of the fore parts of birds or quadrupeds.

According to Dr Stary, the helmet bearing a round cap surmounted by a knob with neck and cheek guards was a Celtic invention. The Celts brought this design with them to Italy and it was rapidly adopted by the Etruscans and then by the Romans. The knob helmet was very suitable for flexible warfare. Whereas the initial Celtic design has cheek guards of three rounded discs in the form of a trefoil, the Etruscans added a sickle-shaped cheek piece.

The Celts also had better shields than the early Romans, large shields which were a better protective covering for the body. They were often carried by a central handle but no forearm strap. The Celtic shield doubled as an offensive weapon because it not only protected the holder from blows of the enemy but could be turned to strike the opponent as well. Examples of shields in early La Tène have been found around 1.1 metres tall but others have been depicted in reliefs as around 1.4 metres, which was the size adopted by the Romans. Diodorus Siculus observed:

> They have man-sized shields decorated in a manner peculiar to them. Some of these have projecting figures in bronze skilfully wrought not only for decoration but for protection.

It is very likely that the Latin word for shield, *scutum*, has its origin in the Celtic word which provides the basis of the

Irish *sciath* and its Welsh equivalent *ysgwyd*, meaning both shield and shoulder. The word *scutum* was used by the Romans particularly for the Celtic-style man-sized shield, which they did not develop until after their first encounters with the Celts. Attempts to explain *scutum* from the Latin root *obscurus* or even a more removed Greek root are not convincing.

The use of body armour by the Celts has been confirmed by archaeological finds and even by Roman representations of Celts in battle. Indeed, yet another Celtic technical innovation was the invention of chain mail around 300 BC. Diodorus Siculus mentions this, and shirts of interlocking iron rings have been found at Celtic sites. These were labour-intensive products and so only leading chieftains or kings probably wore them. Such shirts could weigh as much as 15 kilograms. The chain mail shirts became highly prized as spoils of war among the Romans who later adopted the idea in their own army. The Latin word *cataphractes* for a chain mail shirt has been argued to come from the Celtic root *cat*, war or battle, rather than the Latin *catena*, a fetter or chain. The word *caterva*, first used for a company of Celtic 'barbarian' soldiers, uses the same root.

Plutarch admits that the Romans soon learned that the Celtic power in battle lay in their swords, and that the Romans had to develop the new-style helmets, the longer shields and the technique of using their javelins to come under the enemy's swords when raised for the downward stroke, during their encounters with the Celtic warriors.

At the same time, Polybius, apparently quoting Quintus Fabius Pictor, claims the Celtic swords were inferior to the Roman swords, 'the Celtic sword being good only for a cut and not for a thrust'. Yet the very word *gladius*, the short Roman sword, is claimed to be of Celtic origin. Certainly, we find this short sword in use among the Celtiberians. The word is cognate with the Irish *claideb* and the Welsh *cleddyf*, a sword.

We learn from F. Vegetius Renatus (fourth century AD) that the Romans had to learn new methods to combat the tactics and equipment of the Celtic warriors. The ancient Romans, he says, had to be taught not to cut but to thrust with their swords. We hear much on the inability of the Celts to thrust with their swords but many of the Celtic swords have been found to have prominent points as well as long parallel cutting edges.

The Celts also gave to the Romans words for a variety of spears and javelins which, had the weapons been inferior, would not have been adopted by the Romans. The word *lancea*, describing a light spear, has remained in English as lance. The *mataris*, from which come *matara* and *materi*, a pike, was also adopted from Celtic. A *gaesum* was a strong heavy javelin, and the root *gae* for spear is still easily recognisable in Irish. There was also a *tragula*, a light javelin, which Pliny says was also the name for a Celtic sledge. Spears from the La Tène period have been found as long as 2.5 metres, together with spear heads whose serrated edges would have been deadly. It is attested that the Celtic warriors also had bows and slings but used them merely as defensive weapons. If their cavalry had to fall back, archers, who had been strategically placed, would support them and cover their withdrawal.

Perhaps the Celtic 'secret weapon' was their use of war chariots and cavalry. The Celtic armies were highly mobile and had developed the use of transport and a transport system, as we shall discuss in Chapter 10.

Martial spoke of the *covinus*, a war chariot, which eventually became the Latin *covincarius* or travelling cart. But the Celtic word *covignos* actually implied a shared transport. As war chariots were 'shared' by the warrior and his charioteer, this is quite acceptable. Martial, however, has the chariot's axles fixed with scythes, deadly *falces* or blades.

Chariots in battle were something new to the Romans.

Chariots as war machines had fallen into disuse in the ancient world centuries before the Roman–Celtic collision. The Celts had retained them or redeveloped them in the light of their innovations with working iron. With stronger wheels and the Celts' ability to open up a transport system, it was easy to move the chariots to where they were needed. As a weapon of war they were used mainly on the flanks with cavalry. In the initial stages of a battle they would drive against the enemy at speed for the purposes of causing panic. A thousand Celtic chariots took part in the battle of Sentium (295 BC) and also at Telamon (225 BC).

Diodorus Siculus comments:

> When going into battle, the Celts use two-horsed chariots which carry the charioteer and the warrior. When they meet with cavalry in war, they throw their javelins at the enemy, and, dismounting from their chariots, they join battle with their swords . . . they also bring freemen as servants choosing them from among the poor, and these they use as charioteers and shield bearers.

Livy admits that, in battle, often the first Roman lines would be trodden underfoot by the rush of cavalry and chariots. Once the lines were broken the Celts used their chariots as a means of transporting the warriors to their combat positions as foot soldiers, just as chariots had been used in Homeric Greece.

After the battle of Telamon the chariot as a war machine fell into disuse among the Continental Celts who came to rely on cavalry and the staying power of infantry. When Julius Caesar, nearly 200 years after Telamon, took his Roman legionaries to Britain, he seemed surprised to find that war chariots were in use there. He wrote:

> In chariot fighting the Britons begin by driving all over the field hurling javelins, and generally the terror inspired by the

horses and noise of the wheels is sufficient to throw their opponents' ranks into disorder. Then, after making their way between the squadrons of their own cavalry, they jump down from the chariots and engage on foot. In the meantime their charioteers retire a short distance from the battle and place the chariots in such a position that their masters, if hard pressed by numbers, have an easy means of retreat to their own lines. Thus they combine the mobility of cavalry with the staying power of infantry; and by daily training and practice they attain such proficiency that, even on a steep incline, they are able to control the horses at full gallop, and to check and turn them in a moment. They can run along the chariot pole, stand on the yoke, and get back into the chariot as quick as lightning.

Caesar confesses that the soldiers of his VII Legion were unnerved by the British chariots.

From early Irish documentation and archaeological remains we find that chariots were also in use in Ireland. Irish mythological texts give fine descriptions of chariot warfare, individual heroic episodes as well as warfare on a greater scale, such as the descriptions of the *Táin* war.

The other powerful weapon of the Celtic armies was their cavalry. They even won begrudging admiration from the Romans, who adopted the Celtic horse goddess Epona as an accepted deity of the empire as well as recruiting cavalry regiments from the Celts. This was the only Celtic deity they adopted and her feast day was held in Rome on 18 December. According to Strabo the best cavalry in the Roman army were Celtic. He says of the Celts: 'Although they are all fine fighting men, yet they are better as cavalry than as infantry and the best of the Roman cavalry is recruited from among them.'

Like the chariots, Celtic cavalry combined mobility and staying power for the cavalryman would not only unnerve the enemy by shock charges but also dismount and fight on foot when the need arose. The Celtiberians were noted for having small pegs attached to their horses' reins so that they could ride into a battle, dismount and fix the pegs into the ground to prevent the horse from straying while they fought as infantry.

Pausanias, in describing the Celtic cavalry at the battle of Thermopylae in 279 BC, has this description of a Celtic cavalry formation:

> To each mounted warrior were attached two servants, who were themselves skilled riders and, like their masters, had a horse. When the Celtic cavalry were in battle, the servants remained behind the ranks and proved useful in the following way. Should a horseman or his horse fall, the slave brought him a horse to mount; if the rider was killed, the slave mounted the horse in his master's place; if both rider and horse were killed, there was a mounted man ready. When a rider was wounded, one slave brought back to the camp the wounded man, while the other took his vacant place in the ranks . . . This organisation is called in their own language *trimarcisia*, for I would have you know that *marca* is the Celtic name for a horse.

Leaving aside the misconception of 'slave' in the description, certainly the word *marca* is accurately recorded as one of the old Celtic terms for a horse. The word is easily recognisable as *march* (Welsh), *margh* (Cornish) and *marc'h* (Breton).

Flavius Arrianus, or Arrian (b. *c*. AD 85–90), a Greek from Nicomedia in Bithynia, who made a career in the Roman army, was much impressed by Celtic cavalry and says that the Romans borrowed their cavalry tactics from the Celts. Talking of witnessing some military manoeuvres, Arrian says that the Celts, on one particular training exercise,

> . . . ride into the mock battle armed with helmets made of iron or brass and covered with gilding to attract the partic-

ular attention of the spectators. They have yellow plumes attached to the helmets, not to serve any other useful purpose than for display. They carry oblong shields, unlike the shields for a real battle but lighter in weight – the object of the exercise being smartness and display . . . and gaily decorated. Instead of breastplates, they wear tunics, made just like real breastplates, sometimes scarlet, sometimes purple, sometimes multi-coloured. And they have hose, not loose like those in fashion among the Parthians and Armentians, but fitting closely to the limbs.

Livy has much to say about the tactics of the Celtic cavalry. The Spartans respected the Celtic cavalry when they fought for them against the Thebans. The Hellenic kingdoms were among the first to hire the services of Celtic mercenaries, specifically cavalry units. The Carthaginians also used Celtic cavalry to good effect and, as we have seen, even the Romans, in spite of their sneering criticisms, eventually employed Celtic cavalry as auxiliaries in their army after they had conquered the Celts of Gaul. Indeed, Celtic cavalry became an essential part of the imperial army of the Caesars.

The Celts were among the first Northern Europeans to evolve a saddle and the Celtic saddles were very intricate. A key technical innovation was the four-pommel saddle. Historians once thought that cavalry could have only a limited effectiveness until the invention of the stirrup. However, in the La Tène period the Celts developed a saddle with a firm seat by means of the four pommels, two behind the rump and one angled out over each thigh. The rider sat in, rather than on, this saddle.

Greek and Roman writers mention the spectacular clothing which the Celts wore in battle. According to Diodorus Siculus, the Celts 'wear colourful clothing, tunics dyed and embroidered in many colours, and garments which they call *bracae* [breeches]; and they wear striped cloaks, fastened by a brooch, thick in winter and light in summer, worked in a variegated,

closely set pattern.' The trousers were particularly worn by
Celtic cavalrymen; being such a strange garment to the toga-
wearing Romans, they were quickly noticed and adopted
whence the Celtic word *bracae* came into the Latin language
and from there made its way into other languages including
English (as breeches).

Linen shirts, tunics and shoes of leather were worn, often
with cloaks of coarse wool. It later became fashionable in
Rome to wear a *sagus* (later *sagum*), initially a Celtic warrior's
cloak. The word was used symbolically by Cicero in the
phrase *saga sumere* or *ad saga ire* – to take up arms or prepare
for war – and *saga poner*, to lay down arms. Another Celtic
cloak used by the Romans was the *caracallus* (hooded cloak).
The word *cacullus* derived from this and eventually gave
English the word 'cowl' with cognates to be found in many
other European languages.

The Celts also liked wearing ornaments to indicate their
status in society, such as gold bracelets or the brooches with
which their cloaks were fastened. Kings and chieftains,
together with warriors and women of position, wore gold
necklets, usually a torc around their necks.

One particular aspect of several of the battles they fought
with the Celts fascinated the Romans. They found that bands
of Celtic warriors went into battle naked. These warrior
bands were wrongly identified as a tribe which the Romans,
using a Celtic word, called the Gaesatae. Polybius describes a
contingent at the battle of Telamon. They went into battle
with only sword and shield. Camillus had earlier captured
some of these naked Celtic warriors and showed them to the
Romans saying, according to Appian: 'These are the creatures
who assail you with such terrible cries in battle, bang their
swords and spears on their shields to make a din, and shake
their long sword and toss their hair.'

The Greeks also encountered these special groups.
Dionysius of Halicarnassus was disparaging:

Our enemies fight bare-headed, their breasts, sides, thighs, legs are all bare, and they have no protection except from their shields; their weapons of defence are thin spears and long sword. What injury could their long hair, their fierce looks, the clashing of their arms and the brandishing of their weapons do us?

At Telamon Polybius gives a totally misleading interpretation:

The Insubres and the Boii wore their trousers and light cloaks but the Gaesatae had been moved by their thirst for glory and their defiant spirit to throw away these garments and so they took up their positions in front of the whole army naked and wearing nothing but their arms. They believed that they would be better equipped for action in this state, as the ground was in places overgrown with brambles and these might catch in their clothes and hamper them in the use of their weapons.

The Gaesatae were not a tribe at all but a group of élite professional warriors who fought naked for religious purposes as they believed that it enhanced their martial karma, their spiritual vibrations in battle. This contact with Mother Earth added to their spiritual aura, ensuring rebirth in the Otherworld if they perished in this one. The word 'Gaesatae' has a cognate in the old Irish *gaiscedach*, a champion or one who bears arms. *Gaisced* is a word for weapons, and *gaesum* is a spear. We have an entire series of words from this root such as *gaisemail* (warlike or valiant), *gaiscemiacht* (military prowess and wisdom) and *gaisce* (wisdom). Was the warrior deemed to be a wise person?

In spite of Dr Simon James' claim that the insular Celts, unlike their Continental cousins, were 'egalitarian farming communities lacking warrior nobles', we find that such warrior nobles did exist. In fact, insular Celtic mythology and record is full of references to such groups. We have the Fianna of Fionn Mac Cumhail – the word means 'warriors', and it appears as an ancient Indo-European term. The cognate in Sanskrit, *vanóti*, means 'to win or conquer'. The word survives in Latin as *venatio*, a hunter, and in English as 'win'. More interestingly, it appears in the Gaulish Celtic tribal name of the Veneti, who gave their name to Vannes in Brittany, and to the Veneti of the Po valley, who gave their name to Venice. We also have the term *feinnid*, a word allied to Fianna, for a band of warriors. *Tréin-fher*, man of strength, described a champion, and *óglach* a young hero. More ancient than these words is *curad*, which, according to Windisch and Stokes, is the root of the name for the warrior élite of the kings of Connacht, Gamanrad. Yet in later texts the name is expressed as Gamhanrhide, using *rhide* or *ridire* meaning 'knight'.

There are other groups of warrior élites such as the Craobh Ruadh (Red Branch) warriors of Ulaidh (Ulster) which Professor O'Rahilly argues was probably a mistranscription of Craobh Rígh (Royal Branch). We also find the Degad, a band of warriors exiled to Munster. The Nasc Niadh were the élite bodyguard serving the kings of Munster. From its beginnings the Niadh Nask (the military order of the golden chain), as it is now called, developed into a dynastic nobiliary honour at the bestowal of the head of the Eóghanacht dynasty. Since the death of Donal IX MacCarthy Mór (1596), last regnant King of Desmond and titular King of the Two Munsters, the order has remained as a valid and legal dynastic honour into modern times. According to the late The Rt Hon. The Lord Borthwick of that Ilk, President of the International Commission for Orders of Chivalry: 'The Niadh Nask is without doubt one of the most ancient nobiliary honours in the world, if not the most ancient!'

In several ancient Irish sources there appears another warrior élite called the Ríglach, or royal heroes. In the *Metrical Dindshenchas*, the *Book of Leinster* and the *Betha*

*Colmáin maic Lúachain*, it denotes a royal bodyguard, meriting a capital letter. In later middle Irish texts the meaning of the word has degenerated first to veterans and then simply to old people.

The Ríglach, as a group of young warriors recruited only from the sons of kings, finds a parallel in the Rajputs of the Hindu culture, who developed into a warrior tribe, their name deriving from *raj*, king, and *putrá*, sons. The Rajputs of India boasted they were all the sons of kings, descendants of royal warriors, and formed the principality of Rajputana in north-west India arising as a powerful force in the seventh century AD. They lost power after Indian independence. In the folk memory of the Ríglach, might we be seeing the basis of that Irish cliché, 'We are all kings' sons'?

In the ancient Celtic world we have overwhelming numbers of names incorporating the royal element, both tribal names such as Bituriges, 'Kings of the World', and personal names such as Dumnorix, 'World King'. We know that after the Claudian invasion of Britain, King Cogidubnus of the Regni, whose territory was in West Sussex, was given the title '*rex (et) legatus Augusti in Britannia*' for his pro-Roman attitudes. His capital Noviomagus, Chichester, was called the 'New Plain'. Regni was not, as some have suggested, a renamed Celtic tribe because their king had been confirmed in his kingship by the Romans. They still bore their old Celtic name – 'King's People' or perhaps even 'King's Sons'!

The Romans even had lessons to learn from the Celts in terms of battle tactics. Livy mentions that at Sentium the Celtic warriors deployed a *testudo* (tortoise) – a battle tactic in which the fighting men locked their shields together to form an impregnable wall. Once the Romans had adopted the Celtic shield, for it is clear that such interlocking could not be achieved with the older Roman round shield or buckler, the *testudo* became regarded as a Roman battle tactic.

If the Celts were initially able to teach the Romans about

warfare, why was it that, with the exception of northern Britain and Ireland, they were eventually defeated and swallowed in the *pax Romana*? Dr Simon James proposes that the explanation lay in the contrasting nature of the two societies. They thought about war and waged it in different ways.

To the Celts warfare was a matter of honour which could begin and end in a personal single combat. It was often a matter of individual courage. Generally, the Celts were not interested in central authority and discipline. They thought and acted as individuals and were natural anarchists. In modern times these attributes are seen as laudable. In ancient times, they were the reason for the downfall of the Celtic peoples.

We find that the excuse for many of the invasions of Celtic territory by foreign forces, who then remained to exploit the Celts, was an invitation from a disgruntled Celtic leader who refused to accept the decision of his fellows. Caesar invaded Britain on the excuse of putting back a prince on his father's throne. Mandubracius of the Trinovantes, chased out of his territory, went to Gaul and sought Caesar's help. Caesar did place him on the throne of his father. But, if Celtic law was being followed, in which primogeniture was not recognised, perhaps Mandubracius had no right to sit there? Mandubracius, ironically, means 'Black Traitor'.

The same internal squabbles, in which the electoral system of the Celtic succession laws was challenged or a deposed king did not accept the ruling of the law, can be seen in many examples throughout Celtic history. Diarmuid Mac Murrough of Hy-Kinsella, deposed as King of Leinster, sought Henry II's aid to put him back on the throne of Leinster with results that still rebound in Ireland until this day. Maol Callum (Malcolm), grandson of Duncan, sought English help to put him on the throne of Scotland, and overthrow the legitimate ruler Macbeth who had ruled for seventeen years. Today it is Macbeth who is the villain and Maol Callum the 'rightful' king.

As an Indo-European people, the Celts used a solar symbol of well-being, which in Sanskrit was called the swastika, a symbol perverted by Nazi Germany in the 1930s. The motif is seen here in a 2nd century BC embossed silver horse harness found at the Villa Vecchia Manerbio.

Generally regarded as 'The Father of the Gods' in Celtic terms, Cernunnos, the horned god, is equivalent to the Irish 'The Dagda'. This is a panel from the Gundestrup cauldron.

A Celtic inscription from Gaul, written in Greek letters, from Vaison-la-Romaine. A Celt named Segomaros states he has dedicated a shrine to Belisma, a Celtic goddess whose name means 'the shining one'. 2nd/1st century BC.

In the Hallstatt period the Celts stylized heads. This bearded head from the 5th century BC is from a bronze ornament on a wooden jug and may well have been that of a king or warrior.

In the Le Tène period, Celtic heads began to be more realistic and this may be a portrait of a prominent leader or chieftain from the 3rd century BC found in Aix-en-Provence.

In trying to denigrate Celtic society, Caesar claimed that the Celts conducted human sacrifices and put victims into a large man-like object made of wicker and burnt them alive. This reconstruction of the idea comes from Aylett Sammes' *Britannia Antiqua Illustrata*, 1676. There was no evidence of such practices.

The Druidic teaching on Celtic afterlife is depicted on the Gundestrup cauldron showing a god dipping the dead bodies in the cauldron of life and restoring them to the world of the living.

An Arch Druid in His Judicial Habit.

From the 17th century, and particularly into the 18th and 19th centuries, Druids were 'reinvented' and seized popular imagination. This illustration from *Costumes of the British Isles* (1821), Meyrick and Smith, shows how people fondly imagined Druids. The reality was quite different.

One of the most spectacular pieces of Celtic military art, the bronze shield found at Battersea, in the Thames, dating from the 1st century BC. Note the swastika designs in the enamelling.

Celtic war helmets were highly decorated. This one, bearing horns, was found in the Thames and is thought to have been placed there as a votive offering. It is dated to the 1st century BC.

A female figure of the early Celtic period in the Po valley, found in Caldevigo.

A bucket found at Aylesford, Kent, made of bronze and wood and dated to the 1st century BC. An essential item for farming and domestic use.

While Celtic farmhouses on the Continent were generally built in rectangular fashion, insular Celtic farm buildings were round. This is a reconstruction of a typical Celtic farm building of the 1st century BC at Castell Henllys, Newport, Dyfed.

In early Celtic society the wheel was an important cosmological symbol, often symbolizing the solar wheel. The 'wheel of the sun' was how the ancient Celts viewed the constellations of the stars. The Gundestrup cauldron depicts a horned helmeted figure holding a spoked wheel.

Because Celtic road builders constructed their roads with wood, Celtic roads have survived only by being preserved in bogland. The Corlea Road, a causeway across a bog in Co. Longford, is a magnificent example and has been radio carbon dated to 148 BC.

Celtic chariots were a popular motif on Celtic coins. This coin, which also shows human headed horses drawing the chariot, is attributed to the Namnetes, dated to the 1st century BC.

It was the Celtic custom, as Diodorus Siculus remarked, when gathered for battle, for a warrior to step out of the ranks and challenge the most valiant champion among the enemy to single combat, brandishing his weapons, boasting of his deeds and those of his ancestors in order to break the nerve of his opponent. Depending on the results of the combat the entire battle could be decided.

The problem was, in battle against the Romans, that cultural differences resulted in different endings. If a Celt was beaten in single combat, often the Celtic army would accept that the matter had been resolved and fade away. If a Celt won the combat then the Roman forces did not go away and merely fell on the Celts in fury to exact revenge.

In defeat, the Celtic leaders who had led their people into such extremity would either seek death in combat or commit ritual suicide. This was not at all unusual among the ancient Indo-European societies. The Roman generals often did the same. Catuvolcus, an ageing joint king with Ambiorix, of the Eburones, 'poisoned himself with yew' when his people's countryside was laid waste by Caesar. When the Gaulish uprising of AD 21 failed, Julius Florus of the Treverii and Julius Sacrovir of the Aedui both committed suicide, as did Boudicca of the Iceni in Britain following her defeat in AD 61.

There is no extensive evidence of women generally taking part in warfare, although there is a strong insular Celtic tradition of female warriors and queens leading their people in battle. Women like Boudicca or Cartimandua certainly did command their people in battle during the Roman conquest. We will discuss their role in detail in Chapter 6.

For the Romans, war was a cold-blooded profession. The legionaries had been trained to fight as units. Unquestioning obedience to the commands of their officers was essential and they relied on their fellows to act with them as a cohesive force. Roman generals wrote and studied military treatises, and planning and method became important. That planning, that ruthlessness, finally gave Rome the military advantage. Indeed, a certain lack of humanity, a devotion to discipline, and a severity of punishment to any who lacked complete commitment to the will of a central power, appear necessary for the growth of an imperial regime. The Roman legionary had to be more frightened of his superiors than he was of the enemy. The same principle has often applied in modern armies.

However, the Roman claim that the Celts never showed any staying power in warfare was not true. In 57 BC, the Nervii at the battle of the River Sambre, a tributary of the Meuse, fought to the death under their chieftain, Boduognatus. Caesar, hardly ever speaking well of the Celts in battle, was moved to report:

> The enemy, even in their desperate plight, showed such bravery that when their front ranks had fallen those immediately behind stood on their prostrate bodies to fight and when these too fell and the corpses were piled high, the survivors kept hurling javelins as though from the top of a mount, and flung back the spears intercepted by their shields. Such courage accounted for the extraordinary feats they had performed already. Only heroes could have made light of crossing a wide river, clambering up the steep banks, and launching themselves on such a difficult position.

The Nervii, Caesar reports, were almost annihilated. Only 500 men were left capable of bearing arms out of the 60,000 who had formed their army. Of 600 nobles only three survived.

When the Celts did fight as an army, they fought as a tribal group and were divided into septs or sub-divisions of the tribe – just as they were at Culloden in 1746. If the model of the Scottish clan army is a model for the ancient Celts, it seems that each sept had an hereditary place in the line of battle.

The 'age of choice', when Celtic males came to manhood,

was seventeen years old, so every male over that age, fit enough to carry arms, would be part of the regiment of his clan or tribe. The chieftain was automatic commander. They marched into battle with pipes, drums and voices raised in war songs or battle cries.

Livy describes how the Celts used such noise and tumult to throw their enemies into confusion and terror. 'They are given to wild outburst and they fill the air with hideous songs and varied shouts.' Further, 'their songs, as they go into battle, their yells and leapings, and the dreadful noise of arms as they beat their shields in some ancestral custom, all this is done with one purpose, to terrify the enemy.' Diodorus Siculus says the Celts had trumpets (*carnyx*) that were peculiar to them. Such trumpets may be seen on the panels of the Gundestrup Cauldron, and fragments have been found at various Celtic sites. The mouthpiece of one trumpet in the shape of a boar's head was found in Banff. Representations of other trumpets are seen on a triumphant Roman arch at Orange in southern France. 'When they blow upon them, they produce a harsh sound, suitable to the tumult of war.'

All in all, then, we see that the Celtic warrior was every bit as sophisticated and well armed, though perhaps not as well disciplined, as his Greek and Roman counterparts.

# 6

# CELTIC WOMEN

Celtic women were the subject of much comment from the writers of Greece and Rome, and there continues to be much speculation and argument about them. Compared with their sisters in the classical world, they enjoyed considerable rights and freedom and, indeed, even political power. Plutarch reports how Celtic women ambassadors intervened to prevent a war among the Celts of the Po valley during the fourth century BC. Women ambassadors from the Celtic Volcae were sent to negotiate a treaty with Hannibal. When the Romans arrived in Britain they found Celtic warrior queens ruling in their own right. Were these exceptions to the rule or did Celtic women have a role in Celtic society which made their contemporaries in Greece and Rome appear primitive?

The evidence from the late Hallstatt and early La Tène graves on the Continent, such as the 'princess of Vix' and the female chariot burial from Rheinheim, shows that some women were regarded as worthy enough to be buried in rich graves with the accoutrements usually reserved for warrior kings. Chariot burials of females have been found in what was the Parisii territory of eastern Yorkshire during the third to first centuries BC.

The classical writers are eager to point out that Celtic women are not as 'womanly' as the Greeks and Romans. Ammianus Marcellinus says:

> A whole troop of foreigners would not be able to withstand a single Celt if he called his wife to his assistance. The wife is even more formidable. She is usually very strong, and has blue eyes; in rage her neck veins swell, she gnashes her teeth, and brandishes her snow-white robust arms. She begins to strike blows mingled with kicks, as if they were so many missiles sent from the string of a catapult.
>
> The voices of these women are formidable and threatening, even when they are not angry but being friendly. But all Celtic women, with equal care, keep neat and clean and in some areas, such as among the Aquitani, no woman can be seen, be she never so poor, in soiled or ragged clothing.

'The women of the Celts,' Diodorus Siculus comments, 'are nearly as tall as the men and they rival them also in courage.'

Our classical sources, however, are not interested in recording any details about Celtic female leaders unless they are exceptional, such as Cartimandua or Boudicca. We know of a ruler called Onomaris, arguably meaning 'Mountain Ash', who was chieftainess of the Scordisci. She is recorded as leading her people in battle against the Illyrians of the Balkans. The Scordisci settled by the Danube and founded their capital at Sinigdunum, which is now Belgrade.

Also from this area emerged 'Queen Teuta' in 231 BC. A group of tribes in the region of modern Kotor on the Illyrian coast were ruled by a king called Agron, the masculine form of Agrona, a Celtic war goddess, whose tradition survived in Wales as 'the Washer of the Ford'. In the autumn of 231 BC

Agron died from pleurisy. He was succeeded by a woman called Teuta. This comes from the Celtic *teutates* (people), cognate to the Irish *tuath* (tribe) and similar to the Gaulish male name or title Toutiorix (King of the People). Teuta may well mean 'The People's Queen'.

Polybius has little good to say about Teuta, mainly because she decided to extend her kingdom by attacking the neighbouring Greek state of Epiros. Whatever else he was, Polybius was a Greek, a prominent member of the Achaean Confederation. Teuta's warriors are clearly identified as Celts. The kingdom of Epiros was employing Celtic mercenaries at the time, and Polybius is very sarcastic about this fact. Indeed, the Celtic mercenaries decided to join forces with their compatriots from Teuta's kingdom. Polybius is scathing about Epiros' decision to entrust its safety to the hands of such people.

Rome decided to take a hand in the affairs of Teuta and sent ambassadors to lecture her. If the arrogance of the Fabii ambassadors towards the Celts at Clusium is anything to go by, perhaps it is no wonder that Teuta, as Polybius puts it, 'gave way to a fit of womanish petulance'. She had the Roman ambassador and his party assassinated. But because the rules of hospitality applied, she waited until the ambassador and his party were already on their ships about to make sail for Rome. It was not a politically wise thing to do. Rome dispatched 200 ships commanded by Gnaeus Fulvius to attack Teuta's kingdom.

Teuta and her people were besieged in Kotor by legions commanded by Lucius Postumius who systematically reduced the rest of her cities. Teuta finally concluded a treaty with Rome, agreed to pay reparation and gave assurances of her good behaviour in the future. Rome's victory was celebrated in 228 BC.

The next major female Celtic figure we come across is Chiomara, wife of Ortagion of the Tolistoboii of Galatia. At the time when the Romans invaded Galatia under Gnaeus Manlius Volso in 189 BC, Chiomara was captured by the Romans. A centurion raped her. When the centurion discovered she was the wife of the Celtic king they were fighting against, greed overcame caution, or perhaps the Roman was arrogant. He sent a ransom note to Ortagion. The exchange took place on a river bank in neutral territory. When the centurion was busy picking up his gold, Chiomara turned, took a sword from those who had come to escort her to her husband, and calmly decapitated him. She then took his head in Celtic fashion to her husband. The exchange of greeting related by Plutarch is fascinating.

'Woman, a fine thing [is] good faith.'
    '[A] better thing, only one man alive who had intercourse with me.'

Professor David Rankin has pointed out that the recorded words 'preserve genuine, gnomic Celtic idiom'.

Plutarch gives information about another Celtic heroine of Galatia. Camma, probably a priestess of Brigantu, the equivalent of the goddess Artemis, was married to a chieftain named Sinatos. Sinatos was murdered by a man called Sinorix (King of Storms) and Camma was forced to marry him. It was a ritual at wedding feasts to drink from a common cup. Camma put poison in the cup and allayed Sinorix's suspicion by drinking first, so accepting death herself so long as Sinorix drank and died as well.

There is not much written about Celtic women rulers until after the Romans invaded Britain in AD 43. We find that in the Lancashire and Yorkshire area there was a tribal confederation called the Brigantes. It is argued that they were named after Brigantia, the Exalted One. They were ruled by a queen named Cartimandua (Sleek Pony) and Tacitus describes her as *pollens nobilitate* (powerful in lineage). She was, he adds, 'flourishing in all the splendour of wealth and power'.

Cartimandua decided to accept Roman suzerainty and become a client king. She proved her loyalty to Rome by betraying and handing over Caractacus (Caradog), the high king of southern Britain, who had made the mistake of seeking asylum with her. In fact, one of the tribes that made up the Brigantian confederation, the Setanti, had, in AD 48, supported Caractacus, presumbly against her wishes. Was this her revenge? Cartimandua was fairly secure until her husband, Venutius of the Jugantes, began to take an anti-Roman view. He was, says Tacitus, 'since the loss of Caractacus, the first in fame and valour and military experience.'

We can only guess at the domestic situation. Cartimandua divorced her husband and asked the Romans to send a legion to help put down Venutius' rebellion. The legion, commanded by Cesius Nasica, was duly sent. She married her former husband's armour-bearer and charioteer, Vellocatus, which has been seen as another form of the name Billicotas (Courteous Warrior). However, Venutius appears to have had some degree of support among the Brigantes and to have driven Cartimandua out of her kingdom. The Romans only just rescued her and her new husband.

In AD 72 Quintus Petilius Cerialis finally caught up with Venutius near Stanwick and defeated him, smashing the powerful Brigantian confederation. Claudius Ptolemaeus, the Greek geographer (c. AD 100–178) placed the Brigantes in Ireland during his survey. This might not be a mistake, for it is possible that some elements of the Brigantes fled, like many other Britons, to seek political refuge in Ireland. In 1927 excavations carried out at Lambay Island, off the coast of Dublin, unearthed artefacts that are untypical of Irish weapons but closer to the finds in cemeteries from the Brigantian area.

Dominating all the women of the ancient Celtic world is undoubtedly the figure of Boudicca, or Boadicea as it is Latinised. The name means 'Victory'. We are told that her husband was Prasutagus, king of the Iceni, in what is now Norfolk. The Iceni were a rich and cultivated people, issuing their own coinage since about 10 BC. When the Romans invaded in AD 43, it seemed that Prasutagus accepted Roman overlordship and became a client king, paying a tax to Rome so long as Rome did not interfere with his kingdom.

In AD 60/61 Prasutagus died, leaving Boudicca a widow. Nero's policy was now one of direct rule. Perhaps because of this Prasutagus, in Roman fashion, had made a will leaving his kingdom and goods to be divided between the Roman emperor and his two daughters 'in equal shares'. This has caused some confusion among scholars: the fact that Boudicca was subsequently accepted as ruler of the Iceni meant that she had to have a bloodline claim in her own right as well as being elected by her family to that position in accordance with Celtic law.

The argument, however, was irrelevant because the civil administrator of the Roman province of Britain, Catus Decianus, extended Roman direct rule over the Iceni. He did so in a particularly brutish way. He marched with some troops into their kingdom, whereupon the Iceni, unsuspectingly, greeted him as an ally with traditional Celtic hospitality. Decianus then turned his troops on the people, seizing goods and leading away citizens as hostages and slaves. Boudicca protested at the ravaging of her people and she herself was stripped and whipped in public while her two teenage daughters were raped in front of her. Others of her relations were taken into slavery and the soldiers confiscated goods, chattels and personal wealth.

Boudicca now emerges as absolute ruler and war leader of the Iceni. 'This is not the first time that Britons have been led to battle by a woman,' records Tacitus. Certainly other tribes came flocking to her banner. The Trinovantes, the Coritani and the Catuvellauni followed her summons. Boudicca began to march her army on the centre of Roman administration, Camulodunum, once the Trinovante capital. The Romans had rebuilt it with a great temple to Claudius, regarded as god as well as emperor.

Catus Decianus was in London now but sent 200 legionaries to reinforce the garrison, which was comprised of retired veterans and auxiliary troops. Quintus Petilius Cerialis, then commander of the IX Hispania Legion at Lindon (Lincoln) in the land of the Coritani, was ordered to hasten south to protect the Roman capital.

Boudicca proved to be a military strategist of exceptional merit. She managed to ambush the IX Hispania – some 6000 legionaries and 500 cavalry. The IX Hispania had a long battle record and had won their spurs in the Iberian campaigns against the Celts before being sent to Pannonia where the legion had helped in the pacification of the Balkans. Boudicca annihilated this élite force except for Petilius Cerialis, his general staff and his 500 cavalry who managed to escape back to their fortress at Lincoln. Boudicca had no time for siege work. She turned back to Camulodunum.

She took the town and burnt it within two days, destroying the buildings raised by the Romans to mark their conquest and domination, including the great Temple of Claudius. Then she turned on Londinium (London). The population of 20,000 consisted mainly of Roman veterans, traders and civil administrators who had followed the Roman armies in their new conquest. It was the financial capital of Roman administration and a large trading port. The II Augusta Legion was ordered to march from the south and defend it but the camp marshal, Poenius Postumus, hearing of the fate of the IX Hispania, refused to march out. He was barely a day's march from the city. After the news of the destruction of

Londinium, Poenius Postumus took his own life rather than face court martial.

Verulamium (St Albans) was at that time the third major Roman settlement in Britain, populated also by retired Roman veterans, settlers, traders and merchants. The local Celts appear to have been driven out into the surrounding countryside. Once again, Boudicca's army smashed into the city and destroyed it.

The only major Roman force left in Britain was the army of the Roman governor and military commander, Seutonius Paullinus, who had the XIV Gemina and XX Valeria Legions with him. He had been campaigning in what is now North Wales. He had turned and marched his legions back to the south-east at the news of the uprising. All depended on how he faced the British Celts, for defeat would mean that the Roman conquest would be turned back.

Roman accounts are to be treated with some degree of scepticism. Suetonius was reported to have 10,000 men. This is reasonable enough, for two legions at maximum strength would number 12,000 men. But Boudicca is credited with 230,000 warriors at her command. Tacitus gives the result of the battle as 80,000 British dead and only 400 Romans. However the figures work out, it was a Roman victory and appears to have been fought north-west of St Albans.

Little is known of Boudicca and her daughters after this. She did not fall into Roman hands. Tacitus believes she escaped the battlefield and then took poison rather than fall into Roman hands. Dio Cassius says she simply fell sick and died, and adds that the Britons gave her a rich burial. What a find that tomb would be if it had, somewhere, withstood the ravages of time and grave robbers. Dio Cassius says that Boudicca was also a priestess of Andrasta, goddess of battle and victory. This seems to be the same goddess as Andarte worshipped by the Vocontii of Gaul.

We have a few more glimpses of powerful Celtic women

from the period. Dio Cassius mentions Veleda, 'a virgin prophetess among the Celts' during the reign of Vespasian. Veleda is clearly a Celtic name deriving from the root *gwel*, to see, a title rather than a name and meaning 'Seeress'. Veleda was said to arbitrate between rulers and prevent war. Dio Cassius says that her successor was a woman called Ganna whose name derives from the Celtic word for intermediary. Ganna, according to Dio Cassius, accompanied Masyos, king of the Senones, of Gaul, on an embassy to the emperor Domitian, the younger son of Vespasian (AD 81–96). Flavius Vopiscus identifies Ganna as being from the Gaulish tribe of the Tungri (whence modern Tongres, near Liège, Belgium).

In the classical sources there are references to women as priestesses and prophetesses. Strabo mentions a priestess called Namnites at the Loire. He also says that such women were married but very independent of their husbands. Aedius Lampridius, one of the authors of *Historia Augusta* , written *c*. fourth century AD, has a Druidess foretelling the defeat of Alexander Severus before he set out on his expedition in AD 235. Flavius Vopiscus has Gaius Aurelius Diocletia (AD 283–305) as a young man residing in the land of the Tungri of Gaul and being told that he would become emperor. Vopiscus says that Lucius Domitius Aurelianus (*c*. AD 215–275) consulted a *Gallicanas Dryades* (Gaulish Druidess) to ask if his children would reign after him. The answer she gave Aurelian was in the negative.

While historians tend to dismiss all references to Irish history prior to the Christian period and deem the personalities mentioned 'mythological', we find among the Irish chronicles two fascinating references to female rulers. Annals record that in 377 BC Macha Mong Ruadh became queen of Ireland and reigned for seven years. The traditions of Macha are, unfortunately, mixed with the traditions of a Celtic war goddess called Macha. Nevertheless, the historical figure and the goddess appear as two distinct entities. This might be said to be a parallel to Brigit, as an historical Christian saint, taking on the traditions of Brigit, the Celtic goddess of fertility.

The chronicles record that Macha's father, Aedh Ruadha, was drowned in the cataract at Béal Atha Sennaidh (Ballyshannon), Co. Donegal. He had been 'King of Ireland' ruling alternately with his cousins Dithorba and Cimbaeth. On her father's death, Macha was elected ruler by the *derbfhine*, an electoral college formed from three generations of the royal family. Dithorba and Cimbaeth disagreed with the decision and wanted to keep the kingship to themselves. Macha promptly raised an army and defeated Dithorba, taking his five sons as hostages. She made them and the prisoners of war build the ramparts of her new fortress of Emain Macha. She came to terms with Cimbaeth and, it is recorded, married him.

Another queen, who certainly has become a mythological character, is the famous Medb of Connacht. There are several Medbs in Irish records and they seem separate personalities but all seem to have traditions associated with a goddess of sovereignty. Medb of Connacht is recorded by the Irish chronicler, Tighernach (*c.* AD 1022–88), abbot of Clonmacnoise, as an historical figure who died *c.* AD 70. Some chroniclers say that she succeeded Tinne as ruler and married Ailill, who is stated to be the commander of the Gamhanrhide or her royal bodyguard. However, the story of the *Táin Bó Cuailgne*, the great mythological epic, has put the historical Medb beyond the reach of historians.

We know something of the role of women in insular Celtic society in as much as their legal position is clearly marked out in the Brehon Laws, whose first recorded codification was in AD 438, and the Laws of Hywel Dda of Wales from the ninth century AD.

The law text, the *Bretha Cróilge*, on the categories of women, includes 'the woman who turns back the streams of

war' (*ben sues srutha cochta for cula*). This has been interpreted to mean a 'war leader'. There is also a 'hostage ruler'
(*rechtaid géill*) whose office has been interpreted to mean a
woman who can legally take hostages or prisoners of war.
The Welsh law, which brings us into medieval times, refers to
the office of *arglwyddes* or a 'female lord' or 'the chieftainess
of a district in her own right'.

What we know of Celtic law before the Christian era is
based on the rather biased writings of Julius Caesar.
However, he does seem to be echoing the insular Celtic
concept of female property rights when he says of the Gaulish
Celts:

> When a Gaul marries, he adds to the dowry that his wife
> brings with her a portion of his own property estimated to
> be of equal value. A joint account is kept of the whole
> amount, and the profits which it earns are put aside; and
> when either dies, the survivor receives both shares together
> with accumulated profits.

So, unlike their Greek and Roman sisters, Celtic women could
inherit property.

However, Caesar goes overboard when he says of the
British Celts:

> Wives are shared between groups of ten or twelve men,
> especially between brothers and between fathers and sons;
> but the offspring of these unions are counted as the children
> of the man with whom a particular woman cohabited first.

This is a total misrepresentation of the polygamous society of
the early Celts.

The Romans seemed preoccupied with the 'liberated' attitude of the early Celts. Dio Cassius comments on the fact that
the empress Julia Augusta criticised what she saw as a lack of

morals in the way Celtic women were free to choose their husbands and lovers and did so openly without subterfuge. The
object of her criticism was the wife of a north British chieftain named Argentocoxos. The encounter took place early in
the third century AD. According to Dio Cassius, the wife of
Argentocoxos turned to the empress and replied with dignity:
'We Celtic women obey the demands of Nature in a more
moral way than the women of Rome. We consort openly with
the best men but you, of Rome, allow yourselves to be
debauched in secret by the vilest.' It is not recorded how the
empress reacted.

In both surviving codifications of Celtic law systems,
women certainly enjoyed considerable rights. A girl under the
age of seven years of any social class in the Irish system had
the same honour price as a cleric. From seven girls were sent
to be educated, just as boys were. They completed their
education at the age of fourteen while boys continued to
seventeen. However, the *Bretha Cróilge* allowed the girl to
continue until the age of seventeen 'if required'.

Women could inherit property and remained the owner of
all property brought into a marriage. They fought alongside
men until Christianity abolished the practice with the introduction of the *Lex Innocentium* at the Synod of Birr in AD
697. In Irish and Welsh law there were nine types of marriage,
which corresponded to the eight types found in the Hindu
Law of Manu. Hindu law closely parallels Celtic law, and
many of the same principles can be found in the Irish and
Hindu texts. Divorce was permitted for a variety of reasons,
and men and women had equal rights to divorce each other.
One reason a woman could divorce in Irish law was if her
husband snored. In Welsh law, if a wife found her husband
committing adultery, she was exempt from any legal punishment if, in a fit of jealousy, she attacked him, his mistress or
even members of their families. The exemption was limited to
a period of three days from the time of learning of her

husband's affair. By that time, so the Welsh law-givers reasoned, the woman would have recovered from any shock which might cause such 'irrational acts'. After that, the matter was deemed to be cold-blooded vengeance.

In both law systems women were protected from rape and, indeed, from sexual harassment. In Ireland, the laws are clear that physical or even verbal harassment was punishable by a whole series of fines.

As the Celts emerged into the Christian period, it is to be remarked upon that many of the leading Christian proselytisers among the Celts were women. Female Celtic saints are numerous and out of all proportion to females active in the early Church in other cultures. It is not the task of this book, on the ancient Celtic world, to deal with the subject, but it is perhaps right that we end with a brief glimpse of a most extraordinary Celtic woman of the fourth century AD.

Elen Luyddog, or 'Elen of the Hosts', was the daughter of a British chieftain or king named Eudaf who ruled from Segontium (near Caernarfon). She became so powerful that, in many traditions, she is said to be the wife of Myrddin (Merlin) of Arthurian fame. She actually married a Romanised Celtiberian named Magnus Maximus, known in British Celtic tradition as Macsen Wledig (*gwledig*, a ruler). He served in the Roman army in Britain and in AD 382 defeated a combined army of Irish and Caledonians. The army in Britain, during a time of instability in Rome, declared him emperor and he took his army to Gaul to defy the emperor Gratian who was captured and slain. Theodosius, the eastern emperor in Constantinople, acknowledged him as co-emperor.

Martin of Tours, father of Celtic monasticism, was a frequent visitor to Magnus' court. Martin became a close friend of Elen Luyddog and is said to have converted her to Christianity, according to Sulpicius Severus in *Dialogues*. Elen not only became a leading figure in the intellectual life of the court but was the mother of many children of the new western emperor.

When Magnus crossed the Alps to Milan in AD 387, the eastern emperor, Theodosius, saw him as a threat to his empire and took the field against him. Magnus was defeated, captured and put to death on 28 July AD 388.

Elen decide to leave Gaul with her children and go back to Britain where she began to work assiduously on behalf of the Christian Church. Place-names attesting to her influence include various Llanelens. Elen occupied a position that caused Celtic leaders, even in the Isle of Man, to acknowledge her as a source of their sovereignty. Certainly her sons and daughters founded dynasties. Leo became king of the Cantii; Cystennin ruled at Segontium in Gwynedd; Owain is said to be ancestor of the kings of Glywsing (South Wales); Demetus founded the dynasty which ruled Dyfed; Antonius is claimed as ancestor of the kings of the Isle of Man. Plebig became a disciple of St Ninian. Her daughter Sevira married Vortigern, the famous king ruling at the time of the Anglo-Saxon invasion. His son, Brydw, was blessed by St Germanus of Auxerre during one of his visits to Britain.

Elen's home is said to have been at Dinas Emrys, a fortress which can still be seen at Bedgelert. We are told by Nennius that Dinas Emrys played a central part in the overthrow of Vortigern, who was regarded as betraying Britain to the Anglo-Saxons. It is named after Emrys (Ambrosius) who is said to have toppled Vortigern. At one time scholars tried to prove that Emrys was the real historical figure of Arthur. However, Arthur and Emrys, in historical record, are clearly two different people. Elen Luyddog was undoubtedly dead by the time Vortigern emerged as the 'overlord' of southern Britain.

Women have played a prominent part in Celtic life, from the mother goddess and the pantheon of female deities down to a whole range of powerful historical female leaders, priestesses and Christian saints. Their role did not stop with the coming of Christianity but continued into medieval times among the insular Celts. As has been pointed out before, a unique piece of 'feminist' literature emerges from twelfth-century Ireland in the form of the *Banshenchas*, a book on the genealogies of leading woman. In fact, this could be claimed as the first European book about women in their own right.

# 7

# CELTIC FARMERS

The economic backbone of Celtic society, which was essentially rural like most ancient societies, was in its farms. Celtic farmers were part of a continuum which archaeologists can trace back to the Bronze Age. Archaeology disproves the popular notion of the Celts being an itinerant people, constantly travelling Europe in great hordes, attacking and looting as they went. Both agricultural and pastoral farming were practised and indeed became highly sophisticated as the Celts combined their technology with other rural knowledge and skills. They were a long way removed from the picture that Caesar would have us believe when he speaks of the British Celts in these propaganda terms: '. . . many of the inland Britons do not grow corn. They live on milk and flesh and are clothed in skins.'

In fact, Celtic farmers, in whatever part of the ancient Celtic world they lived, could have taught the Romans a few lessons on farming. Their wheeled transport was superior to the Romans' and their technology allowed them to produce the first harvesting machine; the Celtic plough, fitted with a mobile coulter, was greatly superior to the Roman swing plough of the same period.

The plough, of course, was the very basis of agriculture. The earliest picture of a Celtic plough is found in a rock carving in the Val Camonica, north of Milan, where the Celts had settled from the start of the Hallstatt period. The Camonica rock carvings are an excellent source of information on the Celts and show the first known rendition of the Celtic god Cernunnos together with wagons, scenes of hunting and so forth. Some of the carvings date from the seventh century BC.

Double ploughing, running a plough twice across the field, seemed a common practice in early European societies for the plough did not entirely turn the sod. However, innovative Celtic technology provided the plough with a coulter, a sharp knife attached to the plough beam which made a vertical cut through the soil at the same time that the share made the horizontal cut and thus the soil was turned over upon itself.

The Celts developed iron shares while their neighbours continued to use wooden ones. The iron provided the Celts with, literally, an 'edge' over their neighbours. The plough was often pulled by two yoked oxen and by this means they were able to open up vast tracts of arable land. The Celtic farmers would penetrate regions previously impossible to plough and cultivate.

Among the British Celts, the iron share and coulter, plus the practice of crop rotating and manuring, seemed to mark a major change in intensive farming before the end of the second century BC. Land was being cleared at an unprecedented rate and some areas, such as marshy, clay soil valleys, were actually being drained and brought under the plough. When the Romans arrived in Britain, in total contradiction to Caesar's assertions, a patchwork of hedged, fenced or walled fields, with others delineated by ditches, and smaller woodlands, would have been the landscape seen by the invaders. In other words, the countryside was not too dissimilar to what we see today.

Throughout the Celtic world the intensive exploitation of agricultural land required manuring to ensure that the soil remained fertile. Classical writers attest to the fertilisation of lands by Celtic farmers using lime and marl, which is a limey clay.

Essential to this agricultural progress was the development of the wheel, and the general purpose wagon and other wheeled machinery helped Celtic farmers to make rapid advances. They evolved the first harvesting machine, the *messor*, later called *vallus* by the Romans. According to Pliny, this was a 'big box, the edges armed with teeth and supported by two wheels, which moved through the cornfield pushed by an ox rather; the ears of corn were uprooted by the teeth and fell into the box.' A stone relief found in Brussels is the best representation of this Celtic harvesting machine.

The introduction of iron obviously helped farmers in that sickles, scythes, spades, forks, axes and billhooks became more powerful and sophisticated. The former socketed hafting was now replaced by shaft-holes, while cutting tools were attached to their handles by means of a sharp spike on the tool going into a wooden handle or haft. The hand tools which we still use today were all anticipated by Celtic crafts-men at least by the first century BC.

The Celtic farmers grew a large variety of crops and these depended on what area of the Celtic world they farmed. Mainly they produced cereals, notably several varieties of wheat such as emmer, spelt and bread wheat. Millet was a major crop in Gaul and Cisalpine Gaul; this was a gramina-ceous plant giving a crop of nutritious seeds. The species of millet called panicum, or panic, was a particular Celtic crop of the Po valley. Barley, rye and oats were produced as well as fibrous plants, such as hemp and flax, the latter grown not only for linen to make clothes but for oil as well.

Crops like pulses, beans, peas and lentils, were also grown. From archaeological evidence, we find that a wide variety of fruits and berries were cultivated. While in northern Celtic climates, from the sixth century BC, wine was imported from Etruscan and Greek sources, and later from Roman merchants, it appears that the Celts of the Po valley and then the Celts of southern Gaul soon began to cultivate the vine and produce their own wines. Even in southern Britain during the Roman occupation, there is evidence of vines being cultivated and wine produced. The Saluvii of southern Gaul also started to grow olives. Archaeologists have found the presence of olive and grape presses at the Saluvii capital of Entremont.

Corn was ground by circular millstones which were turned by hand, and then dried in kilns or stored in large granaries. These querns were often worked by two people, sitting facing each other, passing the handle or both handles from one to another. Even so quern grinding was tedious work, for it would take about an hour to grind 5 kilograms of meal in this fashion. This type of grinding was found throughout the Indo-European world; an ancient word in Irish for the quern was *meile*, cognate with *melyn* in Welsh, *mola* in Latin and *mylen* in Anglo-Saxon.

Where the Celts had water power they adopted the water mill. In the *Dindshenchas* there is a story of how the water mill supposedly came to Ireland. We are told that King Cormac mac Art (said to have reigned AD 254–277) fell in love with a woman whose job was grinding corn. In order to relieve her from her task, the king sent 'across the sea' for a millwright (*saer-muilinn*) and asked him to construct a mill on a stream called the Nith (Ir. *nemnach*, sparkling) beside the royal palace at Tara. Whether this is true or not, water mills were in general use in Ireland by this time.

In a world without refrigeration, storage was an essential in case of crop failure, war or some other disaster. The Celts were great salt producers and salting was their chosen method

of preservation, especially of meats. Celtic salt pork, from
Gaul, was an early export to the peoples of the Italian peninsula.

The main method of storage was by the use of pits. A large
number have been found and for a long time they provided
archaeologists with a problem. Charred grain had been discovered in many of them but the idea that such holes in the
ground could be safely used to store grain or vegetables in a
dry condition seemed nonsensical. However, experiments,
particularly those at the Butser Celtic Farm, Hampshire,
suggest that if the pit was sealed, the grain in contact with the
damp walls would germinate, using available oxygen and
releasing carbon dioxide. This would cause the rest of the
grain to go into a form of suspended animation so that it
lasted in perfect condition for many months.

These pits are often called souterrains and in Cornwall they
are given the Cornish name *fougou*, meaning a subterranean
chamber. There are similar structures in Ireland, also called
souterrains. These are built of dry-stone walling surmounted
by large lintels forming the roof. Some of them are quite
lengthy in that the passages connect with elaborate small
chambers. Those at Carn Euny, Sancreed and Boleigh, in
Cornwall, are good examples that have survived. While local
folklore imagined all sorts of dark practices taking place
within these narrow passages and chambers, they were
nothing more than winter storage places.

As well as agriculture, the Celts practised pastoral farming.
They kept sheep, cattle and pigs, but their varieties were very
different from modern-day domestic farm animals. The bones
of sheep discovered by archaeologists show that the breeds
kept by the Celtic farmers were small and goat-like, rather like
the modern Soay sheep from St Kilda, in Scotland. The wool
of this breed is short, coarse and usually dark. They were
exploited for their wool and milk rather than meat. The production of woollen goods from Britain was well known in

Caesar's time for such items were part of a thriving export business from Britain to Rome.

The cattle – the now extinct Celtic Shorthorn, which was smaller than modern breeds – were also bred to produce powerful oxen for pulling ploughs and wagons. The modern Dexter cattle seem to be the closest approximation of the early breeds used by the Celts. Physical knowledge is based on archaeological finds of bones at Celtic sites and settlements. From this we know that cattle were not only draught animals but supplied meat and milk. Cattle occur as the most frequent of domestic animals. Certainly, from early Irish literary sources we find that the number of his cattle was the indicator of the wealth and social status of a man and his family. Early Irish units of exchange were based on a *séd*, which was the value of one milch cow. Three *séd* made a *cumal*, being the value of three milch cows. A *cumal* was also a unit of land measurement.

Because of the importance of cattle in Celtic society, bulls played a major role in Celtic culture. Images of bulls begin to appear in the Hallstatt culture and they are frequently connected with sacrificial rituals, one of which is mentioned by Pliny. We have already referred to the royal *tarbhfeis*, or bull ritual, in connection with kingship. This is described in the *Serglige Con Culainn* and *Togail Bruidne Da Derga*. The significance of bulls can be seen in insular Celtic mythology, particularly the Irish saga of the *Táin Bó Cuailgne*. Over forty images of mystic three-horned bulls have been discovered in Gaul together with a relief showing what appears to be a deity called the 'Bull with the Three Cranes' – Tarvos Trigaranus – from Paris. In this inscription, the Celtic word for bull is recognisable, cognate to old Irish *tarb* and Welsh *tarw*, also the word *tri* (three) and the Welsh cognate *garan* for crane.

Pigs were the second most common domesticated animals in the Celtic world. Pigs and boars came to have a religious significance among the Celts and they were assigned to aristocrats as part of their grave goods. Pigs also play a prominent role in insular Celtic literatures. In the Welsh epics, Pryderi possesses a herd of pigs acquired from Arawn who ruled Annwfn, the Otherworld. In Irish myth, in the story of *Scéla mucce Meic Dathó*, we find the dissection of a gigantic pig playing an important role. Celtic warriors also appear with symbols of boars on their helmets, and sculptures of boars and pigs occur frequently in Celtic art. The boar became one of the royal symbols among the early Irish kings.

Horses and dogs were bred for both hunting and warfare. There seems no trace of the use of donkeys and mules before contact with the Italian peninsula. Chickens and cats were also found in Celtic farmsteads. Caesar says of the British Celts: 'Hares, fowl, and geese they think it unlawful to eat, but rear them for pleasure and amusement.'

The construction of farmhouses, which we will discuss in Chapter 12, varied in design through the Celtic world. In Britain and Ireland, houses tended to be circular. Caesar, in a slip from his usual propaganda about barbaric Britons, says that the houses in southern Britain were no different from those in Gaul. 'The population is exceedingly large, the ground thickly studded with homesteads, closely resembling those of the Gauls, and the cattle very numerous.' In Gaul, the Celtic houses were predominantly rectangular, as they were among the Celts of the Po valley. They were usually half-timbered constructions. Such two-storey rectangular houses were certainly being built by the Celts from the second century BC.

One of the interesting things in Ireland is the survival of ancient boundary pillar stones, used to delineate farm boundaries. Cormac mac Cuileannáin's *Sanas Chormaic*, his tenth-century 'Glossary', refers to these boundary markers as *gall* and *gallan* because, he says, they were first erected by Gaulish Celts when they arrived in Ireland. True or not, the Brehon Laws, as one would expect, have some stringent rules about farmers and their duty to the land and community.

From Irish sources we learn the names and uses of implements which are similar to those we know were used in other parts of the Celtic world. We know that the ancient Irish had mastered the art of manuring (*ottrach*) and that they used dung-heaps (*crum duma*). We know that they understood the importance of irrigation. We also learn that in Ireland the plough was drawn not only by oxen but by horses, for we are told in the ninth-century *Féilire* of Oenghus that the Munster religious Ciaran kept 'fifty tamed horses for tilling and ploughing the ground'.

The picture that archaeology reveals of a stable Celtic farming economy is certainly a different one from the popular notion of itinerant war bands.

# 8

# CELTIC PHYSICIANS

A small family cemetery has been uncovered at Obermenzing near Munich dated to the third or early second century BC. In one of the graves, described as Grave 7, a sword and iron scabbard was found whose chagrinage and bird-headed triskel make it a noteworthy item of Celtic artwork. But the most remarkable discovery in Grave 7 was a whole range of surgeon's equipment which promptly caused it to be labelled by the archaeologists 'the warrior-surgeon's grave'. The surgical instruments included a retractor, probes and a trephining saw, a cylindrical skull drill.

According to Dr Simon James: 'In medicine, as in so many other areas, the Celts stand favourable comparison with the classical world.'

We do not know much about specific medical practices among the Celts until the start of the Christian era when such information was committed to writing. However, we do know that surgical medicine was advanced in the Celtic world. The 'surgeon's' grave at Obermenzing is not the only one in which surgical instruments of bronze and iron have been discovered.

We know from the skulls of several skeletons that the Celts often did neurosurgery and were adept at the trephining operation, making circular cuts into the skull in order to relieve pressure in the case of head injuries or, it has also been suggested, psychological disorders. Several times we find skulls which have been trephined as many as three times.

The best-known example demonstrating the success of ancient trephining operations was found in January 1935, off the coast of Ovingdean, Sussex, when a fisherman trawled the skull in his nets. 'The Ovingdean Trephined Skull' is now in the Brighton Museum, Sussex. The skull has two large round holes cut into it over the brain pan. It is dated to the second or first century BC. The remarkable thing about this skull is that the ancient Celtic surgeons had cut into it on two separate occasions; the healing of the bone around both holes indicated that the patient survived both operations but eventually died of sepsis some weeks after the second. Similar skulls have been discovered on the Continent where the patient has survived the infections and the shock of such operations. One found at Katzesdorf, Austria, actually shows three attempts at trephining. Two holes were completed but the third was not, and there are no signs of healing. Obviously this patient died on the operating table.

The first native Celtic record of the trephining operation appears in an account of the battle of Magh Rath or Moira in AD 637. An Irish chieftain named Cennfaelad had his skull fractured by a sword blow. He was taken to the medical school of Tuam Brecain (Tomregan) and had the injured part of his skull and a portion of his brain removed. On his recovery, it was said that his wits were as sharp as ever and he became a great scholar and author of *Uraicept na n-Éces* (*Primer of Poets*), a work still existing in copied form.

We know, from early Irish sources, the Irish Celtic names of some of these surgical instruments. Early Irish physicians carried a stethoscope, a horn called a *gipne* or *gibne*, explained in Cormac's Glossary with the words *adarc lege* (physician's horn). The surgical probe was called a *fraig*.

In the ancient Celtic world, water was the source of health as well as of life. The link with water, the divine waters from heaven from which the Celtic peoples, according to their philosophy, had their origin, was all-pervasive. Therefore we find that rivers and springs were the focus of ritual practices designed to ensure well-being. Like their fellow Indo-Europeans, the Hindus, the Celts regarded water with veneration and they had their sacred rivers. They bathed in them and offered votive gifts to the deities of the springs and rivers; these offerings included wooden models of themselves or the affected part of their limbs, together with all manner of treasures.

Most Celtic river names are identified with goddesses. The Marne, for example, comes from Matrona, which means 'mother'; the Severn in Britain is named after Sabrina; the Wharfe is sacred to Verbeia; the Boyne in Ireland is named after the goddess Boann; while the Shannon takes its name from the goddess Siannon. Sequana was the goddess of the Seine, and the source of the river on the Châtillon plateau, north-west of Dijon, was where she was particularly worshipped with votive objects being cast into the river to ensure well-being and health. Among these were solar wheel amulets. A healing shrine was established at 'Fontes Sequanae' (The Springs of Sequana) and the Romans took over the site and built two temples and other structures there.

Sequana seems to have been particularly prayed to and given offerings in connection with various diseases of the organs. Some of the votive offerings are wooden and stone images of limbs, organs, heads and complete bodies, many images showing blindness or swollen eyes. The images were offered to her with coins and items of jewellery. This does not mean, of course, that the people placed their faith in the offering to the goddess alone but that, as well as placing themselves in the hands of their physicians, a prayer to their gods and goddesses would not come amiss. In fact, there was little difference in their attitude to our attitude today.

The offering of images of limbs and organs was by no means confined to the Celtic world. The practice occurred among the Greeks, and even in medieval times in certain Christian communities. But certainly it was widespread in the Celtic world, and many such images are to be found at the healing shrines in Britain. One fascinating example is a pair of sculptured breasts which were offered to the goddess Sulis at Aquae Sulis (Bath). Presumably a young woman was suffering, perhaps from breast cancer, and sought to invoke the aid of the goddess. Sulis was a major deity of healing and her sanctuaries were found in Britain and in Gaul.

We find, in the Irish medical tracts, that baths were frequently prescribed for healing. Fingin, the Druid physician of Conchobhar Mac Nessa, cured the wounded warriors by baths of medical herbs. In Cormac's Glossary such a medicated bath was called *fothrucad* and most often given for leprosy – *doinnlóbru*.

A hot air bath was used in Ireland as a cure for, among other things, rheumatism. It was called a *tigh 'n alluis*, or 'sweating house'. One such ancient structure survives on Inishmurray, in Donegal Bay, and several have been described in nineteenth-century sources which have now been vandalised and destroyed. The 'sweating house' was a stone cabin, around 2 metres long. A turf fire was kindled inside and the place heated like an oven. The fire was removed. The patient, wrapped in a blanket, went inside and sat down on a bench. The door was closed up. The patient remained until a profuse perspiration developed and then, on leaving, they plunged in cold water before being rubbed dry. The patient was encouraged to meditate (*dercad*) to achieve a state of peace (*sitcháin*). This process has been found in many cultures in the world, even among the Native American peoples, and has the same religious connotations as in the Celtic world.

The fame of the Irish baths spread to the Continent. Professor Henry Hennessy observed, in 1885, that 'it is remarkable that what are called Turkish baths in Ireland and Great Britain have been designated Roman-Irish baths in Germany and Bohemia'.

There were also male deities connected with healing. Lenus was the physician-deity of the Treveri, worshipped at Trier and Pommern, where the spring and a small set of baths were situated. He seemed to look after children particularly, and many images have been found with children holding out gifts, specifically of doves, to him. Lenus was also worshipped among the British Celts, at Caerwent in Gwent, and Chedworth in Gloucestershire.

Belenus, the name meaning 'bright' or 'brilliant', was a sun deity who probably represented the sun's curative powers. Vindonnus, whose sanctuary was at Châtillon-sur-Seine in Burgundy, was invoked in the case of eye afflictions for there are bronze plaques there depicting the eyes. He is, significantly, a god of light and his name is argued to mean 'clear light'.

Grannus was a healing deity who, according to Dio Cassius, was invoked by the Roman emperor Caracalla who went to his temple sanctuary. We are unsure which sanctuary this was, for his cult was found from north-east Gaul (Brittany) as far east as Hungary, and a pot discovered at Vestmanlung in Sweden bears a dedication to Grannus. This pot probably arrived in Sweden by means of trade or plunder. The name means 'sun' and at Trier the god is depicted driving a sun chariot.

Only in Irish mythology do we have a god of medicine clearly defined. This was Dian Cécht who, with his daughter Airmid, guarded a healing spring which restored the dead and wounded to life. After Nuada, the leader of the Tuatha Dé Danaan, lost his hand in the first battle of Magh Tuireadh, Dian Cécht supplied him with a silver hand, earning Nuada the nickname Nuada Airgetlámh. However, this blemish excluded Nuada from kingship and Bres, the half Fomorii, became king. Dian Cécht's son, Miach, proved himself a better physician by providing Nuada with a new hand of flesh and blood and allowed him to regain his kingdom.

Dian Cécht grew increasingly jealous of his son especially when Miach and his sister sewed a cat's eye into the socket of the one-eyed porter of Nuada's palace and gave him sight. In rage Dian Cécht killed his son. Airmid gathered the herbs that grew on her brother's grave and laid them out on her cloak in order of their various healing properties. Dian Cécht, still jealous, overturned the cloak and hopelessly confused the herbs so that no human would learn the secret of immortality by their use.

Pliny was the first classical writer to give an account of Celtic medical knowledge, and he pointed out that it was the Druids who possessed these skills. As the Druids were the Celtic intellectual caste, it was natural that the professional role of healer would be one of those assumed by them. It has been asserted that the medical knowledge of the Druids was what gave them power in Celtic society, although this is a matter for debate. Pliny, in the first century AD, also stressed that the Druidic physicians were possessed of 'magical lore', something he was particularly interested in when writing his *Naturalis Historia*.

When records begin in insular Celtic, the Druidic physicians are regarded as skilled in the prescription of herbs as well as in surgery; among the operations they performed were Caesarean sections, neurosurgery and straightforward amputations. We even find an entire medical corps accompanying the army of Conchobhar Mac Nessa during the *Táin* wars under the direction of Fingín Fáithliaig. It is no coincidence that the name is a compound of *fáith*, a seer, and *liaig*, a physician.

We know from later European sources that the Irish physicians were renowned for their skill in medical botany, including the production of herbal sleeping potions (*deoch suaim*).

Of course, the use of poisons was known. A herb called *éccinél* was recorded as a deadly poison but, alas, we are not sure to what this word refers. It corresponds with the old Irish word for hurtful, unkindly and unnatural. We are told that the poet Cridenbél was poisoned *tre luib éccineol*.

It is Pliny who links the Druids with mistletoe, saying: 'They believe that mistletoe given in drink will impart fertility to any animal that is barren, and that it is an antidote to all poisons.' In the modern pharmacopoeia, mistletoe is reputed to be beneficial to sufferers of insomnia, high blood pressure and certain malignant tumours. Pliny tells us that the smoke produced by burning the selago plant was thought to be good for all diseases of the eye.

In the pre-Christian period, in most European societies, even those of Greece and Rome, little provision was made for the treatment of the ailing poor. The sick, feeble and elderly were often put to death as the ultimate remedy for their ills. Disease was regarded as a curse inflicted by the supernatural powers. These powers had to be propitiated rather than the sick cured. There was no 'system' of health care. It is now part of European cultural folklore that the first hospice in Europe for the sick and needy, the first hospital, was established by the Christian matron, St Fabiola (d. *c.* AD 399) at Porto near Rome.

Such institutions had, however, been established by the Indo-Europeans of India. The *Charaka-Samhita* (*Annals of Charake*) tell us that Asoka (*c.* 273–232 BC), the emperor of India, sickened by war and the struggle for power, turned to Buddhism and professional non-violence, establishing the first hospitals in India for the ailing poor.

What is overlooked, in a European context, is that Irish sources refer to the establishment of the first hospital in Ireland by the semi-legendary queen Macha Mong Ruadh (d. *c.* 377 BC). She is said to have established a hospital called Bróin Bherg (House of Sorrow) at Emain Macha, Navan in

Armagh. It is reported that this hospital remained in use in Navan until its destruction in AD 22. Legendary foundation or not, we do know that such hospitals were in existence by the time of the Christian period in Ireland, some for sick people with general ailments, and others serving specialist needs, such as leper hospitals. The Brehon Laws indicate the existence of an advanced and sophisticated medical system, for they ordered that hospitals be made available in all tribal areas. This implies a long tradition of medical practice. References by Pliny to the reputation of Gaulish physicians such as Crinias and Charmis and the use of astrology as an aid to medical diagnosis – a system Charmis was especially known for – show how progressive the Celtic system was. Martial refers to Alcon, a famous Roman surgeon who had studied at the Gaulish medical colleges. Gaulish Celtic physicians and orators certainly had an excellent reputation.

Joseph O'Longan (in an unpublished MS in the Royal Irish Academy) shows that the use of astrological observations as an aid in medical diagnosis and prognosis was universal among Irish physicians. This was a standard practice throughout Europe in the medieval period. It is worthy of mention that one of the last books in Irish on astrological medical skills was written by a Jesuit priest from Donegal, Father Maghnus Ó Domhnaill, in 1694. Father Ó Domhnaill had studied at the Irish College in Salamanca University, which disbanded its faculty of astrology in 1777, the last university to do so.

The Irish language contains the world's largest collection of medical texts in any one language prior to 1800. There are translations of works credited to Hippocrates, Galen, Herophilus, Rhazes, Avicenna, Seapion, Dioscorides and many other European medical scholars in addition to the native books of learning. The majority of surviving texts date from between the fourteenth and sixteenth centuries, such as the books of the O'Hickeys (1352), O'Lees (1443), O'Shiels and the 1512 Book of Mac Anlega (Son of the Doctor). The oldest surviving medical textbook in Ireland dates from 1352, now in the Royal Irish Academy, but it is a copy of a far older book. Even older medical texts are kept in the British Museum and the University Library, Cambridge. This wealth of ancient medical material has, to the shame of scholars, scarcely been examined.

Under the Brehon Laws the provision of sick maintenance, including the price of curative treatment, attendance allowance and nourishing food, was made available for everyone who needed it. Expenses for the treatment of wounded people, those injured unlawfully, were paid out of the fines which the perpetrators of the deed had to pay. The *Law of Torts* says that 'full sick maintenance [must be paid] to a worker injured for the sake of unnecessary profit . . .'

The Brehon Laws make it clear that only qualified physicians could treat the sick and there were severe penalties if unqualified physicians were found practising. The qualified physicians were responsible for the treatment of their patient and if, through negligence or ignorance, they caused a patient's condition to worsen, they had to pay compensation. Each qualified physician undertook by law to maintain four medical students and train them. Every so often the physician was allowed, under law, to take a sabbatical and devote himself to catching up on new knowledge and techniques.

Each territory had to maintain a hospital. The law is exact on the conditions under which it was to be built and maintained. It should have four doors, be placed by a stream of running water, and be maintained free of charge or taxation by the local assembly. The existence of such hospitals is attested by the names of towns or places such as An Spidéal (Spiddal, Spital etc.). The local physician and his students were in charge. There was a full-time caretaker or hospital manager who was employed to keep away stray dogs, mentally sick people, who had their own institutions, and anyone liable to cause the sick or injured distress.

The Irish laws relating to medicine and the fragmentary evidence from the Continent demonstrate that ancient Celtic society was concerned with protecting its sick and ailing poor at a time when tending the ill was not a priority in neighbouring societies.

# 9

# CELTIC COSMOLOGY

In speaking of the Druids, Julius Caesar remarked:

> They also hold long discussions about the heavenly bodies and their movement, the size of the universe and of the earth, the physical constitutions of the world, and the power and properties of the gods; and they instruct the young men in all these subjects.

Pomponius Mela (c. AD 43), author of the earliest surviving Latin work on geography, which offers explanations for the actions of the moon and the tides and the midnight sun in the north, mentions that the Celts had a reputation for their 'speculations from the stars'. He states:

> They have, further, their eloquence and their Druids, teachers of wisdom, who profess to know the greatness and shape of the earth and the universe and the motion of the heavens and of the stars and what is the will of the gods.

And Hippolytus (*c.* AD 170–*c.* 236), in *Philosophumena*, gives us one of the clearest statements by saying that the Celts foretold the future from the stars by ciphers and numbers after the manner of Pythagoreans.

From the very beginning of time the human species has been perceptive of natural phenomena. Early societies noticed that the sun and moon together affected the tides, and the sun regulated the seasons, giving light and heat which fructified the harvest. They also noticed that the motions of the moon could in some cases affect men and women and their mental attitudes. From these initial observations there developed a belief that the motions of what were then thought of as 'stars' influenced individuals and events on earth.

Astrology was initially an integral part of astronomy. Indeed, Aristotle used the word 'astrology' rather than 'astronomy' to describe the whole science. It was only as late as the seventeenth century that astronomy and astrology really parted company with the dawning of the so-called 'Age of Reason'.

Historians of astronomy and astrology generally argue that the science had its origins in ancient Babylonia and made its way from Babylonia into Europe via Greece. Yet in fact we find that astrology did not have its 'birth' in any one place and that all societies, in whatever part of the world, evolved a system of cosmology, of looking at the heavens; they all developed a theory of the phenomena and the laws which govern them and, on the basis of seasonal observations, learned to predict the future by the movements of the planets. The Celts were no exception to other societies, but how did they view the heavens and relate to them?

That the Celts were highly competent in astronomy is proved by the fact that they originated their own calendrical system. The earliest surviving Celtic calendar is from Gaul and dated to the first century BC. This is the Coligny Calendar, now in the Palais des Arts in Lyons. It is a lunar calendar on engraved bronze plates and was discovered in November 1897. The language on it is Gaulish Celtic. Seymour de Ricci's analysis in the *Revue celtique* at the time of the discovery pointed out that the calendar confirmed Pliny's comment about the Celtic thirty-year calendrical cycle. Professor Heinrich Zimmer, a leading Celtic scholar as well as a Sanskrit expert, studied the calendar within months of its discovery and was the first to point out in his *Altindisches Leben* that it had many parallels to Vedic calendrical computations. He specifically cited the *Taittirya Samhita*.

There have been many studies of the calendar but in 1992 Dr Garrett Olmsted's seminal work, published in Germany, substantiated the Celtic parallels to the Vedic system. Olmsted was both a Celtic scholar and a qualified astronomer. While accepting that the surviving calendar was manufactured in the first century BC, Dr Olmsted went further and demonstrated by astronomical calculus that the calendar must have originally been computed in 1100 BC. In other words, we have a Celtic calendar that dates back three millennia, endorsing the comments of the classical sources regarding the long tradition and sophistication of Celtic calendrical methodology.

Professor Eoin MacNeill, when he examined the calendar in 1924, posed the question: 'Is it possible that the Coligny Calendar preserves the older Indo-European tradition of the Celts?' He felt the answer was in the affirmative. Every study of the calendar has inclined to support this.

Certainly far more work is due to be done in this field and comparisons with early Vedic records as well as records in Hittite need to be completed. The Hittite records, written in cuneiform on clay tablets dating from around 1900–1400 BC, are the earliest example of an Indo-European language being committed to a literature. The material is rich in cosmological records. As a relative of Vedic Sanskrit and Celtic, its cosmological philosophies provide fascinating comparisons. It is suggested that these Hittite records were

merely translations of Babylonian texts. But if there are philo-
sophic and linguistic parallels between these early Indo-
European remains, then we might indeed be on the path to an
understanding of ancient Indo-European cosmology.

The Coligny Calendar is far more elaborate than the rudi-
mentary Julian calendar and incorporates a highly sophisticated five-year synchronisation of lunation with the solar
year. It is a masterpiece of calendrical calculation. Against
the months are subscribed either the letters MAT or ANM.
One does not need to be an expert linguist to recognise these
as the equivalent of *maith* (Irish) or *mad* (Welsh) meaning
'good', and of *an maith* (Irish) or *anfad* (Welsh) meaning 'not
good'.

The months are named in Gaulish Celtic with Giamon as
the midwinter month and Samon as the midsummer month.
Both names can be recognised in the surviving Celtic languages. What is significant here is that the old Irish name for
November was Gam. Today November has been erroneously
renamed Samhain which was originally the name for the feast
of the god Samhain on 31 October/1 November. Samhain has
nothing to do with the word *sam* meaning summer.

It is by misunderstanding and misuse that this name was
extended to the whole month of November and thus confused
people as to why a dark month should bear the element of the
name of summer in it. To get round this one observer has suggested that Samhain must mean 'end of summer'. A good try.
However, in thinking that Samon was the name for November
another error was perpetuated by unwary commentators on
the Coligny Calendar when they placed Giamon (winter) as
the May month. The May month was clearly called in old
Ireland Cet-Samhin, the first of the summer period. Cet-
Gamred was November, the first of the winter months or
black period, and it is still so called in Scottish Gaelic. So, in
the Coligny Calendar, we have a black half of the year and a
light half of the year and in between the two halves is the

Gaulish Celtic word *atenvix*, which translates as 'renewal', as in the old Irish word *athnugud*.

There are sixty-two consecutive months in the calendar, divided into periods of twenty-nine or thirty nights each. In Celtic fashion, the calendar reckons periods by nights. Caesar observed· 'They count periods of time not by the number of days but by the number of nights; and in reckoning birthdays and the new moon and the new year their unit of reckoning is the night followed by the day.' Pliny implies that it was by the moon that the Celts measured their months and years and also 'ages' or thirty-year periods. Presumably, the thirty years was regarded as a generation.

Dillon and Chadwick comment:

> The Calendar of Coligny is evidence of a considerable degree of competence in astronomy, and may reflect the learning of the Druids. Moreover, in the division of the year into a bright and a dark half, in the month of thirty days with a five year cycle, at the end of which an intercalary month was added, this Gaulish calendar resembles that of the Hindus.

The Vedas and Upanishads show that the Hindu year was indeed divided into two halves in a fashion analogous to the Celtic year. The Vedic references, such as the *Bhadaranyaka*, indicate that the Vedic calendar was lunar, with a variable 354/355 days, included intercalary months and followed a thirty-year cycle like the Celtic one. Plutarch mentions a thirty-year festival among the Celts when Cronus (Saturn) entered the sign of Taurus.

It is clear that by the first century AD the majority of the Continental Celtic peoples had adopted the new forms of astronomy and astrology that were used in the Graeco-Roman world. These had emerged from Babylonia into Greece and thence to Rome. The older methods used by the Celts, once

common to Indo-European society, were swept away. Evidence
for the pre-Graeco-Roman (Babylonian) concepts appears in
fragmentary form in early Irish cosmological writings.

Pliny refers to the reputation of Gaulish Celtic astrologers
in the first century AD. But by the time they emerge into historical scrutiny they were, as Hippolytus tells us, using the
Graeco-Roman forms. We know that Favorinus of the Volcae
Arecomii, born in AD 80, had a reputation in the Roman world
for his astrology. The Aedui astrologer Caecilius Argicius
Arborius, of the third century AD, was another astrologer of
note and he drew up a birth chart for his grandson, the poet
Decimus Magnus Ausonius of Bordeaux. We know this from
Ausonius' *Parentalia* in which he also tells us that Arborius
was of the Druid caste. Perhaps the name Arborius, linking
him with sacred trees, is an indication of this connection?

Another Celtic astrologer was Anthedius, a friend of the
Gaulish Celtic bishop, Apollinaris Sidonius. And a fourth-
century Gaul wrote a Celto-Latin comedy play entitled
*Querolus* (*Complaint*) whose main character is a Celtic
astrologer named Mandrogente, meaning 'born of a horse'.
The Roman biographer Flavius Vopiscus observed drily that
'superstition based on astrology always prevailed over the
Celts'.

It is from the sixth century AD that we begin to find a wealth
of written evidence from the insular Celts concerning cosmology. From it we find that Irish cosmology falls into four
historic phases. The pre-Christian phase, of which we have
only fragmentary knowledge, indicates that the Celts shared
the Indo-European knowledge of numerology, astronomy and
astrology which emerges in the Vedas. Then, as the Celtic
world entered the Christian period, the new Graeco-Latin
learning arrived from Babylonia. In the earliest Irish evidence,
the cosmology shows the influence of the Alexandrian
Claudius Ptolemy, second century AD, whose teachings on
astronomy and astrology were accepted until the arrival of

Arabic influences and the work of Copernicus. From the eleventh century, the Irish astronomers and astrologers used the Arab forms which had entered Europe.

In Britain there is a sculpture showing the zodiacal signs dating from as early as the third century AD. It was found in Housesteads, at the northernmost edge of Roman influence, and is now in the museum at Newcastle on Tyne. One of the earliest surviving texts in old Welsh is a tenth-century discussion about the zodiac which is called *seraul cichol*.

Aibhistín, an Irish astronomer writing in AD 655, shows a masterful display of computational skills and in his text we find evidence of an ancient lunar-based astrological system which appears to have similarities to the twenty-seven lunar mansions of the Vedic system, called the Nakshatras. Aibhistín is the earliest medieval writer to discuss the relationship of the tides to the phases of the moon. He is also the first Christian writer to proclaim that the Three Wise Men in the Gospel of St Matthew were astrologers.

In the late 1980s an important discovery was made when the 'lost' Irish calendrical eighty-four-year Easter table, covering the years AD 438–521, was found in the Biblioteca Antoniana in Padua (MS.I.27). The table is linked with early Irish calendrical systems and it is the very calendrical study which was used by St Columbanus to argue the dating of Easter with Pope Gregory the Great in the early seventh century. A preliminary study has been published in *Peritia, Journal of the Medieval Academy of Ireland*, Vols 6–7, 1987–88.

Our first Irish astrological chart survives from the eighth century. This was found in the library at Basle in Switzerland. From the 'Ptolemaic' period we have Diciul's classic *De Astronomiam*, a text on astronomy and astrology, written in AD 814. Diciul, a famous Irish geographer, was taught by Brother Fidelmid of Fermanagh who, it is reported, went to Egypt to measure the pyramids which he did with great accuracy.

As a demonstration of early Irish sophistication in matters of astronomy we may cite the Irish annals. Dr Dan MacCarthy of Trinity College, Dublin, recently examined twelve of these annals and chronicles, collating all observations made of astronomical phenomena between AD 442 and 1133. What emerged was a body of records of eclipses, comets, aurorae and even a supernova, carefully and accurately set down.

It appears that, following the introduction of Christianity into Ireland, when the great ecclesiastical universities displaced the bardic colleges, the latter became the centres for studying the heavens, particularly those at Durrow and Clonmacnoise. Through the medieval period, astronomical observation was a sustained activity in many Irish monastic schools. A comparison of the Irish records with Continental records shows that the former tend to be trustworthy while the latter are often badly transcribed, wrongly recorded and inaccurate. Between AD 627 and 1133 some thirty astronomical observations were found to exist only in Irish records. No other European textual evidence for these events was found, but they corresponded to many non-European sightings, from India, China and Japan, and when calibrated the Irish records were in precise accord.

As one example, in AD 1054 the Italians recorded what appeared to be a supernova in the Crab Nebula dating it to 19 April 1054 – significantly, the date of the death of Pope Leo I. But the Irish sources dated it nearly eight weeks later. Who was right? The answer was found in Chinese and Japanese records, comparison with which demonstrated that the Irish date was accurate. The Italians had adjusted the date to coincide with Pope Leo's death.

The system used by the Irish astronomers and astrologers changed again in the eleventh century AD when new Arabic learning, mathematics, medicine, astronomy and astrology entered Europe through such universities as Montpelier and

Bologna. Irish professors teaching there at the time doubtless brought the new knowledge back to Ireland. We find a rich source of manuscript texts and books about astronomy and astrology written in Irish between the twelfth and sixteenth centuries AD, including translations from Arabic, Greek and Latin as well as native texts. But, by this time, the ancient ideas had more or less been filtered out.

The identification of parallels between Celtic cosmology, predominantly surviving in early Irish texts, and the cosmology of the Vedas is important. If, as some Western authorities on astronomy and astrology claim, the Vedas had really borrowed wholesale from the Babylonians via Greece at the time of the invasion of Alexander of Macedonia, then we should not be able to see similarities between old Irish and Sanskrit in the fields of linguistics, cosmology and numerology. Why? Because Babylonian culture would have introduced a completely alien element into Vedic culture and there would be no parallels in the Celtic culture. Babylonian culture derives from two non-Indo-European sources: Sumerian, the oldest recorded language, dating to 3500 BC and unrelated to any other known group, and Hamito-Semitic. Certainly we could not expect parallel cognitive terms and ideas to exist in two diverse branches of Indo-European culture if one of them had been heavily influenced by non-Indo-European learning.

This area of Celtic studies is only just opening up to scholarship; through it we may discover not only the realities of Celtic cosmology but also how the original Indo-Europeans viewed their universe.

# 10

# CELTIC ROAD BUILDERS

In discussing classical commentaries on the Celtic use of heavy wagons and chariots, Dr Anne Ross observed: 'That some provision for all this activity and coming and going must have been made in the way of roads is clear; and it is an aspect of Celtic life which cannot simply be ignored.' Prior to 1970 the evidence for roads was scanty although Dr Ross, myself and several others argued that an efficient network of roads must have existed throughout the ancient Celtic world and that the Romans only improved on it.

The evidence in classical works was there for the discerning reader. Diodorus Siculus talked about merchants using heavy goods wagons in the Celtic lands. Strabo actually mentions the roads in Narbonensis. Then we have the heavy wagons found among the grave goods of the Celtic princes of the Hallstatt period. It is also significant that many of the words connected with roads and transport in Latin are Celtic loan words. The late Professor Stuart Piggott estimated that there were no fewer than nineteen Celtic words connected with roads and transport adopted into pre-empire Latin. In his study, *The Earliest Wheeled Transport*, Professor Piggott points to 'the rich vocabulary of Celtic loan words' and says:

> The Celtic vehicle words in Latin seemed roughly divisible into two groups, the majority being those absorbed in the language at a relatively early date and then used for a variety of Roman wagons, carriages and two-wheelers; a plausible origin would be among the Cisalpine Gauls.

When the Celts first swept down the Italian peninsula and won their early victories over the Roman armies, moving vast distances with their war chariots, wagons and other vehicles, they were clearly used to such transport and the road systems required to move it. According to Roman sources, however, the Romans did not begin to build their own road systems until nearly eighty years after the Celts arrived at the gates of Rome. This road building was initiated in 312 BC by Appius Claudius whose first major construction was named after him – the Appian Way.

The wheel had appeared in prehistory and reached all parts of Europe long before the emergence of the Celts. Through the Bronze Age it had developed from a single cast piece to a hub, usually with eight spokes, set into a wooden curved section in the circumference of the wheel, a felly, made up of two strips bent into the circle with overlapping ends secured in place.

For the Celts the wheel became a solar symbol. Indeed, from 1500 BC the spoked wheel had become a religious symbol in most northern European societies, particularly as representative of the sun. The Celts often buried models of bronze wheels with their dead, perhaps as a means of lighting their journey to the Otherworld. Wheel models have also been found at Celtic shrines, and the symbol appeared on Celtic warrior amulets, helmets and coins.

The Celtic wheelwrights created a new and highly sophisticated concept in wheel-making during the seventh century BC.

They gave the felly a double thickness. The inner felly was made of a single piece of wood bent into a circle. The outer felly consisted of several separate sections bent into an arc following the curvature of the inner felly. They were then joined with iron clamps. In addition to this, and to make the wheel rigid, the ends of the spokes penetrated the inner and the outer felly and the whole was bound with an iron tyre attached with large-headed nails; the nail heads formed the running surface of the wheel, giving that extra purchase.

What was particularly intriguing was that this iron tyre was made too small for the wheel but it was then heated. The Celtic smithies knew that iron expanded with heat. Once expanded, it was forced over the wheel and burnt itself into position. On cooling, the iron contracted and bound the wheel tightly.

The Celts were now able to produce wheels that could carry a range of weapons and chariots far superior to those of their neighbours. Julius Caesar's preoccupation with the movement of British Celtic heavy war chariots, which initially appeared to his soldiers as the first tanks must have appeared to German infantry in the 1914–18 war, certainly implies the existence of a good road system in Britain. Caesar shows that even his cavalry had difficulty facing the British chariots:

> The cavalry, also, found it very dangerous work fighting the charioteers; for the Britons would generally give ground on purpose and after drawing them some distance from the legions would jump down from their chariots and fight on foot, with the odds in their favour.

Caesar points out that after his legions had crossed the Thames into the territory of Cassivellaunus, the British king,

> disbanding the great part of his troops, . . . retained only some four thousand charioteers, with whom he watched our

line of march. He would retire a short way from the route and hide in dense thickets, driving the inhabitants and cattle from the open country into the woods wherever he knew we intended to pass. If ever our cavalry incautiously ventured too far away in plundering and devastating the country, he would send all his charioteers out of the woods by *well-known lanes and pathways* [my emphasis] and deliver very formidable attacks, hoping by this means to keep them afraid to go far afield.

The remains of such chariots have been found in the Parisii graves in Yorkshire. But heavy, iron-tyred chariots could not have been used in the manner that Caesar described without good roads, and evidence for the sophistication of Celtic roads was discovered in the mid-1980s.

The Corlea bog, near the village of Kenagh, Co. Longford, was at the southern extremity of a raised bog covering an extensive area of central Ireland. While the bogland was being explored by Bord na Móna (the Irish Turf Board) in the early 1980s, traces of a roadway were discovered. It was wooden-based but preserved by the anaerobic conditions. Archaeologists began excavations in 1985 and the timbers from the roadway were sent off for dendrochronological analysis. All the samples pointed to a tree-felling date of 148 BC.

This was not the first discovery of a Celtic roadway, but it was the first to attract publicity and impinge on the minds of scholars. In fact, in 1957, in Derraghan More, over a kilometre away, a similar roadway had been discovered and a tree-ring date of 156 BC plus or minus nine years was given. It was obvious that both roadways were part of the same major highway, which proved what had been argued for some years – that the ancient Celts were sophisticated road builders but that, because they used the materials which came naturally to hand, the great forests of northern Europe, only in bogland conditions was any evidence of them preserved. Most of the roads had been overlaid by Roman engineers, working with more enduring stone. Everyone had assumed that it was the Romans who had initially constructed these roadways, whereas in fact they were merely strengthening an existing road system laid out by the Celts.

The Corlea roadway of 148 BC shows that highly sophisticated planning and organisation were needed, together with a massive quantity of timber and a large labour force. Oak and birch were the principal woods used in the construction together with alder, elm, hazel and a few yew trees. Birch formed the substructure, supporting the weight of the upper timbers. Oak planks were put on the birch runners. The roadway was consistently 3–4 metres wide and the oak planks were often carefully adzed to ensure a smooth, flat surface.

To build a roadway crossing a bogland, strong enough to take wagon transport, was a difficult feat in the second century BC. The Celtic engineers showed a brilliance of ingenuity. Professor Barry Raftery, the leading Irish archaeologist, has said:

> The road at Corlea was no ordinary road . . . The construction of the Corlea road was a gigantic undertaking comparable to the effort involved in the erection of the linear earthworks or in the building of the great royal centres.

Corlea is the largest stretch of early Celtic roadway which has survived. But it is not unique. Similar roads have been found in other parts of the Celtic world such as in Dümmer, south of Oldenburg, in Lower Saxony, where the road, in former peatland, shows remarkable similarities of construction. This survival also seems to date from the second century BC. The oldest Celtic roadways have been found in Gwent, in southern Wales; these are also of wooden construction and are laid across the mudflats adjacent to the Severn. The first of these to be found, called the Upton track, has been radiocarbon-dated to around 410 BC.

Evidence for early Irish roads, bridges and causeways abounds in early Irish literature. The five main roads leading to Tara are mentioned in the oldest manuscripts and these were called *slige*, significantly from *sligim*, I hew. Cormac's Glossary says that such roads were built so that two chariots could pass each other comfortably on the road. These five great roads were often referred to in the annals as well as other literature. The Slige Asail ran north-westerly; the Slige Mudluachra went northwards from Tara in one direction and southwards in the other. The Slige Cualan ran southeast through Dublin across the Liffey by the hurdle bridge which still gives the Irish name to Dublin – Baile Atha Cliath, Town of the Hurdle Ford. The Slige Dála ran south-west from Tara to Ossory, Co. Kilkenny. The fifth road, the Slige Mór, ran south-west from Tara to join the Eiscir Riada, a natural ridge running across the whole country from Dublin to Galway. Significantly the name means 'Sandhill of Chariot Driving'.

There is an abundance of terms for a road in old Irish, each name apparently denoting the size and the quality of the road, rather like modern M, A and B categories in England. The ancient Irish were more particular and used no fewer than seven categories ranging from the *slige* to a *lámrota*, a term for a small byway literally meaning a hand-road, from *lámh*, hand, and *rót*, a small road which is defined as being made for a single-horsed chariot.

The Brehon Laws state that the king or chief of the territory through which the road ran was responsible for its upkeep. If a traveller was injured on the road, compensation had to be paid. If the traveller himself did damage to the road, he had to pay damages to the king or chief. All roads had to have three major renovations, during the winter, at the time of the fairs or horse racing, and during a time of war.

There was also a system of bridges and the *Senchus Mór* lays down precise rules on the construction of these bridges. The ancient word in Irish was *droichet*. As well as bridges, causeways or *tóchar* were built. Caesar refers to bridges in Gaul during his conquest of the country.

Long before Caesar's time, the Latin language had adopted many Celtic words connected with transport and forms of transport, even the measure of distance – a league, entering Latin as *leuca* or *leaga*.

One of the earliest and most popular Celtic words for a chariot entered Latin as *carpentum*. It came from the Celtic root *carbanto*, describing a two-wheeled carriage, and was later used by the Romans specifically for a baggage wagon. From this evolved such words as carpenter, car and cart in a number of European languages. The original Celtic word may be seen in such place-names as Carbantorate, Carpentorate and Carbantoritum. Florus uses the word to describe the silver-mounted vehicle in which the Arverni king Bituitus was paraded after his defeat in 121 BC. By Caesar's day it was in general use in Latin for a civil vehicle built especially for women.

There was the *carruca*, a four-wheeled carriage, and the *carrus*, a four-wheeled goods wagon. The *essedum* was a war chariot and the warrior who fought from it was an *essedarius*, from the Celtic *ensedo*, implying something for sitting in. The *essedum* became a Roman pleasure vehicle and during the time of Seneca they were all too common in Rome. Professor Piggott points out that 'we are in a world where foreign names are in use for wholly Roman vehicles, like nineteenth-century London when gentlemen might discuss the relative comfort of the beline or landau as against brougham and tilbury.'

The *reda* or *rheda* was a four-wheeled carriage used for long distance journeys, driven by a *redarius*, and the *petorritum* was an open four-wheeled Celtic wagon. It was Martial, himself an Iberian Celt, who introduced another Celtic loan word – *covinus*, a war chariot, which eventually became a Roman *covinarius* or travelling cart. The word is from the Celtic *covignos*, implying a shared transport.

Another Celtic term for a wagon, *plaustrum* or *ploxenum*, was applied to a vehicle used among the Cisalpine Gauls. Catullus, Cato, Varro and Virgil all describe it as a heavy duty wagon drawn by oxen, asses or mules, with disc wheels and iron tyres. Ovid, curiously, says that *plaustrum* was the Celtic name for the constellation Ursus Major (the Great Bear).

Celtic words pertaining to horses were also borrowed, including *caballus* itself – originally a pack horse but eventually evolving into similar words in many languages, for example (in English) cavalier, cavalry and cavalcade. One of the towns of the Aedui was called Cabillonum, now Châlon-sur-Saône.

This high preponderance of Celtic words in Latin at so early a stage is indicative of Celtic pre-eminence in the field of roadways and transport in their early contacts with Rome.

Obviously the Celtic world was open to land trade and the movement of goods in heavy wagons. Additionally, however, the Celts built river-going craft and traders moved easily along the great Celtic river routes, along the Danube, the Rhine, the Rhône, the Seine, the Loire and the Po. The question that springs to mind is whether the ancient Celts were also a sea-going people.

At least one area of the Celtic world was, otherwise we would have great difficulty explaining the presence of Celts in the north-western islands of Ireland and Britain. The traditions of migrations from the Iberian peninsula and the later migrations of the Belgae would have been impossible if the Celts were unable to master the turbulent seas off Europe's north-west coastline. But to what extent were the ancient Celts ship builders?

Apart from insular records, we have to rely for our most detailed account on Julius Caesar. He says:

The Veneti are much the most powerful tribe on this coast [western Gaul]. They have the largest fleet of ships, in which they traffic with Britain; they excel the other tribes in knowledge and experience of navigation; and as the coast lies exposed to the violence of the open sea and has but few harbours, which the Veneti control, they compel nearly all who sail those waters to pay toll.

Caesar is telling us that the Celts of this coast all have fleets but that the Veneti have the largest and are very skilled in navigating the western seas. Caesar goes on:

The Gauls' own ships were built and rigged in a different manner from ours. They were made with much flatter bottoms, to help them to ride shallow water caused by shoals or ebb-tides. Exceptionally high bows and sterns fitted them for use in heavy seas and violent gales, and the hulls were made entirely of oak, to enable them to stand any amount of shocks and rough usage. The cross-timbers, which consisted of beams a foot wide, were fastened with iron bolts as thick as a man's thumb. The anchors were secured with iron chains instead of ropes. They used sails made of raw hides or thin leather, either because they had no flax and were ignorant of its use, or more probably because they thought that ordinary sails would not stand the violent storms and squalls of the Atlantic and were not suitable for such heavy vessels.

We know that the use of flax and linen was well established, so Caesar's second explanation appears the more likely. Caesar says the Celtic sea-going vessels were solidly built and weathered the storms easily. They could not be damaged by ramming with the Roman vessels. Caesar's description of the Veneti ships is endorsed by Strabo.

Unfortunately, archaeologists have not discovered any

surviving examples of these sea-going vessels though they have come across remains of river craft, a typical example being a large dug-out type from Hasholme, in East Yorkshire, dated to the third century BC. However, a vessel remarkably like the one described by Caesar, with high prow and stern, appears on a Pictish cross slab from Cossans, Angus, known as St Orland's stone.

Certainly, the insular Celts and their Gaulish sea coast neighbours were advanced in this area. In the early centuries of the Christian period the Picts were famed for their fleet, just as the Veneti had been. The *Annals of Tighernach* allude to the might of the Pictish navy. There are descriptions of a warship from the Dàl Riada kingdom in Argyll – a small compact vessel which, when not under sail, was propelled by twenty-eight oarsmen seated on seven benches with seven oars on each side.

Caesar himself makes it clear that there was much intercourse between Gaul and Britain during his time. He met several Britons in Gaul who probably gave him false information about the poverty of Britain in order to dissuade him from invading, for not everything he wrote could be put down to sheer propaganda.

There was trade with the Celts of Britain and Ireland long before Julius Caesar and the Romans made their first military voyages. As has been mentioned, during the century before Rome's major conquest of Britain, the period in which southern Britain seemed to be under the high kingship of Cunobelinus, Britain's trade with the Mediterranean world was much valued. Wheat, cattle, gold, silver, iron, leather goods, hides and hunting dogs were the main exports. Indeed, Strabo (60–24 BC) argued that trade with Britain produced more revenue for Rome than would accrue if the island were to become a Roman province and the Roman treasury had to pay for a standing army and civil service to run the country.

Ireland, too, had sea-going vessels and it was obvious that

there was much contact between Ireland and Britain and Ireland and Europe. Tacitus tells how an Irish king visited Britain and was taken hostage by Agricola, the Roman governor, and, incidentally, Tacitus' father-in-law, who planned to invade Ireland. A war in northern Britain forestalled him.

The Brehon Laws list three types of ship: the *ler-longa* or sea-going vessels, the *barca*, or small coastal vessels, also called *serrcinn*, and lastly the river vessels or *curragh*. The *longa* is not a loan word from Latin *longus* or Saxon *long*, but merely a cognate, as is *barc*. The Irish word is used in the earliest manuscripts. Certainly in the early Christian period the Irish were making many expeditions to Britain, travelling to Cornwall and establishing larger colonies, such as the kingdom of Dyfed, in what is now Wales, and the kingdom of Dál Riada, in what is now Scotland. Irish traders and missionaries were also making their presence felt in Europe.

The discovery of early wine amphorae from the Continent in south-western Ireland indicates the extent of the trade. Certainly we know that Phoenician and Greek traders were visiting Ireland several centuries BC and there is no reason not to suppose that Irish traders were making reciprocal visits. As the early Irish texts speak of their ancestors arriving from the Iberian peninsula, and as the Iberian peninsula was settled by the Celts by the start of the first millennium BC, the use of seagoing ships must have been well established among the Celts.

In the early Christian period we know that groups of Irish missionaries and settlers had reached Iceland before the Norse and were on the Faroes by the time Diciul was writing in the eighth century. In 1976 explorer Tom Severin and his team reconstructed a sixth-century Irish ship using ethnographic, literary and archaeological sources. They built a leather-covered boat some 11 metres long with a beam of 2.5 metres and fitted with sails and oars. Using the Irish classic *Navigatio Sancti Brendani Abbatis*, which is said to be a factual account of a voyage made by St Brendan of Clonfert (*c.* AD 486–578), and the earliest manuscript copies of which survive from the tenth century, Severin traced the voyage from Galway, sailing on 17 May 1976, travelling by way of the Hebrides, Faroes, Iceland and Greenland, and making landfall in Newfoundland on 26 June 1977. He thus proved that the Irish of this period would have been capable of crossing the Atlantic as the *Navigatio* had apparently recorded.

The ability of the ancient Celts to travel great distances has been underestimated, in spite of the knowledge of their movements through Europe. Henri Hubert has demonstrated that the various Celtic societies in the ancient world not only shared a sense of common origin but were in communication. He cites two instances from the Second Punic War. When the Romans found that Hannibal proposed to march from the southern Iberian peninsula, through southern Gaul, across the Alps and into Cisalpine Gaul, they sent ambassadors to prevent the Celtic tribes supporting Carthage, but found that all these tribes shared a sense of unity against Rome. Shortly afterwards, the Greek Senate of Massilia (Marseilles) asked their Celtic neighbours to contact the Celts dwelling in Galatia (the central plain of Turkey) and ask them not to act with hostility towards Lampsacos. Hubert argued:

This solidarity of the Celtic peoples, even when distant from one another, is sufficiently explained by the sense of kinship, of common origin acting in a fairly restricted world, all the parts of which were in communication.

For that ancient world to be in communication to the extent which these references imply, it would have been essential that the Celts had an efficient transport system, via roads and shipping.

# 11

# CELTIC ARTISTS AND CRAFTSMEN

Polybius makes an extraordinary statement when he writes about the Celts of the Po valley: 'Their lives were very simple, and they had no knowledge whatsoever of any art or science.' Here we see the 'superior' Roman attitude dominating. I say 'Roman' advisedly, although Polybius (*c*. 200–after 118 BC) was a Greek, born at Megalopolis in Arcadia. He became a tutor to the children of Publius Scipio in Rome and was an unashamed Romanophile. In his work charting the rise of the Roman empire he is unquestioning in the belief that Rome was the greatest nation on earth and its constitution 'perfection'. Polybius waxes lyrical about his pursuit of 'truth' and how he was writing a *pragmatike historia*, a factual history. However, it is hard to imagine that a man of his learning really believed his own comments on the state of Celtic art and craftsmanship. His audience were the upper-class Romans, who were able to read Greek, and he was writing at a time when the Romans were in the middle of a colonisation programme of the Celts of northern Italy having conquered them in a series of bloody wars.

Archaeology has given the lie to Polybius and the Roman propagandists, revealing the brilliance of early Celtic art and craftsmanship. Indeed, Celtic art, described by Dr Simon James as representing 'an aesthetic sense fundamentally different from the classical canon which framed the Renaissance and modern Western conceptions of art, was one of the greatest glories of prehistoric Europe'.

It is, of course, by the distinctive patterns of surviving arte-facts that archaeology traces the emergence of the Celts before written records. The brilliance of metalwork, jewellery, weapons, utensils, wagons and other items shows that the Celtic artists and craftsmen were exceptionally skilled and sought technological perfection in their work.

Celtic arts and crafts began to evolve in the distinctive form we recognise today during the early Hallstatt period. The decorative art is identified by geometric designs, such as chevrons, parallel lines and concentric circles. Archaeologists have iden-tified the centres of the developing Celtic art as being the Hallstatt royal sites such as Hohenasperg, west of Ludwigsburg in Swabia, where there are many princely graves, and Heuneburg.

Celtic art was basically a design-centred technique develop-ing in the later period with many zoomorphic emblems and representations. There are very few representations of com-plete human figures on a realistic level such as occur in Greek and Roman art. However, there are stone sculptures of figures such as those at Hirschlanden and Glauberg.

Human faces did become a popular motif but they are generally given an almost surreal appearance. There is some evidence that Celtic artists were also capable of realistic por-trayals but they appear to have rejected this approach. The bronze head of a Celtic war goddess from the first century BC, from Dineault, Brittany, is a realistic representation, as is the Celtic warrior appearing on a brooch, dating from the second century BC, and reckoned to be of Iberian Celtic workmanship. There is also the figurine of a goddess from the first century AD, from Chalmalières, now in the Musée Archéologique, at Clermont Ferrand. Dr James has suggested that, in the light of the obvious Celtic ability to make realistic representations of the human body, 'perhaps human figures and scenes were taboo'. This seems a likely explanation. In Moslem art, too, human representations are taboo; the accent is on design because of religious proscription and not because of an inability on the part of the artists.

As the Hallstatt period came to its later stages and trade with Etruscans, Greeks, Phoenicians and the Latin world opened up, the Celtic artists were undoubtedly influenced by the new concepts from the Mediterranean world, but they were highly selective as to what they took from these sources.

The La Tène period of art began to flourish with a continuation of geometric motifs whose intricate detail and ornamentation fascinates modern viewers. Many people think that the intricacy and inexplicable symbolism might have had a religious connotation – again, much as similar motifs are used in Moslem art.

A great deal of La Tène art concentrated on jewellery and items of personal domestic use such as mirrors and combs, as well as weapons and decorated harnesses for horses. One of the richest expressions of Celtic art, however, is to be found in the production of Celtic coinage.

The Celts had developed their own distinctive coinage by the late fourth century BC. It is safe to say that it was inspired by Greek coinage and had resulted from Celtic trade with the Greek world. Greek coinage had come into being at the end of the seventh century BC. To put the Celtic development of coinage into context, the Insubrean Celts of the Po valley were minting their own coins some fifty years before Rome started to do so; Roman coins also resulted from contacts with the Greek city states of southern Italy and were based on the same weight standard as that used by the Greeks.

Dr Daphne Nash is inclined to believe that Celtic coinage arose because of the payment in Greek coinage to Celtic mercenaries selling their services to the Greek states from the fourth century BC. She is not inclined to take into consideration the continuous trade between the Celts and Greeks which dated back to the seventh and sixth centuries BC. I consider this to be an omission.

Coinage is to be found in all parts of the ancient Celtic world, with the significant exception of Ireland. No native coinage appeared to have developed here until the Christian period was well under way. Some Roman coinage has been discovered. Early references imply that gold rings were used as currency. Caesar had said of first-century BC Britain: 'For money they used bronze, or gold coins, or iron ingots of fixed weights.' Certainly coinage was being used in Britain by the second century BC, with each major tribe and its king issuing stamped coins.

Throughout the Celtic world, coins were minted by first casting the metal, which was generally gold, silver or bronze, in moulds of burnt clay that had been prepared beforehand. This resulted in the production of coins of exactly equal weight. The pieces were then finished manually, by hammering them between the two stamps. Most of these coins bore images which could have been of religious significance.

We are extraordinarily lucky in that a great many of the Celtic coins survive, although what has been lost by melting down the gold and silver of many hordes can only be guessed at.

When names or human heads begin to appear on the coins in the mid-second century BC, they are personal names of rulers, comparable with the names of Roman consuls of the republican period and the emperors of the later period. We have the coins of many famous Celtic kings and rulers such as Cunobelinus (Cymbeline), who was issuing his coinage in the years before the Roman Claudian invasion. We have coins, and

The Desborough Mirror, a British Celtic bronze mirror, one of several such decorated mirrors showing the curvilinear art style for which the Celts were famous.

*Above*: The Snettisham Torc. Celtic nobility and elite warriors (males and females) from all parts of the Celtic world wore these gold neck pieces. This is one of the finest examples.

*Left*: Celtic artists excelled in metalwork. This flagon, one of a pair from Basse-Yutz in the Moselle, dated to the 5th century, with its stylized animals and coral and red glass, depicts a pack of dogs chasing a duck which 'swims' into the pouring wine.

The remains of the broch of Carloway on the Isle of Lewis, Scotland,
which is one of the 500 brochs that have survived and are visually some
of the most exciting remains of early Celtic architecture.

Graggaunowen, Co. Clare, is a reconstruction of a 'crannog'. These are circular, timber framed thatched houses built on an island in a lake or estuary or marsh. The island was often man-made with a man-made causeway for security. They were occupied from 1000 BC and provide a fascinating glimpse of Celtic architectural ingenuity.

The 'Father of the Gods', Cernunnos, equivalent to the Irish 'The Dagda', from the Gundestrup cauldron.

This section of the Gundestrup cauldron is thought to depict Danu, the mother goddess, incorporating the solar wheel symbol and various cult animals.

One of the most fascinating cult pieces from the ancient Celtic world, a 7th century BC bronze wheeled cauldron which is supported by a goddess (Danu?) while around her appear to be hunters or warriors with two stags.

This gold model ship from the 1st century, found in Broighter, Co. Derry, is argued by some to be a votive offering to the sea god Manannán Mac Lir, or to be the ship in which Donn gathers the dead for the voyage west to the Otherworld.

The Cerne Abbas Giant,
Dorset, standing 55 metres
high and 51 metres wide,
carved on a hillside, steps
directly out of the Celtic
myth. 'The Dagda' of Irish
myth is depicted in like
manner and he is equated with
Cernunnos. The Cerne Abbas
figure is almost a replica of a carving
found at Costopitum (Corbridge,
Northumberland). He is the famous
Dis Pater, the Father of the Celtic Gods.

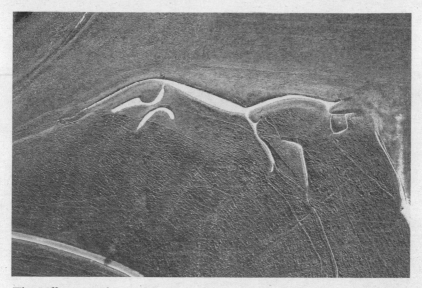

The Uffington White Horse, one of the most spectacular hill carvings, 365 feet from nose to tail, dated from the 1st century BC, is thought to be a product of Belgae craftsmanship. The exact same stylization appears on many Celtic coins, including a gold coin of the Aulerci (1st century BC).

One of the spectacular plates from the Gundestrup cauldron which is replete in Celtic mythological and religious symbolism.

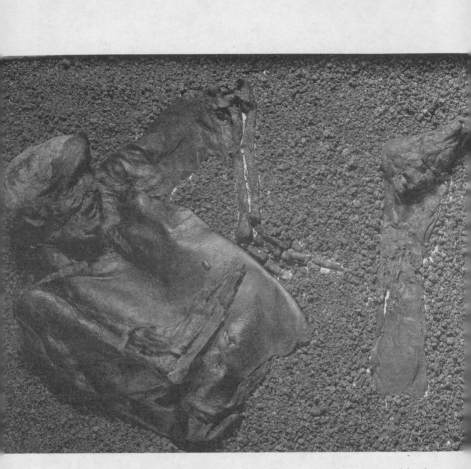

One of the most intriguing finds in recent years was the preserved body of a young man found in a peat bog near Winslow, Cheshire, England. The man had been hit on the back of the head, strangled and had his throat cut. His manicured fingernails pointed to him being of a high social caste. Known as Lindow Man, some have argued he was the victim of a ritual threefold death sacrifice.

some rare gold coins, of Vercingetorix, the great Gaulish king who fought Caesar and is considered the last ruler of the 'free Gauls'.

The majority of the late Celtic coins have heads on one side and a pattern based on an animal on the reverse. Some experts consider the heads to be gods or goddesses. I am more inclined to believe that the heads are those of the actual rulers, male and female. Early coins do have representations of deities but it is always quite clear what they are. For example, a second-century BC bronze coin of Belgic Gaul, issued by the Remi tribe, shows a figure in a lotus position holding accoutrements very much like the figure on the Gundestrup Cauldron. The heads of deities seem clearly to be identified as such. The later heads are of bearded and unbearded males and of females with elaborate individual hairstyles.

The animals on the reverse are often horses, sometimes with a chariot, and even a charioteer. Sometimes a horseman is represented. The next most popular figure is a boar. Less frequently coins carry representations of lions, bears, cattle, goats and ravens. The zoomorphic emblems are usually accompanied by other artefacts above or below them. These undoubtedly possessed a symbolic significance which we can longer discern. The man-headed horse and the goat-headed snake are particularly Celtic and are found in many pieces of artwork. Severed human heads also abound.

No examination of the Celtic world is complete without a consideration of these coins, whose sheer exuberance and artistry illustrate so many Celtic concepts. Their composition also gives us invaluable information about the metallurgy and metrology of the period.

While Greek and Latin terms have subsequently been given to these coins (such as *stater* and *tetradrachme*), Dr Bernhard Maier has rightly pointed out that we do not know what the Celts named their coinage. The only native evidence we have is from early Irish sources from the time the Irish kings started to use a coinage system. The value of currency in eighth-century Ireland, the period from when our evidence comes, was fixed on the cow. A full-grown cow or ox was the general standard of value not only in Ireland but throughout the Celtic world. Greek coinage developed from the value of an iron cooking spit (*obelos*), hence the *obol*, six *obols* being equivalent to one *drachma*. For the Irish the value represented by one milch cow was usually called a *séd*. Cormac's Glossary lists a classification of the *séd* from the milch cow (the top value) to a heifer (called a *dartaid*) or the worst value. The Irish law system later seems to have adopted a *miach*, or sack of corn (oats or barley), as a general standard of currency.

In early times we find a native coin called a *crosóc*, whose tabular weight was entirely different from later coins. It was reckoned to be eighteen grains of wheat (13.5 troy grains). This coin was marked with a cross, but we should not immediately conclude that this was a Christian symbol for the Celts used cross motifs as solar symbols, including the swastika-style cross which evolved into Brigit's cross. The *crosóc* fell out of use when the *screpall* and *pinginn* came into being around the fourth and fifth centuries AD.

These two coins were both of silver. The *pinginn* weighed eight grains of wheat or 6 troy grains while the *screpall*, also called a *sical*, weighted twenty-four grains (18 troy grains). It has been pointed out that the words *screpall* and *sical* must undoubtedly have been borrowed from the Latin (*scrupulus* and *siculus* in turn derived from the Hebrew *shekel*). But on closer examination we find there are several native names for these coins (*puingcne, opuingc, oiffing, faing* and *fang* were all alternative names for the *screpall*, and *píss* was an alternative for the *pinginn*).

The evolution by the Celts of metalworking was the foundation of their technological advancement. Their proficiency in iron working was a significant step in European progress. How the Celts came by these techniques is impossible to say. It may simply be that they developed them through the process of working other metals. The first peoples to emerge as advanced in such techniques, in the late second millennium BC, were the Indo-European Hittites. Iron ore was abundant in the Anatolian mountains where they had settled, and iron became a valuable metal among the Hittites. It was worked by a few skilled craftsmen. King Anittas received as tribute from the city of Puruskhanda an iron sceptre and an iron throne. Iron swords began to be produced here but not in such quantity as to make a significant difference in warfare. However the Celts, experimenting over many centuries with smelting and forging techniques, probably arrived at their knowledge without outside influence.

In ancient Celtic society, the smiths were accorded a high status. They were considered to rank with the professional intellectuals and were thus part of the intellectual caste of society. Perhaps this was because they were regarded as possessing some Otherworld knowledge; some magical skill in that, by means of fire, water and their art, they produced strong metal from the rough iron ore.

The Celtic god of smiths seems to bear a single name throughout the Celtic world, represented by Goibhniu in Ireland and Gofannon in Wales. In Ireland, the smith god appears as a triune god, as Goibhniu, Luchta and Credhne. In some texts the trinity is Goibhniu, Cian and Samhain. Goibhniu was the smith, Luchta the wright and Credhne the metalworker; all three combined to produce weapons or wheels or whatever other artefact came from their combined skills.

In the famous battle between the children of Danu and the gods of the Underworld, the Fomorii, each of the gods made a different part of the weapons: Goibhniu made the blade, Luchta the shaft and Credhne the rivets. Goibhniu's weapons were always accurate and inflicted a fatal wound. Curiously enough he was also made host of the Otherworld feast in which he provided a special ale and those who drank of it became immortal.

In Welsh myth, Gofannon, the smith god, was the son of Dôn, the equivalent of Danu, who features in the Tale of Culhwch and Olwen.

The Celtic god is clearly the equivalent of the Greek Hephaistos, who also prepares the feast of the gods while his ale preserves their immortality, and the Roman Vulcan. Figures of smith gods are found throughout the Celtic world but they are particularly prevalent in northern Britain. While the Continental name for the smith god does not seem to have survived in epigraphy, we may speculate from the insular Celtic forms. There are many representations of the god Sucellus carrying a long-shafted hammer or mallet, and the name has been interpreted as 'the good striker'. Yet the immediate identification of Sucellus as a smith god could be an over-simplification, for his hammer might symbolise something entirely different.

Celtic craftsmen were also skilled in the production of glass and in enamelling. The Celts had learned how to make glass by the sixth and fifth centuries BC but it is only from the fourth century BC that the first traces of Celtic glass-producing workshops survive. Glass was used chiefly in the production of jewellery and other artefacts, particularly coloured beads and ornaments. Glass animals abound from this period. A fascinating example of how advanced the Celts were in making coloured glass figurines may be seen in the miniature glass dog found in Wallertheim, Germany, dating from the second century BC. The technique used was spinning semi-molten ribbons of variously coloured glass on a rod.

Glass beads were very popular during this period, as were glass bangles. Several statues and Celtic heads were clearly made with glass eyes, such as the figure from Bouray, Essome, dated to the first century AD, who is seated in the lotus position, a torc around the neck, and with a blue and white glass eye – the only one remaining *in situ*.

The production of glass and enamel in Britain and Ireland had become extremely sophisticated by the first century BC. The enamelling technique would eventually influence the gospel illumination of the Christian period in these areas.

In 1987 archaeologists uncovered a spectacular third-century BC sword at Kirkburn in Yorkshire. It is now in the British Museum in London, and demonstrates the high degree of craftsmanship among the Celts. It is of iron, bronze and enamel with patterns engraved on it, and the pommel is of horn. It was found to have been assembled from over seventy components, each item crafted with considerable skill. The overall length was 697 millimetres with a blade of 570 millimetres.

Enamelling was also carried out among the Continental Celts. The craftsmen had learned how to fuse the glass on to the surface of copper alloys, creating a true enamel working. They used a variety of colours but the favourite was red. A typical example of this type of work is the late-fourth-century BC bronze helmet from Amfreville-sous-les-Monts, Eure, France, which is stylistically decorated with gold and red enamel. Another example, from a bronze belt chain of the second century BC, is a pendant in the shape of a dragon-type animal, which has red enamel inlays. This was found in Nové Zámky, in the Czech Republic.

Some of the most outstanding examples of Celtic art may be found in the mirrors, especially as represented by the Desborough, Northamptonshire, bronze mirror, dated to the end of the first century BC. The bronze back surface is engraved with fascinating Celtic designs that could only have been achieved with the aid of a compass. The Holcombe, Devon, mirror of the same period is similar in style. Very few Celtic mirrors have survived on the European mainland but we are lucky in having a whole series of insular Celtic mirrors found mostly in Britain from East Anglia across to Cornwall.

Celtic potters had progressed to the use of the wheel from

the end of the Hallstatt period. They fired their pots in technically advanced kilns which were designed to allow oxygen to be introduced; the potter could thus control the colour of the vessel, depending on its clay. By the La Tène period, the potters often stamped their pots with animal designs. Later the pots were painted with bands of red or white or black patterns such as cross hatching. This was done by applying liquid clay before firing. Some Celtic potters added graphite to the clay to achieve a metallic appearance.

The insular Celts tended to make their pots by hand, particularly the north Britons. In fact, both the north Britons and the Irish appeared to produce very little in the way of pottery at all, preferring, it seems, to use intricate metalwork bowls or carved wooden vessels, which were much more labour intensive but durable. The evidence shows that the Celts even used lathes to turn out wooden bowls and tool handles.

Woodworking was advanced among all the Celtic peoples, which is not surprising as wood was their environment. Great forests covered all the Celtic lands and once iron had been introduced into their tools the Celts fell to work with a will to fell the forests for constructional work in building their homes, towns and roadways. Celtic carpenters were as skilled as their metalworkers. The great trees were felled with axes and split into planks using wooden wedges. From the early La Tène period some constructional timbers have been recovered up to 12 metres in length along with a variety of woodworking tools. These included small saws and even adzes.

Celtic woodworkers were little different from their Roman counterparts in using mortises and tenons or pegged joints. There are traces of elaborate wooden structures, such as gates to towns, or doors to buildings and so forth. There are even references in some classical works to elaborate wooden bridges being found in Gaul across the rivers.

We will deal with the construction of houses in the next chapter and have already remarked on the building of ships and land vehicles in which carpenters played a central role. But the Celtic woodworkers also produced an intricate range of portable objects, including metal-bound wooden buckets, or barrels, such as those found at Aylesbury in Britain or Manching in Germany.

We have seen that the Celts were skilled in the production of fabrics, and that the British woollen cloak or *sagum* was the height of fashion in Rome in the second and first centuries BC. Cassius Dio, in his description of Boudicca, says that 'she wore a tunic of diverse colours over which a thick mantle was fastened by a brooch.' Unfortunately, fabric only survives in exceptional circumstances, but we do have a fur cape and a wrap-around skirt from the fifth century BC, preserved in a bog at Huldrenose, Denmark. The skirt is of a fabric similar to tartan. Other finds from the Hallstatt period include check patterns and the colours, although faded, are reminiscent of the tartan so characteristic of Celtic clothing according to the descriptions in classical sources. Wool and linen were the main fabrics for clothing although silks, obviously imported, have also been discovered.

Leather working was widespread and leather sandals, shoes, belts and other accoutrements have been found throughout the Celtic world. Combinations of wood and leather were also used by the Celtic shoemakers.

Once again, we have to conclude from the remarkable evidence left from the ancient Celtic world that the Roman descriptions of barbaric savagery are less than fair to a society highly advanced in the field of arts and crafts.

# 12

# CELTIC ARCHITECTURE

There are two popular views of Celtic builders and both are erroneous. The first is that the Celts constructed the great megaliths of western Europe but, as these were built in a period long before we can safely identify a Celtic culture, we must disregard this theory. Jacquetta and Christopher Hawkes have suggested that the megaliths might have been built by an early Indo-European people and that these people were proto-Celts, but as we simply have no way of proving this it remains an hypothesis. The second view is that the ancient Celts lived in wattle huts, often huddled behind earth ramparts, and did not build anything substantial at all. That is how the Roman propagandists would have us see them. That also is untrue.

Celtic architects and builders, in their northern homelands, were faced with problems which their Greek and Roman counterparts did not have to contend with when it came to constructing buildings that would last. Nevertheless, despite the test of nature and time and the destructive intervention of subsequent generations, remnants still exist. There are constructions in Scotland, for example, originally built in the fifth century BC, which still stand to a height of 12 metres.

Early Celtic Hallstatt culture was basically rural and many of the constructions were wooden farmhouses. For the Celts, dwelling among the vast European forest regions, wood was the major source of building material. On the other hand, the great royal centres had begun to spring up. Strongholds such as Heuneburg, in the sixth century BC, and Entremont developed into cities, with a royal residence surrounded by clusters of houses and set out on street patterns with shops and other places of business.

Archaeologists call these royal sites, enclosed by fortifications, *oppida*, the plural of the Latin word for town. Built from the sixth and fifth centuries BC, these *oppida* differed from early sites in their size and in the fact that they were centres of trade and crafts as well as providing means of protection in case of threat.

At the open air museum of Asparn, near Vienna, one can see reconstructions of the typical Continental Celtic farm dwellings, rectangular houses that would not be out of place among modern Canadian log cabins. These rectangular Celtic houses varied from a single large room to great multi-room buildings with a central corridor leading to the various chambers. It was not uncommon to have a second storey on these buildings.

There is an interesting contrast between early Continental Celtic housing and insular Celtic housing for the constructions in Britain and Ireland were mostly round houses, as demonstrated by the recreations at Butser Farm and the Chiltern Open Air Museum. These museum constructions were based on the plan of a house excavated at Pimperne, in Dorset. The idea of the round house came from the older Atlantic coast tradition of building. The British and Irish Celtic round houses continued into the late La Tène period with exceptionally large constructions such as that at Navan, Co. Armagh, built about 94 BC.

As the La Tène period progressed on the Continent we find half-timbered houses often two storeys high and sometimes even rising to three storeys. A Celtic village excavated at Monte Bibele in the Apennines has revealed a site occupied by the Celts between 400 and 200 BC with a possible population at any one time of 200–300 people. They lived in some forty or fifty houses, which were built of stone and timber, probably thatched, and arranged in a systematic pattern. The timbers show that they were houses of two storeys. The excavated houses were destroyed by fire about 200 BC and we can hypothesise that this happened during one of the Roman incursions into the area for the site fell within the territory of the Boii tribe dwelling south of the Po River.

In the second century BC, the Celtic settlements throughout Europe began to change pattern and a system of cities emerged. One of the biggest was Manching, 8 kilometres south of Ingoldstadt, Bavaria, close to the Danube. It was a walled city, with a circumference of 8 kilometres, and the walls stood up to 5 metres high, enclosing some 380 hectares. Within the walls there was a system of well laid out streets and an orderly arrangement of the mainly timber buildings.

Manching was the capital of the Vindelici and a centre of arts and crafts, including pottery. There was even a mint for striking coins. The Romans attacked and destroyed the city in about 15 BC. Excavations began in 1938 and still continue, and in 1988 a museum was opened on the site. Previous finds are divided between the Prähistorische Staatssammlung in Munich and the Stadtmuseum of Ingoldstadt.

The great walls of Manching were built of a box structure of criss-cross timbers laid horizontally. A stone wall was built on both sides with the ends of the cross timbers inserted. The centre was then filled with rubble and stones. Caesar mentions finding such great wall constructions in Gaul proper and he called them *muri Gallici*. He was particularly impressed with the capital of the Aedui, Bibracte (Mont Beuvray), which was surrounded by a wall 5 kilometres in circumference and 5 metres in height. Bibracte was not destroyed by the Romans for the Aedui were initially pro-Roman. Its business life continued, with iron workers, jewellers and other craftsmen working in their shops along the main streets and its royal palace dominating the city. Bibracte did not fall into disuse until after 5 BC when the Romans and Romanised Celts built a new city, Autun, nearby.

Numantia was another great Celtic town, situated overlooking the River Douro in Spain. It was the capital of the Arevaci, occupied from ancient times but achieving the height of its prosperity in the third century BC. It covered some 20 hectares with a well-defined street system and houses of stone or stone foundation, timber and clay brick. In 133 BC the Roman general P. Cornelius Scipio threw up siege works around the town and starved the inhabitants into surrender. The town was then systematically destroyed by the Romans and the occupants were sold into slavery.

Maiden Castle, Dorset, and Danebury, in Hampshire, are among the best known of the British Celtic townships. They were originally built as hill-forts and grew over the years. The fortifications at Maiden Castle are immense and it seems they were constructed around 350 BC. The town walls enclosed some 19 hectares. Over the years the fortifications were added to with ramparts reinforced with limestone blocks. The inner rampart itself was a vertical barrier of 15 metres. Danebury was built on a lesser scale, but its exterior fortifications enclosed a site of 11 hectares. It was occupied from 650 to 100 BC. Danebury has been carefully excavated over the years, and the Museum of the Iron Age in Andover shows many artefacts and reconstructions of life in these fortified towns. Both Maiden Castle and Danebury were destroyed by the II Augusta Legion under Vespasian who subsequently became emperor.

The most important sites of cities and towns in the ancient

Celtic world, from an archaeological viewpoint, were Alesia, Bibracte and Gergovia in France, Heidengraben and Manching in Germany and Staré Hradisko and Závist in the eastern Celtic area. Alesia occupied some 100 hectares on the slopes of Mont Auxois, near Alise-Sainte-Reine. It was here that Vercingetorix had to face the starvation of his people or surrender to Caesar. The site was apparently so important that it was still used after Vercingetorix surrendered it to Caesar, and was not abandoned by its inhabitants until the Middle Ages.

Gergovia, the home town of Vercingetorix and an Arverni stronghold, enclosed 75 hectares and did not fall to Caesar's siege tactics. Even more spectacular was an unnamed town at Heidengraben, on the Swabian Alb north-east of Urach. The site covered an incredible 1660 hectares and was defended by walls and gates. An area of 153 hectares in the southern part of the walled-in site was given additional protection by ramparts and pits and was, perhaps, the aristocratic or royal quarter. Finds suggest it was built in the second century BC but, sadly, no full-scale excavations have yet been made. No evidence of when it fell into disuse has been found but it seems likely that the Celts who occupied it formed part of the great Helvetian confederation and that they abandoned it when they began their westward migration around 58 BC.

Staré Hradisko, 18 kilometres east of Prostejov in Moravia, was a site of 40 hectares but surrounded by a chain of fortifications some 3.2 kilometres in circumference. It appears to be one of the most important eastern Celtic towns. Závist, south of Prague, at the confluence of the Beraun and Moldau, was another important eastern Celtic town and the site of a Celtic religious sanctuary. Its earliest fortifications date back to the sixth and fifth centuries BC. By the second century BC the town covered 170 hectares. In the last decades BC, as the Celts were being forced westward by the pressure of the incoming Germanic tribes from the north and Slavs from the east, the town was burnt, presumably either in an attack or by the Celts themselves. Caesar says that when the Helvetii and their allies moved westward they adopted a scorched earth policy rather than leave their townships and immovable wealth to the invaders.

The evidence in both Gaul and Britain is that the fortified sites had generally fallen into disuse during the late La Tène period. Having no enemies, the Celts often lived in unwalled farming communities or in the great cities. Then, firstly with the threat from the Romans and then with the threat from the Germanic tribes, the Celts reoccupied the fortified sites and strengthened them.

The excavation of these fortified towns or hill-forts leaves one open-mouthed at the craftsmanship of the Celtic architects and builders. There are literally hundreds of hill-forts and thousands of ring-forts throughout the ancient Celtic world. The work involved in moving such colossal amounts of earth and stone is absolutely breath-taking. Of course, we must allow for centuries of burning and destruction by the Romans and Germanic tribes before we can understand what the face of Celtic Europe really looked like.

While the vast majority of constructions were of wood, the ancient Celts also built in stone and many examples have survived. One of the best-preserved early Celtic villages built in stone is Chysauster, at Madron, in Cornwall. It appears to have been built in the century before the Roman invasion in the south-east of Britain, and to have been peacefully occupied until the fourth century AD. There are eight houses in the village, four on either side of a street, while a ninth house lies down an alleyway. The stone houses are oval in shape; an entrance passage, often 6 metres long, leads into a courtyard out of which a series of doors open into circular and rectangular rooms. The floors were stone-faced. Some of these rooms were for living in, others apparently for working. One of the houses had underfloor drainage, showing that the

Romans were not the only Europeans possessed of such ingenuity. It seems that the courtyards were left open to the sky but the houses were either corbelled or thatched. Near the houses is a *fougou*, or underground storage chamber, some 15 metres long. Terraced and walled garden plots are situated behind the houses, a field system is close by and a track leads to a stream where tin working was carried out.

Scotland seems to have more surviving stone constructions than many other places. The Celts probably built in stone here because of the weather conditions. The most visually exciting survival of early Celtic architecture is the broch, or defended homestead. Over 500 have been recorded with only a dozen of these outside northern Scotland and the western and northern islands. They are therefore considered to be an innovation of the Celtic tribes who later emerged under their Roman nickname Picti (past participle of *pingere*, to paint).

Dr Ian Armit maintains that the first identifiable ancestors of the brochs are a series of thick-walled dry-stone round houses that began to appear around 600 BC. The Bu round house, on Orkney, was divided into rooms by tall flagstones.

The typical broch was a dry-stone structure, with walls usually about 5 metres thick and with an internal diameter of 10 to 13 metres. Their tapering shape was designed to give them great strength. There is a single entrance, a door, chambers and one or more staircases leading to galleries. Inside were ovens, cupboards and stairways leading to the various levels.

The most famous example is that of Mousa (Shetland) where the walls remain about 15 metres high. Another spectacular broch is Dun Twelve, Inverness, where the walls stand up to 10 metres and are 4 metres thick. Many artefacts were discovered here and are now in the National Museum of Scotland. A reconstruction has been made of the Clickhimin broch which was in use from the end of the second century BC to the second century AD. It has been conjectured that they came into being as a visual expression of the power of the maritime trading tribes. Dr Armit believes that there were more than twenty 'broch villages' in Caithness alone and that such groups of broch houses represented the architectural embodiment of social control. The petty king or chief ruled from the exceptionally tall and imposing structure, which was surrounded by a series of cellular stone buildings in which those of lesser rank dwelt. The broch would take its place as the equivalent of the local château or castle dwelling of the lord of the territory.

The ancient Celts also built circular, timber-framed thatched houses on artificial islands in lakes, estuaries or marshland, called crannogs. The majority have been excavated in Scotland but there are also several in Ireland, mainly in the north, and some have even been found in the fens of East Anglia, in England, while there is a solitary example in South Wales. Most crannogs were built at the start of the Hallstatt period.

The crannog is further evidence of the ingenuity of Celtic architects and builders. Once the site was located – say, in a lake – large boulders were rafted to the position and sunk until, eventually, an island broke the surface of the lake. Great numbers of wooden piles, beams and stakes were cut and incorporated into the boulders as foundations, and a wooden platform was built just above the water level. On this, the house was built, sometimes as large as 15 metres in diameter. A quay was added and, sometimes, a planked walkway to the shore which usually incorporated a drawbridge as a means of protection. The main purpose of these houses was to provide their occupants with protection from any sudden attack. Through Loch Tay there have been some fifteen crannogs identified.

The Celtic builders in Ireland used similar techniques. Ring-forts, or enclosed farmsteads, and fortified dwelling places of varying sizes are found throughout Ireland. It has been estimated that some 30,000 to 40,000 sites have been identified. As well as crannogs there are also over fifty major hill-forts, including the spectacular stone-built Dun Aengus. One of the most impressive examples of Celtic stone building is Staigue fort in Co. Kerry. Built in the fifth century BC, the fort is strategically situated at the head of a valley around which the hills form an amphitheatre. It is also surrounded by a ditch. The circular walls, of dry-stone construction, still stand at 4 metres in height and are 2.5 metres thick in places, with steps and walkways around the interior circumference and two inner chambers. The entire structure is 27 metres in diameter. The door faces down the valley and has sloping jambs.

When the Brehon Laws were codified in Ireland, the position of builder carried professional status. The Ollamh (surviving as the modern Irish word for a professor) builder superintended the craftsmen in their work. Kings – both petty and provincial kings and the high king – employed an Ollamh builder, who received a yearly 'retainer' of the value of twenty-one cows. The law even classifies the work which the Ollamh builder could undertake – nineteen classes in all – and the payment he would receive for such work. For example, if he was required to build a new kitchen his fee was the value of six cows. Obviously, this was no ordinary kitchen but the kitchen of a king or a chief.

The ancient law text, the *Crith Gablach*, deals with offences against buildings and the penalties they incurred. The ancient Irish recognised the offence of damaging buildings. If straying cattle ate the thatch of a house, if someone broke down the door of a house and especially if someone set fire to a house, there was a whole list of fines and compensations to be paid. There are references in the surviving law texts to a lost text entitled *Bretha Forloiscthe*, 'judgements of arson'. According to the surviving commentaries on it, this text distinguished between accidental fire, fires caused by negligence and fires caused by deliberate arson. It laid down the penalties for causing death or injury to people and to domestic animals in such fires. St Patrick in the fifth century AD is said to have preached strongly in support of the law against arson.

Once again we see that the popular notion of ancient Celtic society as consisting of itinerant hordes, constantly on the move from one area of Europe to another and living in hastily constructed wood or mud huts, is entirely erroneous.

# 13

# CELTIC RELIGION

When they speak of 'Celtic religion', many people are referring to the insular Celtic mythology of which we have written records, albeit in a bowdlerised Christian form. However, religion is not merely mythology, although the sacred traditions of the latter often account for beliefs relating to ritual practices and festivals. There is, admittedly, a fine line between what is mythology and what is religion, by which we mean the cults of deities, and the rites and beliefs associated with them.

As the ancient Celts did not leave us written records of their beliefs in a systematic form, some have expressed the belief that it is impossible to summon the pre-Christian Celtic religion from the grave and have simply left the field to those who have conjured the inventions of the seventeenth, eighteenth and nineteenth-century romantics to claim all manner of weird rituals for the ancient Celts. However, when we examine the evidence, there is much we know about Celtic religion.

Like almost all the religions of the ancient world, Celtic religion was polytheistic. There are over 400 names of Celtic deities, male and female, recorded but the vast majority would appear to be local deities, tribal gods and goddesses. However, that leaves some hundred or so who are to be found throughout the Celtic world; indeed, many of the deities are clearly the major deities of the Celts.

Julius Caesar commented that the Celts were a very religious people, a characteristic still evident among modern Celtic peoples. As a Roman, Caesar saw the Celtic religion as something exotic, alien and barbaric. However, the themes of the common Indo-European inheritance are still there to be observed, and the pantheon of Celtic deities is not far removed from the pantheon of Latin, Greek or even Hindu deities. If we may overlook the Irish Christian bowdlerisation of their gods and goddesses, as they appear in the written mythology, they were as fallible, unpredictable and subject to all the human vices as were the deities who dwelt on Mount Olympus in Greek culture or the Hindu gods as depicted in the epics the *Mahabharata* and the *Ramayana*.

Our problem is that the Greek and Roman observers have added to our confusion by attempting to equate the Celtic deities with their own and also by comments which seem at odds with the evidence. We find a school of thought which claims that the Celts did not make images of their deities in human form until late in the Iron Age because, according to Diodorus Siculus, when the Celts stormed the Greek sanctuary of Delphi, their leader Brennus is reported to have laughed at the idea of gods and goddesses being represented in human form. 'When he came only upon images of stone and wood he laughed at them, to think that men, believing that gods had human form, should set up their images in wood and stone.'

Yet Caesar on the other hand says that the Celts believed that the deities were their ancestors and not their creators, so, surely, they had human form? And, indeed, we have an image of Cernunnos, clearly in human form albeit with horns coming out of his head, from the fourth-century BC rock scratching at Paspardo in the Val Camonica, a long time before Brennus reached Delphi. Confusion lurks everywhere for the unwary. Cernunnos was certainly a major god. The name seems to indicate 'the horned one' and he is often depicted with the symbol of stag's antlers – which remained a royal symbol among the Irish kings, particularly the Eóghanacht dynasty of Cashel. It has been argued that the Cernunnos of the Continental and British Celts is The Dagda (The Good God) of Irish mythology.

At Nautae Parisiaci both his name and his description are given on a monument dating from around AD 14–37. It was found in March 1711, beneath the Cathedral of Notre Dame in Paris. He is bearded, with stag's antlers from which hang hero's torcs. While the lower part of this figure has been lost, indications are that Cernunnos is sitting in the lotus position. There are over 300 figures of gods found in the Celtic world adopting this classic meditation position so closely associated in the modern mind with the Buddhist or Hindu religions. Again, in this we see an Indo-European common practice. Cernunnos, of course, appears on the famous Gundestrup Cauldron where he also sits in the lotus position. He is sometimes accompanied by a ram-horned snake. On one relief found in Haute-Marne he is depicted as feeding this snake. In other carvings he has a female consort – in examples found at Clermont-Ferrand and at Besançon she is antlered as well.

In Britain the god appears at Cirencester in a small stone relief whose legs are turned into the ram-horned snakes themselves which rear up, tongues protruding. On either side of the god are open purses of money. Cernunnos also appears on a Celtic silver coin dated c. AD 20, of the Belgae Remi, found at Petersfield, Hampshire. Here, between the antlers, the god bears a solar wheel. It is now in the British Museum.

Clearly Cernunnos is a major god in the Celtic pantheon. Scholars have argued that his zoomorphic accompaniment indicates that he was 'Lord of Animals'. Shiva, in the Hindu pantheon, was also called Pasupati, meaning 'Lord of Animals'. When Sir John Marshall was excavating at Mohenjodaro, in north-west India, he found a seal on which Pasupati was represented. 'The general resemblance between the Cernunnos panel and the Mohenjodaro seal [now in the Delhi Museum] is such that one can hardly doubt their common origin,' commented Professor Myles Dillon.

The Dagda carries a club which can destroy at one end and restore to life with the other. If The Dagda is also Cernunnos and a cognate with Shiva, then we can see vague similarities to the Hindu triple forms of Brahma (Creator), Vishnu (Preserver) and Shiva (Destroyer). The famous hill-figure carving of the Cerne Abbas Giant in southern England, some 55 metres high, carrying a club and with penis erect, is argued to be Cernunnos and therefore the British Celtic equivalent of The Dagda. The figure is almost a replica of a carving found at Costopitum (Corbridge, Northumberland) now in the Newcastle upon Tyne Museum of Antiquities. It certainly has all the attributes of Cernunnos. Shiva is also regarded as the male generative force of the Vedic religion whose symbol was the *linga* or phallus. In Greek and Roman perceptions this would equate with Heracles, whom they often saw as progenitor of the Celts.

We saw in Chapter 1 that the Celts believed their origins lay with the mother goddess, Danu, 'divine waters from heaven'. She fell from heaven and her waters created the Danuvius (Danube), having watered the sacred oak tree Bíle. From there sprang the pantheon of the gods who are known as the Tuatha de Danaan (Children of Danu) in Irish and the Children of Dôn in Welsh myths.

It has been argued, not with any degree of conviction, that Anu, occurring in both Continental and Irish Celtic forms, is unrelated to Danu. *Sanas Chormaic* in the tenth century clearly describes Anu as 'Mother of the Irish Gods'. In an etymological list, the *Cóir Anmann* (*The Fitness of Names*), the earliest form we have is from the fourteenth century. Anu was a fertility goddess and patroness of the Eóghanacht kingdom of Munster in Ireland; the term *Iath nAnann* (Land of Anu) was a name given to Ireland, reinforcing the Eóghanacht claim to the kingship of all Ireland. In Co. Kerry there are two hills called Dá Chích nAnann (Paps of Anu).

Anu appears in an inscription at Vaucluse where Professor John Rhys argues that the name occurs in dative form Anoniredi, translated as 'chariot of Anu'.

Most of the major Celtic deities were venerated in the form of triune gods and goddesses – that is, they had three aspects called by three names, and many representations of them are given three faces or three heads. The triads through which the Druids taught, and the sacredness of the number three, are highly important and a very common feature of the Indo-European tradition. Examples of such triple representations of deities include the janiform head from Leichlingen, Germany, dating from the fourth century BC, the stone triple head from Wroxeter, Shropshire, and the head from Reims in France. There is even a triple image of Cernunnos, with his antlers, on a bronze statuette from Étang-sur-Aroux. The pre-Roman Celtic coins of the Remi (of Reims) depict a triple-headed deity.

This triune or triple form of deity was not confined to the Celts but, as we have said, permeates the Indo-European cultures. In Hindu belief the Trimurti consisted of Brahma the Creator, Vishnu the Preserver and Shiva the Destroyer. Ancient Greeks used three as a symbol of deity and also had their triune aspect in Zeus (heaven), Poseidon (sea) and Pluto/Hades (underworld). There are, of course, three Fates, three Furies, three Graces, three Harpies; the Sibylline books are numbered as three times three, as are the Muses.

Ireland was represented by a female triune goddess – Éire, Banba and Fótla – and there were three craft gods, Goibhniu, Luchta and Credhne. The Mórrígú, triple goddess of death and battles, appeared as Macha, Badb and Nemain, embodying all that is perverse and horrible among the supernatural powers. The Dagda himself was worshipped in triune form.

This philosophy can go even deeper for the Celts saw *Homo sapiens* as body, soul and spirit, the world was divided into earth, sea and air, the divisions of nature were animal, vegetable and mineral, and the cardinal colours were red, yellow and blue. It might also be remembered that it was a Gaulish Celt, Hilary, bishop of Poitiers (*c.* AD 315–367), regarded as one of the first native Celts to become an outstanding philosophical force in the Christian movement, whose great work *De Trinitate* defined the concept of the Holy Trinity for the first time; a triplicity that is now so integral to Christian belief.

We have mentioned some of the major Celtic deities whose surviving inscriptions appear throughout the Celtic world. Another important god was Lugus, found throughout the Continent in both inscriptional form and in the place-names of towns such as Lyons, Léon, Loudan and Laon (in France), Leiden (in Holland), and Leignitz (in Silesia). He also appears in insular Celtic place-names, for example in the original form of Carlisle (Luguvalium). His festival (1 August) marked the beginning of the harvest season and the name of this festival, Lugnasad, survives as a name for the month of August in modern Irish as Lúnasa, in Manx as Luanistyn and in Scottish Gaelic as Lùnasad.

Lugh and his Welsh equivalent Lleu appear in the insular Celtic myths. He is portrayed as a warrior god of shining light. He is a master of all crafts and skills. Caesar says that the Gauls worshipped 'Mercury' as 'inventor of all the arts'. Caesar's Mercury could well have been Lugus. Nuada, ruler of the gods in Ireland, surrenders his rule to Lugh. Lugh is also called Lugh Lámhfhada (of the Long Hand/Arm) in Ireland and Lleu Llaw Gyffes in Welsh (of the Skilful Hand). In the Hindu pantheon the god Savitar is called Prthupani (of the

Large Hand) in the Rig Veda. Both Lugus and Savitar are claimed as solar deities. 'The god with the great hand stretches up his arms so that all obey.' The god of the large hand is an Indo-European concept and known from Ireland and Sweden to the Punjab.

Another of the Celtic pantheon is the god of eloquence, literacy and learning. Ogmios on the Continent is also found in Britain as Ogmia and in Ireland as Ogma. Ogmia in Britain is represented on a pottery piece from Richborough as a figure with long curly hair and sun rays emanating from his head with his name inscribed below. Ogma in Ireland is a son of The Dagda and he is credited with the invention of the Ogam script, which is named after him. The Greek writer Lucian (*c.* AD 115 after 180) identified him with Heracles, and this is confirmed in our insular mythological sources, where his parentage and adventures are in many ways comparable with those of Heracles, the son of Zeus, father of the Greek gods. Zeus, of course, is cognate with Dyaus in Sanskrit and The Dagda in Irish.

Camulos was a male god known throughout the Celtic world and an inscription at Bar Hill, on the Antonine Wall in Scotland, identifies him in Latin as 'the god Mars Camulos'. It would seem, therefore, that Camulos was a war god. The same link is made in dedications in Reims, Rindern and Dalmatia. There are votive inscriptions to the god stretching from Rome to Mainz. Camulos gave his name to the chief city of the Trinovantes in Britain, hence Camulodunum (Fort of Camulos, now Colchester) which became, for a brief time, the capital of the Roman province of southern Britain. The name is found as the original name of Almonbury in Yorkshire, and in southern Scotland in the place-name Camulosessa, argued to be 'seat of Camulos'. In Ireland, the name of the god may be seen in the name Cumal, father of the famous Fionn Mac Cumhail. The word *cumal* in old Irish also meant 'warrior' or 'champion', which could fit in with the image of a war god.

(This form of the word does not appear to be related to *cumal* used as a unit of currency nor *cumal* used as the name for a female servant.)

One of the most famous Celtic gods had a fertility festival which is still acknowledged today as the feast day of a saint that bears her name, St Brigit. The name means 'Exalted One' and it is suggested that she was another personification of Danu. Her name, as Brigandu or Brigando, is found in Valnay. She is identified as the Celtic equivalent of the Roman goddess Minerva. As Brigantia she is identified with Minerva on a relief from Birrens in southern Scotland, now in the National Museum of Antiquities in Edinburgh, which portrays her with Minerva's accoutrements. Brigantia was worshipped in Britain, primarily in the north of the country. The tribal confederation of the Brigantes seem to have adopted her and seven votive inscriptions are found in their area. However, her name also occurs in the names of the rivers Brent (in Middlesex) and Braint (in Anglesey).

In Ireland, as Brigit, she appears in the myths as the daughter of The Dagda with two sisters, also called Brigit. She was associated with the art of healing and the craft of the smithy and was a patroness of poetry. Overall, she was a goddess of fertility. The Christian saint who bears her name, Brigit (*c*. AD 455–*c*. 525), not only took over the feast day of the goddess, the traditional commencement of spring, or Imbolc in old Irish (1 February), but also encompassed the veneration of fertility and light. St Brigit's cross, when examined, is a solar wheel, a symbol of good fortune which appears throughout Indo-European culture and in Hindu culture as the swastika, a symbol perverted by the Nazis. In Vedic Sanskrit *svastika* derived from *sú*, good and *asti*, being.

The difficulty about the Celtic pantheon – if indeed we can accept that there was a single pantheon, merely varying among the Celts of differing areas – is that there is no way of identifying a rigid structure of the gods.

The Romans feigned shock and horror at the Celtic practice of taking and preserving the heads of people they admired, whether they were friend or foe. Most of the classical sources refer to the Celts taking the heads of their enemies after they had fallen in battle and it is noted as early as 295 BC, after the Senones smashed a Roman legion at Clusium, that:

> They cut off the heads of enemies slain in battle and attach them to the necks of their horses. The bloodstained spoils they hand over to their attendants and carry off as booty, while striking up a paean and singing a song of victory; and they nail up these first fruits upon their houses . . . They embalm in cedar oil the heads of the most distinguished enemies, and preserve them carefully in a chest and display them with pride to strangers, saying that for this head one of their ancestors, or his father, or the man himself, refused the offer of a large sum of money. They say that some of them boast that they refused the weight of the head in gold.

But the Celts believed that the soul reposed in the head. Strabo, among others, says that the Celts believed that the human soul was indestructible. Thus the head was venerated as the source and power of the human spirit. It was a mark of great respect to take the head of one they admired, to embalm it in cedar oil and offer it up in a temple or keep it as a prized possession. Dr Simon James, however, argues: 'By keeping the head of an enemy, they may have thought that the spirit was also controlled.' We are told by Livy that the Boii, having killed the Roman consul Lucius Postumius, in 216 BC, took his head to their temple. The Celts also put heads into sacred rivers as votive offerings.

It is quite wrong to interpret this as evidence that the Celts were 'head hunters'. They did not go out looking for heads. Decapitation only took place after the victims were slain in battle or died, and then only if they were deemed worthy of respect.

Archaeological evidence from various sources supports the information on temple offerings. A number of skulls have been found in Celtic shrines, for example at Roquepertuse, Nages and Entremont. At Roquepertuse in Provence there is a skull portico dating to the fourth and third centuries BC. The skulls in this portico are of adult men, most of whom were obviously slain in battle as scars and sword damage to the bone demonstrate. The sanctuary itself was constructed as early as the sixth century but fell into disuse after the Roman conquest of the area in the second century BC. At Entremont, capital of the Saluvii, fragments of a statue have been recovered and a reconstruction shows a figure seated in the lotus position bearing on its lap six severed heads. The figure wears a conical war helmet and a torc around his neck.

Entremont was destroyed by the Romans in 124 BC. Excavations of the shrine have shown that it was on the highest part of the hill and approached by a pathway lined with statues of heroes and heroines. Within this shrine stood a tall pillar carved with twelve heads. Entremont is remarkable for a large array of severed head sculpture.

One of the most interesting severed head sculptures comes from Noves in southern France, a stone sculpture dating to the third or second century BC. It is of a fearsome-looking scaly beast which squats on its hind legs. It has apparently devoured a human being, for an arm protrudes from its mouth. Under its forepaws it holds the severed heads of two people who are bearded and apparently wearing caps.

Heads have also been uncovered at a shrine in Cosgrove, in Northants, while a coin of the British king Cunobelinus shows a warrior brandishing a human head that he has taken after a battle. Skulls have been found placed in pits, and some excavated from fortresses where they had been fixed on poles on the walls or over gateways.

A large number of skulls from the Celtic period have been discovered in the River Thames at London, at the point where the Walbrook flows into it. The Thames was probably considered, like most rivers, to be sacred. But why were the votive offerings placed near the mouth of the Walbrook?

When the Anglo-Saxons took over London, the evidence is that they did not occupy the old city but built more to the north, in the vicinity of Moorgate. It is obvious, simply from the place-name, that the Celts clung to the area of the Walbrook, hence *Weala-broc*, the brook of the foreigners. *Welisc* (foreigners) was the name that the Anglo-Saxons gave to the British Celts. But why did the Celts hang on here of all places? And why were there so many skulls and other votive offerings? It is clear that this was a sanctuary which the Celts were loath to leave. Fascinatingly, the major gate from the city, facing on to the river, was called Bíle's gate (Billingsgate) and Bíle was a god of the dead who transported souls to the Otherworld. The Celtic dead of the city were probably taken out of the gate to commence their last journey on the Thames, just as their fellow Indo-Europeans are carried to the Ganges for burial. Maybe just the heads of the important citizens were taken through the gate to be deposited at the sanctuary now marked by the Walbrook?

The mythological traditions of Ireland and Wales are full of references to the importance of the head. Heads were endowed with the ability to live on once separated from the body, confirming the idea of the soul reposing there. In the *Mabinogion*, Bran Bendigeidfran is mortally wounded by a poison. He orders his men to cut off his head before the poison reaches it, and to take the head back to Britain. On the journey, the head talks, jokes and gives advice to them.

Heads often talk once stricken from the body. The famous decapitation game in *Sir Gawain and the Green Knight* has its origin in Celtic myth and appears in one of the Red Branch tales with Cúchulainn in the role later assumed by Gawain.

Cúchulainn takes the heads of his enemies without compunction and, like the Celts mentioned by Diodorus Siculus, he hangs them from his chariot: '. . . terribly, he comes. He has in the chariot the bloody heads of his enemies.'

This reverence for the head was not displaced by Christianity for many centuries. The doorway from Dysert O'Dea and the doorway from Clonfert, Ireland, both Romanesque, display a preoccupation with heads. Professor Barry Cunliffe has remarked that it is often impossible to distinguish pre-Christian and Christian Celtic head carvings. The gargoyles, corbels and other decorative forms on churches, particularly down to the eleventh and twelfth centuries AD, owed much to the Celtic belief that the soul dwelt in the head.

The Celts believed in an afterlife. The Gaulish teaching was that the soul was immortal. According to Diodorus Siculus it was Polyhistor who first mentioned that the 'Pythagorean doctrine' prevailed among the Gauls. The Alexandrian school of writers, as we saw in Chapter 4, spent much time debating whether the Celts had taken the doctrine of the soul's immortality, its reincarnation, from Pythagoras or whether Pythagoras took it from contact with the Celts. But how close were their teachings? Pythagoras, of course, wrote nothing down or, if he did, nothing has survived even in copies. From later writers we hear that he taught that the soul was immortal, a fallen divinity imprisoned in a body. The soul, by its actions, determined how it would be reincarnated in human, animal, or even plant form. Eventually, the soul would obtain its release from worldly cares by keeping itself pure, which involved an austere regime of self-examination, abstention and so on. This theory of metempsychosis was alien to Greek philosophical traditions at this time.

However, in other Indo-European cultures, notably in India, it was believed that due to its karma a soul transmigrated from one life to another in a never-ending cycle which could only be broken in Nirvana. Nirvana was the state of supreme bliss which, once achieved, liberated the soul from the repeating cycle of death and rebirth.

The Celtic idea of immortality was that death was but a changing of place and that life went on with all its forms and goods in another world, a world of the dead, or the fabulous Otherworld. When people died in that world, however, their souls were reborn in this. Thus a constant exchange of souls took place between the two worlds; death in this world took a soul to the Otherworld, death in that world brought a soul to this. Philostratus of Tyana (c. AD 170–249) observed correctly that the Celts celebrated birth with mourning for the death in the Otherworld, and regarded death with joy for birth in the Otherworld. So firm was the Celtic belief in the Otherworld, according to Valerius Maximus writing in the early first century AD, that 'they lent sums of money to each other which are repayable in the next world, so firmly are they convinced that the souls of men are immortal.' As we have seen, rich grave goods, personal belongings, weapons, food and drink were buried with the dead to give them a good start in the Otherworld.

My view is that the Celts did not borrow their philosophy from the Greeks, nor did the Greeks borrow it from the Celts. The evolution of the doctrine of immortality of the soul was a parallel and differing development in several Indo-European cultures, and might originate from an earlier common belief.

We have used the term 'Otherworld' for this world of the dead because it has become so popular. The insular Celts themselves had numerous names for the Otherworld – all euphemisms, for the Celtic languages are filled with euphemisms. We find over half a dozen names for the sun and the moon, with prohibitions as to when those words could be used. Doubtless this was the case with the Otherworld. In old and middle Irish we find the words *cenntar* as meaning 'this world' and *alltar* meaning the 'Otherworld'.

To take Irish mythology alone we find, among the synonyms for the Otherworld: Tír na nOg (Land of Youth); Tír Tairnigiri (Land of Promise); Tír na tSamhraidh (Land of Summer); Magh Mell (Plain of Happiness); Tír na mBeo (Land of the Living); Magh Da Cheo (Plain of Two Mists); Tír fo Thuinn (Land Under the Wave); Hy-Breasail (Breasal's Island); Hy-Falga (Falga's Island) and Dún Scaith (Fortress of Shadows).

Insular Celtic literature is filled with stories of voyages or journeys to the Otherworld, such as Cúchulainn's trip to Hy-Falga, or the Voyage of Bran, or that of Mael Duin, or the journey of Pwyll to Annwn in Welsh literature. One of the most famous sojourns in the Otherworld in insular literature was that of Oisín who rode off on a magical horse with Niamh, the daughter of the sea god, Manannán Mac Lir, and stayed there for 300 years.

The Otherworld, for the brave traveller who undertook the journey, could be reached by various means, through a cave, in a lake, but most popularly by voyaging across the great sea to the south-west or west. Even in modern English we have a survival of this – when someone was killed in wartime he was referred to as having 'gone west'. One Irish name, Hy-Breasail, Breasal's Island, was so accepted in people's minds as a real land to the west that it was marked on medieval maps. When in 1500 the Portuguese explorer Pedro Alvares Cabral reached South America, he thought he had discovered Hy-Breasail and thus named the country Brazil.

The gathering place of the souls of the dead was always regarded as a small island to the south-west of Ireland and a similar belief was held in Wales. The souls were then transported by the god of the dead to the Otherworld.

The actual location of the Otherworld, whether in this world or a spirit world not of this earth, has caused some confusion. The poet Lucan, in *Pharsalia*, refers to it as *orbe alio*, implying that it was merely a different area of the world known to us. Furthermore, there are many different concepts of what the Otherworld was like, ranging from dark and brooding places to happy, rural paradises.

There was one day of the year when the Otherworld could become visible to this world: on the feast of Samhain, the eve of 31 October to 1 November. This was a time when the supernatural boundary between the two worlds was broken down and people, the dead and living, could move freely between the two lands. It was a time when those who had been wronged by the living could return and haunt them. Christianity, unable to suppress the belief, adopted it. 1 November became All Hallows Day or All Souls' Day and the evening before, 'Hallowe'en'.

In Irish myth there are two 'gatekeepers', the deities who escorted souls to the Otherworld: Bíle, the one-time consort of Danu, and Donn, although Donn is often confused in the texts with Bíle. Tech Duinn (House of Donn) was the name given to the assembly place of the dead off the south-west of Ireland.

Who administered the religion of the Celts? Pomponius Mela states that the Druids 'profess to know the will of the gods'. Caesar says: 'The Druids officiate at the worship of the gods, regulate public and private sacrifices, and give rulings on all religious questions.' But it is clear that this is only one small part of what a Druid did. As we have seen, the Druids were the intellectual caste and incorporated the priesthood within their ranks. This is why the Greeks and Romans are not consistent in using the word Druid for a priest and why Druids are not referred to in many parts of the Celtic world while the intellectual professions are mentioned. Even in areas where Druids are referred to, such as Gaul, other words for priests are used: *gutuatri*, for example, perhaps incorporating the Celtic word for 'voice' which survives in the Irish *guth*. The office of *gutuater* is referred to in inscriptions at Mâcon, Haute-Loire and Autun. Livy talks of the priests of the Boii as *antistes templi* while Ausonius speaks of the *aedituus Beleni*.

Having established that the ancient Celts believed in a pantheon of gods, whom they saw as ancestors and not as creators, and that they believed in an immortal soul and in the Otherworld, can we now find evidence of their moral code? Diogenes Laertius observed that the chief maxim was that the people 'should worship the gods, do no evil and exercise courage'. From the various insular sources, comparing them to classical writers' comments, we may argue that the Celtic priesthood taught that the ideal was for people to live in harmony with nature and themselves, accepting that pain and death were not evils but essential parts of the divine plan, and that the only evil was moral weakness. As Professor Myles Dillon has pointed out, the notion of Truth as the highest principle and sustaining power of creation pervaded all early Irish literature.

The old Irish word for 'truth' is the basis for the linguistic concepts of holiness, righteousness, faithfulness, as well as for religion and for justice. Even in modern Irish one can say: '*Tá sé/sí in áit na fhírinne anois*' when a person dies. This literally means: 'He/she is in the place of Truth now.' This basic philosophy of pre-Christian Celtic religion has many parallels with eastern Indo-European concepts and we find an exact parallel in the Persian-Iranian religion of Parseeism. In the Hindu Vedas we find that Truth (*rta*) is a land in the highest state of paradise and the source of the sacred Ganges. The Vedas say that 'by means of Truth the earth endures'. The same concept is expressed in the famous *Audacht* or will of the Brehon, Morann mac Cairbre, who left instructions for the high king, Feradach Finn Fachtnach (AD 95–117), which are recorded in *Leabhar Laignech* (*Book of Leinster*).

The Celtic religion was based on a moral system which distinguished right from wrong. In old Irish the terms were *fas* and *nefas*, what was lawful (*dleathacht*) and unlawful (*neamhdleathacht*), and the teachings were impressed on people by a series of taboos (*geasa*). Moral salvation was the responsibility of the individual. The Celtic Christian theologian Pelagius (*c.* AD 354–420) was accused of reviving pre-Christian Celtic philosophies, specifically the 'Natural Philosophy of the Druids'; he argued that men and women could take the initial and fundamental step towards their salvation, using their own efforts and not accepting things as preordained.

Augustine of Hippo had taught that mankind took on Adam's original sin and had no free will in effecting its own salvation. Whether people did good deeds or bad deeds in life, they were already fated, everything was preordained. Pelagius argued that Augustine's theories imperilled the entire moral law. If men and women were not responsible for their good or evil deeds, there was nothing to restrain them from an indulgence in evil-doing on the basis that it was preordained and they were not responsible.

Pelagius' arguments were an echo of the more progressive aspect of pre-Christian Celtic philosophy. But Augustine of Hippo prevailed and Pelagius was declared a heretic. For many centuries, the Celtic Christian movement was considered to be imbued with Pelagius' teachings. It was not that the Celts consciously accepted Pelagius' teachings, but the belief that men and women had free will and were responsible for their actions was an essential part of the Celtic culture. Curiously, although Christianity finally accepted Pelagius' teachings, Augustine of Hippo is still regarded as a saint and Pelagius as a heretic.

Concurrently with Pelagius, there were several other Celtic philosophers writing tracts which are now all lumped together as 'Pelagian'. They shared a common set of philosophies. It is not surprising that we can identify them as Celts and their early writings also showed a social philosophy which has distinct echoes in insular Celtic law systems. The British Celtic bishop Fastidius, writing *De Vita Christiana* (*The Christian Life*) about AD 411, argued:

Do you think yourself Christian if you oppress the poor? . . .
if you enrich yourself by making others poor? if you wring
your food from other's tears? A Christian is a man who . . .
never allows a poor man to be oppressed when he is by . . .
whose doors are open to all, whose table every poor man
knows, whose food is offered to all.

The hospitality of Celtic kings and chieftains is well docu-
mented in mythology and stipulated in law. The rights and
duties of a ruler to see that no one, particularly strangers in
his land, went hungry, the law forbidding the exploitation of
workers, the fines in Irish law for anyone profiting from
causing injury – all these point to the fact that Pelagius and the
other 'Pelagian' writers shared a particular cultural background.

We know that, like most ancient peoples, the Celts practised
divination, foretelling the future or will of the gods by the
presence of good or bad omens. The Greeks and Romans
claimed that the Celtic priests searched for prophetic signs in
the entrails of sacrificial animals and in the flight of birds.
Augury, or bird flight, was a method particularly used by the
Etruscans who, like the Romans and other civilisations, also
looked for signs in animal entrails. This was known as *harus-
pices* (auspices) and the art was called the *Etrusca disciplina*.
A college of Etruscan augurs was established in Rome.

Both Strabo and Diodorus Siculus, using as their only
source Poseidonius, claimed that the Druids (or Druidic
priests) divined from the death throes of human victims.
Caesar repeated the information. They described the Celtic
priests as plunging a dagger into a victim and watching his
death throes. Tacitus, echoing these earlier writers, says: 'The
Druids consult the gods in the palpitating entrails of men.'
Indeed, the reputation of the ancient Celts as indulging in
human sacrifice relies on several Roman-orientated writers,
who can all be traced back to one informant only – the source

of all 'human sacrifice' tales is Poseidonius. Those who mention human sacrifice all explain that it was only used in divination or to propitiate the gods. Cicero among others repeats this: 'they find it necessary to propitiate the immortal gods and defile their altars and temples with human victims.'

Of course, human sacrifice in religious matters was certainly practised in the ancient Indo European world and we may ask why the Celts should have been singled out for criticism in this way. Yet we have only the unsupported word of Poseidonius as the basis for all these accusations. We also have to bear in mind that the Romans had an agenda of their own in denigrating the Celts and making them less than human. The curious thing is that the Romans practised human sacrifice themselves. For after Hannibal's victory at Cannae in 216 BC, the Romans sacrificed two Celtic prisoners and two Greek prisoners by burying them alive in the Forum Boarium in Rome to propitiate their gods.

Roman writers loved to talk about Celtic savagery, the quality of being fierce, cruel and uncivilised. By Rome's own bloodthirsty standards, any Celtic cruelty seems to have been quite mild. Ritual killings were a way of Roman life and in the Tullianum, at the foot of the Capitoline Hill, state prisoners were ceremonially executed to appease the gods of war. What else is this but human sacrifice? Vercingetorix, who surrendered to save his people in 52 BC, was incarcerated for six years before being ritually slaughtered to celebrate Caesar's triumph.

The view of Roman society as advanced and moral, and the acceptance of their condemnation of human sacrifice among the Celts, based on a single authority who was then repeated *ad nauseam*, is curious to say the least. In 264 BC Marcus and Decimus Brutus decided to mark the death of their father by having three pairs of slaves fight to the death as a sacrifice to the Roman gods and with the approval of the priests. Julius Caesar in 46 BC, so disapproving of human sacrifice among the

Celts, had slaves fight to the death to commemorate the funeral of his daughter Julia.

This form of sacrifice reached its peak in the fourth century AD. Diocletian (AD 284–305) is recorded as having had 17,000 men, women and children slaughtered in the arena in one month alone. By the first century AD most Roman writers, even if begrudgingly, agreed that human sacrifice among the Celts was a thing of the past. They obviously could not repeat Poseidonius' comments as applying to their own time; a time when tens of thousands were being ritually slaughtered in the Roman arena for the sake of entertainment.

It is certainly true to say that in the insular Celtic literatures there is no tradition, no shadow of a tradition, of human sacrifice. As this material was written down by Christian clerics, who would have taken any opportunity to denigrate the pagan beliefs of their ancestors, it must be argued that had there been any such practice it would have come under fierce attack.

In terms of divination of the future, Greek and Roman writers observe that the Celts were renowned for their 'speculation from the stars', which meant that they practised astrology and were adept at astronomy. We have already considered this aspect of Celtic culture in Chapter 9.

# 14

# CELTIC MYTH AND LEGEND

The evidence of the myths and legends of the *ancient* Celts is, strictly speaking, scanty. The reason for this is that those myths and legends were not committed to a written form until the Christian period when they were given a Christian 'gloss' and when the ancient gods and goddesses were adjusted to new roles to fit in with the precepts of the new religion.

Even with this caveat, the Celtic languages contain one of Europe's oldest and most vibrant mythologies. What do we mean precisely by mythology? It is a sacred tradition embracing a whole set of concepts covering the philosophical beliefs of a given culture. Some have argued that myths are parables to explain ideas on imponderable questions. Basically, the function of mythology is to give an account of the religious ideas, including the concept of creation, and the fortunes of a people. It leads, almost seamlessly, into the legends of a culture, that is the oral history of the people from the distant past. Again, there is a fine line between legend and the historical reality.

When the insular Celtic traditions were first committed to writing about the sixth century AD, it was a development of a far earlier and highly sophisticated oral tradition. Those entrusted with handing on the myths orally had to be word perfect and, as Julius Caesar remarked, it sometimes took twenty years for trainees to learn the lore before they were regarded as 'qualified'. Therefore, the traditions contained an echo of voices from the dawn of European civilisation. The late Professor Kenneth Jackson once described the Irish *Táin Bó Cuailgne* as 'a window on the Iron Age'.

Certainly the Irish myths still have a particular vibrancy as Ireland was the only Celtic land to escape Roman conquest and was relatively uninfluenced by contact with Rome until the Christian period. Then, however, Latin culture was the vehicle by which the new religion was imported. The Christian scribes tended to bowdlerise the pagan vibrancy of the myths and give them a Christian veneer.

Some of this veneer is quite blatant. For example, the sea god Manannán Mac Lir, in one story, foretells the coming of Christ to save the world. In another, the great hero Cúchulainn pleads with St Patrick to intercede with Christ to save him from the 'Fires of Hell', out of which the saint has summoned him to prove a point to a pagan Irish monarch. As the stories were set down by individuals, working at varying times and copying more often than not from older books as well as oral tradition, the pre-Christian vitality in Irish myth has not been entirely obliterated.

Irish mythology has been categorised into four sections. 'The Mythological Cycle' relates to the various 'invasions' of Ireland, from that of Cesair, at the time of the Deluge, through the invasions of Partholón, Nemed, the Firbolg, the Dé Danaan and the sons of Milesius, the progenitors of the Gael. In the background lurk the ancient deities of Ireland, the Tuatha Dé Danaan, the Children of Danu. This group of tales are the closest to the creation myths in any Celtic language. We find the gods and goddesses, the Children of Danu, have arrived in Ireland from their four fabulous Otherworld cities, to overthrow the Firbolg and claim Ireland for their own. However, the real villains are the Tuatha de Domhain, the Children of Domhnu, who are also called the Fomorii (fo, under, morii, sea, so 'undersea dwellers'). It becomes clear that the Children of Danu are the deities of light and good, while the Children of Domhnu are the deities of darkness and evil. The cycle ends with the arrival of the mortals in Ireland, the sons of Golamh, known in Latin as Míle Easpain (Soldier of Spain) or Milesius. He is identified as an Iberian Celt who has wandered the world selling his military services. He has served Nectanebus, the pharaoh of Egypt, and married his daughter, Scota. This is a device to explain the word 'Scotii' as applied to the Irish of this period and eventually the name 'Scotland'. There is another Scota in Irish mythology who was the daughter of the pharaoh Cingris and became the wife of Niul, mother of Goidel.

The old gods and goddesses are defeated and are forced to retreat underground, dwelling in the hills (sídhe). Eventually, they are called 'people of the hills' and the sídhe become 'fairies' in folklore. The best known is the banshee (bean sídhe, woman of the fairies) who wails outside the home of the family to whom she is attached when one of that family is about to die. The great god of arts and crafts, Lugh, was demoted to Lugh chronáin (stooping Lugh), Anglicised as 'leprechaun'.

The second group of tales are called 'The Ulster Cycle'. These are the stories of the deeds of the 'warriors of the Red Branch', the military élite of Ulster of whom Cúchulainn was the great champion. This group of tales contains the famous epic Táin Bó Cuailgne, often regarded as the Irish equivalent of the Iliad. This is the story of the campaign waged by Medb, the masterful queen of Connacht, to capture the famous Brown Bull of Ulster. She leads a vast army against the kingdom of Ulster whose warriors are prevented from defending it by a strange debility inflicted by the war goddess Macha. Only the youthful hero Cúchulainn is able to carry on a single-handed resistance against her army.

The *Táin* is the longest and most powerful of all the Irish myths. It is a separate story from the *Táin Bó Fraoch*, which tells how the handsome warrior Fraoch sets out to woo Findbhair, the beautiful daughter of Medb of Connacht. The other stories of the cycle are enlargements on themes occurring in the *Táin*, preparatory tales leading up to the epic, romances that were added later to fulfil people's desire to know the subsequent fortunes of the main characters, and, of course, a group of entirely independent tales but with related characters.

The third group of tales is 'The Cycle of the Kings', and these might usefully be called legends, although there are many supernatural motifs in the stories. The stories relate to semi-legendary kings, kings who undoubtedly had a real existence in remote Irish history but who had become the subject for romanticising so that we no longer know where reality ends and the story-telling begins. For example, Niall Noíghiallach, Niall of the Nine Hostages, who is recorded as being high king from AD 379 to 405, is regarded as the progenitor of the Uí Néill dynasty, the kings of Ulaidh (Ulster). He is recorded as raiding Britain and Gaul during the time of Theodosius the Great and encountering the Roman general Stilicho. The story of Niall is a typical case in which history and myth are combined in the minds of the story-tellers. Symbolism is used to mark his birth; signs are given to point the way to his being the lawful king; he survives attempts to destroy him by those seeking to evade the prophecy given by Flaithius (Royalty), obviously a goddess of sovereignty, that he will be the greatest high king. Flaithius has appeared as an ugly hag, with black skin and green teeth, demanding that Niall and his companions have intercourse with her. Only Niall does so whereupon she turns into the beautiful goddess.

The fourth, and last, group of stories is 'The Fenian Cycle'. These are the adventures of Fionn Mac Cumhail and the warriors of the Fianna, the élite bodyguard to the high kings of Tara. The Fianna are said to have been founded in 300 BC by Fiachadh and consisted of twenty-five battalions raised from Clan Bascna and Clan Morna. Fionn Mac Cumhail (who has subsequently often appeared in Anglicised form as Finn mac Cool), son of Cumal, the ruler of Clan Bascna, becomes the leader of the Fianna during the time of the high king Cormac Mac Art. The stories of Fionn and his Fianna are innumerable, covering his birth to his death. These stories were highly popular in late medieval Ireland and although the Irish had produced their own native Arthurian saga, many tales of which are not translated into English, nor even acknowledged by 'Arthurian scholars', the stories of Fionn and the Fianna were not displaced as the great hero tales of Ireland.

The Fenian Cycle is sometimes known as the Ossianic Cycle. The first bold synthesis of the eight major parts of the cycle into a cohesive whole appeared in the twelfth-century work *Acallamh na Senórach* (*Colloquy of the Ancients*). Next to the *Táin Bó Cuailgne* it is one of the longest medieval compositions.

The oldest surviving sources of Irish mythology are the *Leabhar na hUidre* (*Book of the Dun Cow*), the *Leabhar Laignech* (*Book of Leinster*) and a book known only by its Bodleian Library reference number – Rawlinson Manuscript B 502. The *Leabhar na hUidre* was compiled under the supervision of Mael Muire Mac Céilechair, who was killed by marauders at the monastery of Clonmacnoise in 1106. The *Leabhar Laignech* (originally called the *Leabhar na Nuachongbála*, named after Noughaval in Co. Leix), was compiled by Aed Mac Crimthainn, abbot of the monastery at

Tír-dá-Ghlas (Terryglass in Co. Tipperary). The Rawlinson Manuscript appears to have been compiled at Clonmacnoise.

Professor Kuno Meyer, in his introduction to *Liadain and Curithir: A Love Story* (1900), listed 400 tales in manuscript, adding another hundred which had come to light since he compiled his list. He thought a further fifty to one hundred tales could lie in libraries still undiscovered. He estimated that scholastic knowledge of Irish myth and legend was based on only 150 tales that had been edited and annotated out of a total of 500–600. Eleanor Hull, in her introduction to *The Cuchullin Saga in Irish Literature* (1898), had made a similar estimation. Professor Gearóid Mac Eoin more recently confirmed that the situation had not changed during this last century. It is incredible to think that what we know of this vibrant mythology is based on 150 stories while a further 450 remain unedited and untranslated.

The world of Irish mythology is remote from the classical world of Greek and Latin myth. Yet one is constantly surprised by the fact that Irish mythology seems to share a curious Mediterranean warmth with its fellow Indo-European cultures. The brooding blackness that permeates Nordic myth is not there and, at times, it is difficult to realise that we are looking at a north-western European culture. A happy spirit pervades the majority of tales, even the tragedies such as 'The Fate of the Sons of Usna' or 'The Pursuit of Diarmuid and Gráinne'. There is an eternal spirit of optimism. Death is never the conqueror and we are reminded, of course, that the Celts were one of the first cultures in Europe to evolve a doctrine of the immortality of the soul.

The real parallels to Irish mythology, as Professor Myles Dillon has so clearly demonstrated in his lecture 'Celt and Hindu' and in more detail in *Celts and Aryans* (1975), lie in Hindu mythology. And to say that a happy spirit pervades the Irish myths is not to say that evil is never encountered. Indeed, as in the real world, good and evil constantly rub shoulders and the malevolent forms of the Fomorii, the gods and god-desses of darkness and death, are constantly hovering on the edge of the northern ocean.

In these stories both the deities and the humans (immortals and mortals) are no mere physical beauties with empty heads. Their intellectual attributes are equal to their physical capa-bilities. They are subject to all the natural virtues and vices, and practise all seven deadly sins. Their world, both this one and the Otherworld, is one of rural happiness, a world in which they indulge in all the pleasures of life in an idealised form: love of nature, art, games, feasting and heroic single combat.

The myths and legends of Ireland are also to be found in the Manx and Scottish Gaelic traditions for these languages did not begin to separate from their old Irish parent until the fifth and sixth centuries, just as the British Celtic language diverged at the same time into Welsh, Cornish and Breton. In Welsh mythology, we can see themes that demonstrate that the Irish and Welsh have a common source; we find echoes of a common Celtic mythological, religious and, perhaps, histori-cal experience. Lugh Lamhfhada of Irish myth appears in the guise of Lleu Llaw Gyffes, Danu is Dôn, Bíle is Beli, Nuada is Nudd and Fionn Mac Cumhail has a Welsh equivalent in Gwyn ap Nudd. The Brythonic forms of Celtic are thought to have diverged from the Goidelic form in about the seventh century BC so it is fascinating to see the parallels. Nevertheless, the Welsh material is nowhere near as extensive or as old as the Irish tales and sagas.

The earliest surviving Welsh mythological texts are from the fourteenth century AD. The tales are collectively known as *Pedair Cainc y Mabinogi* (*The Four Branches of the Mabinogi*). The term 'Mabinogi' originally meant 'a tale of youth' and has since become simply 'a tale'. The tales come from three major textual sources: the *Llyfr Gwyn Rhydderch* (*White Book of Rhydderch*, compiled *c.* 1300–1325); the *Llyfr*

*Coch Hergest* (*Red Book of Hergest*, compiled 1375–1425) and the Peniarth Manuscript (*c.* 1225–35). Scholars believe that the texts were copies from earlier manuscript sources.

There are twelve tales which comprise the Mabinogi: the stories of Pwyll, Branwen, Manawydan, Math, Culhwch and Olwen, The Dream of Macsen Wledig, Lludd and Lleufelys, The Dream of Rhonabwy, Peredur, Owain, Geraint and Enid, and the story of Taliesin.

The story of Pwyll, lord of Dyfed, echoes the 'Holy Grail' theme for Pwyll adventures in Annwn, the Otherworld, and searches for a magic vessel. Bran and Branwen is a tale of love, epic battles interwoven with a supernatural background. Bran is the son of Llyr, the Welsh equivalent of Lir, ruler of the Island of the Mighty, and brother of Manawydan, the equivalent of Manannán. Bran's sister Branwen marries Matholwch of Ireland and is ill treated by him. The Britons then go to war to punish Matholwch, a war in which only seven, if we include Bran, Britons survive; these are Pryderi, Manawydan, Taliesin, Gluneu son of Taran (Taranis was the old Celtic god of thunder), Grudye and Heilyn. Bran himself is mortally wounded and asks his companions to cut off his head, which remains alive until it is taken back to Britain.

Culhwch's search for Olwen is thought to be one of the earliest surviving native Arthurian sagas while The Dream of Rhonabwy is regarded as a close second.

One of the most interesting stories is *Hanes Taliesin*. Taliesin was a poet who flourished in the Celtic north of Britain in the sixth century AD. He is mentioned in the *Historia Britonum* and the fourteenth-century *Book of Taliesin*, a group of twelve poems which some believe to represent his authentic work. *Hanes Taliesin* is a highly mythologically oriented tale which represents Taliesin as the child of a goddess, Ceridwen, who goes through a number of trans-migrations (or reincarnations) before he reaches the state of being Taliesin. One of his songs resembles the invocation of

Amairgen, the first Druid, on landing in Ireland and also bears a more than passing resemblance to a passage from the Hindu *Bhagavadgita*. Sir Ifor Williams believed that *Hanes Taliesin* was developed in North Wales sometime during the ninth or tenth centuries but had its roots in Welsh culture long before then. Certainly if Taliesin did live in the sixth century this would be so. Other poets identify him as the court poet to King Urien of Rheged (the north-western British Celtic kingdom covering what is now Cumbria) and to his successor King Owain ab Urien. He certainly appears in other Welsh myths, such as the story of Bran and Branwen. His name is frequently coupled with that of Merlin and given as an authority on prophecies.

Since the only complete Celtic mythological texts to survive are from the insular Celts, we do not know nearly as much about Continental or Gaulish Celtic mythology. Dr Miranda J. Green's *Dictionary of Celtic Myth and Legends* relies heavily on archaeology to develop her themes, including the names of gods and goddesses, albeit often in their Latin forms, which are found on inscriptions throughout the Continent. Some fragments do seem identifiable with their insular counterparts. Mainly, however, the gods of Gaul can only be glimpsed through Roman eyes. Caesar, as we have seen in our section on Celtic religion, was content simply to give Roman names to the gods – Mercury, Jupiter, Mars, Minerva, Apollo and Dis Pater (Pluto). This unfortunate *interpretatio Romana* has merely confused their identification and functions.

No Greek or Latin writer has made clear the origin myths of the Celts on the Continent, though we may deduce these from a compendium of evidence and a comparison with Hindu mythology; we have already discussed the similarity of themes based on the 'divine waters' of Danu.

In the fabulous and epic histories of Livy we can see some similarities with the insular Celtic stories. We must bear in mind that Livy was born in Patavium (Padua), between the territories of the Veneti and the Cenomani Celts. He was therefore raised in Cisalpine Gaul, soon after the Roman conquest and settlement. It is entirely possible that his family were among the early Romanised Celts. Camille Jullian has suggested, in his *Histoire de la Gaule*, that Livy's histories, which are unlike the usual straightforward Roman accounts, were influenced by Celtic oral epics he heard in his youth. We can point to a fascinating example.

In 348 BC the Celts, apparently encouraged by the Latin cities which were trying to break free of Roman dominance, were threatening Rome again. The consul, Lucius Furius Camillus, marched his legions 60 kilometres south of Rome into the modern area of Pontine. He was worried about meeting the Celts in open battle as the Romans were still smarting under previous Celtic defeats.

We are told by Livy that during this campaign a Celt approached the Roman picket lines and announced himself by striking his spear on his shield. He was a champion of outstanding size and wore armour. The Celt, according to Livy, employed an interpreter to issue a challenge for any Roman champion to come forth and meet him in single combat. A tribune named Marcus Valerius, then twenty-three years old, sought permission from Camillus to answer the challenge. Livy then recounts a combat which has remarkable resonances with insular Celtic mythology.

> The duel proved less remarkable for its human interest than for the divine intervention of the gods, for as the Roman engaged his adversary, a raven suddenly alighted on his helmet, facing the Celt. The tribune first hailed this with delight, as a sign sent from heaven, and then prayed for the good will and gracious support from whoever had sent him the bird, were it god or goddess. Marvellous to relate, not only did the raven keep the perch it had once chosen, but as often as the struggle renewed it rose up on

its wings and attacked the enemy's face and eyes with beak
and claws, until he was terrified at the sight of such a
portent; and so bewildered as well as half blinded, he was
killed by Valerius. The raven then flew off out of sight
towards the east.

Valerius then took the cognomen of Corvus, being the word
for crow or raven.

Cassius Dio (c. AD 150–235) repeats this story mentioning
Livy as his source. Now this symbolism is scarcely Roman. We
know that one of the personae of the Celtic war goddess was
in the form of a raven. This is particularly evident in Irish
mythology. Indeed, Dr Henri Hubert points to the combat at
the ford where the Red Branch champion Cúchulainn fights in
single combat. He has rejected the amorous advances of the
war goddess the Mór Ríoghain (or Mórrígán, Great Queen),
the personification of the triune war goddess. In some versions
she assumes the form of a raven of battle and, as a revenge,
attacks Cúchulainn during his combat against the champion
Lóch. Cúchulainn realises that he does not stand a chance
when the great crow or raven stands before him and croaks of
war and slaughter. The portent means: 'My life's end is near;
this time I shall not return alive from the battle.' Like the
unknown Celtic warrior in Livy's story, he eventually suc-
cumbs and, mortally wounded, ties himself to the pillar stone,
so that he can die standing up. The goddess, still in raven form,
perches on his shoulder and drinks his blood.

I have argued elsewhere that Livy's story, instead of being a
'lift' from a particular mythological tale, could be a recounting of Celtic symbolism. Ravens warn the god Lugh of the
approach of a Fomorii army. Lugdunum (Lyons), named after
Lugh, once issued a coin with a raven on it. The Celtic goddess
Nantosuelta and also the horse goddess Epona are sometimes
accompanied by, or depicted as, ravens. In the Welsh story, the
Dream of Rhonabwy, we find a raven army raised by Owain

ap Urien. Raven symbols are found on Celtic war helmets from the third to second centuries BC.

This was not the first time that Celtic symbolism entered Livy's work. One of his best-known accounts is of the Celts climbing up the Capitol in Rome at night with the sacred geese of Juno cackling a warning to the Roman garrison. Juno, the wife of Jupiter, was goddess of women and marriage and mother of Mars (Area), the god of war. Now Livy says, and he is echoed by subsequent generations of writers, that these geese were kept as a sacred totem in the temple. In fact, the Roman geese were not sacred to Juno but kept in the Capitol's temples for ritual slaughter during divination practices. If the geese were not sacred to Juno, one cannot help wondering if there is any other reason why Livy introduces them into the epic. It could well be that he is recounting simple fact. On the other hand, as he was raised among Celts, was possibly even a Celt himself, there could be a link with Celtish symbolism here.

Dr Miranda Green, in her *Animals in Celtic Life and Myth*, has pointed out that geese are most commonly associated with war in Celtic iconography. Because of their watchful and aggressive natures, the birds were used as an appropriate symbol or companion to the gods and goddesses of battle. On top of the skull sanctuary of Roquepertuse, in Provence, is a great free-standing goose gazing attentively as a sentinel. A first-century BC figurine of a war goddess, found in Dinéault, in Brittany, shows her with a helmet surmounted by an aggressive goose. An altarpiece from Vaison shows a Celtic god of war with a goose and a raven as his companions.

Caesar noted that the goose was sacred in Britain and he pointed out that there was a taboo on eating the creatures. The same taboo was found in Ireland until medieval times when it was forbidden to eat the barnacle goose on certain holy days. The exiled Irish soldiers who had to leave Ireland, after their defeat by the English, and serve in the Irish Brigades of countries like France, Spain and Austria were known as *na Géanna fiáne*, the Wild Geese, a reference to the military symbolism of the goose rather than to its migratory habits.

The goose as a warlike symbol, aggressive and watchful, is found in Celtic culture long before the sack of Rome. The geese in the Capitol were there as sacrificial birds. Are we witnessing a factual incident in that these geese cackled a warning, changing Roman perceptions, or have 'the sacred geese of Juno' come into Latin mythology from a Celtic source? Thereafter, we are told, the Romans carried the geese on litters, with purple and gold cushions, in an annual ceremony in Rome and their feeding was made the responsibility of the censors. As part of the same ritual, dogs were crucified on stakes of elder, to remind the people they had not barked a warning of the Celtic attack. It was a ritual which lasted in Rome well into the Christian epoch.

Henri Hubert believes that two of Livy's sources were the mainly lost works of the Insubrean Celtic writer, Cornelius Nepos (*c.* 100–*c.* 25 BC), and the Vocontii Celt, Trogus Pompeius (27 BC–AD 14). It was from these Celtic historians, writing in Latin, that Livy learned the Celtic tradition of how the Celts started their expansions through Europe. He gives as a reason for this expansion the fact that the Celtic heartland had become so populated that the main ruler, Ambicatus, encouraged his nephews to take pioneers with them and move east and south in search of new lands to settle.

Perhaps we should not leave this section on Celtic mythology without reference to two comparatively recent developments in the area. To the modern popular mind, the most famous of Celtic mythological figures is Arthur. He was undoubtedly a historical person, living during the late fifth and early sixth centuries AD. Within a few centuries after his death, this British Celtic 'war chief', fighting the Anglo-Saxon invasions of Britain, had become firmly embedded in mythology. The first literary reference to Arthur comes in a poem attributed to Aneirin, written in the late sixth century. In Y *Gododdin*, Aneirin writes of an attempt by 300 élite warriors, led by Mynyddawn Mwynfawr, chieftain of the tribe whose capital was at Dineiddyn (Edinburgh), to recapture Catraeth (Catterick) from the Anglo-Saxons.

Historical references to Arthur can also be found in Gildas (AD 500–700), the British Celtic monk who wrote *De Excidio et Conquesta Britanniae* (*Concerning the Ruin and Conquest of Britain*); in Nennius (*c.* AD 800), another Celtic historian, in his *Historia Britonum*, who credits Arthur with twelve major victories over the invading Anglo-Saxons; and in the *Annales Cambriae* (*c.* AD 955), a Latin history of the rise of Cymru (Wales), which records Arthur's victory at Mount Badon and states that Arthur and Medraut (Mordred) fell at the battle of Camluan in the year AD 537.

As it seems to be a tendency that Celts make their heroes into gods and their gods into heroes, over the next few centuries, following the death of the historical Arthur, the Celts embellished his story with earlier mythological themes, giving him a special circle of warriors, who later became Knights of the Round Table, but were originally closer to the Fianna of Fionn Mac Cumhail. In fact, many of the Arthurian tales seem to have been embellished with themes from the Fenian Cycle. Christian themes soon began to replace the intrinsically Celtic elements; for example, the search for the magic cauldron of plenty from the Otherworld developed into a search for the Christian Holy Grail. Other elements, however, remain in their pure Celtic form – the magic sword of Arthur, now popularly known through a Latin corruption as Excalibur, was, in fact, the Welsh Caladfwlch (Hard Dinter) which seems to have been taken from the Irish form Caladcholg, the sword of the hero Fergus Mac Roth in the Red Branch Cycle.

Geoffrey of Monmouth (*c.* 1100–1155) developed Arthur into something approaching his popular heroic image in his *Historia Regnum Britanniae*. Since Geoffrey's developments, a great body of literature has sprung up. Arthur was an accepted character in both Welsh and Irish mythology. There are at least twenty-five identified Arthurian tales in Irish from the medieval period but, as we have pointed out before, they never displaced the popularity of Fionn Mac Cumhail as a hero in Irish imagination.

A second world-famous myth developed out of the Celtic world: the story of Tristan and Iseult. There was an historic king Marc'h of Cornwall, identified as Marcus Cunomarus. Marc'h comes from the Celtic word for horse, not from the Latin name Marcus, and the second name means 'Hound of the Sea'. A writer lets slip that Mark, to use the modern accepted form, had ears like a horse. His capital in Cornwall was at the hill-fort of Castle Dore, occupied from the second century BC to the sixth century AD. King Mark had a son, Drustaus or Drustanus, which scholars claim is a philological equivalent of Tristan. A mid-sixth century AD stone inscription at Castle Dore records: 'Drustanus hic iacit Cunomori Filius', Here lies Drustanus son of Cunomarus.

However the myth developed, the basis is that Mark of Cornwall married Iseult, daughter of an Irish king. He sent Tristan, his nephew in the myth, to fetch her and Tristan fell in love with her. They eventually fled from Mark's court. The core motif is a traditional Celtic elopement tale known in Irish as *aithedha*, and most of the essential elements are to be found in other Celtic stories, such as the elopement of the king's wife with the king's nephew. The tales of Diarmuid and Gráinne and of Noísu and Deirdre are comparable.

There are many different versions of the tale written in practically every European language but scholars have traced them back to one extant manuscript written by Béroul in the middle of the twelfth century. It was said that Béroul, writing in French, copied the saga from a Breton source. The source could, however, equally have been Cornish. Our earliest Cornish textual evidence, as distinct from its British Celtic parent, is from the tenth century AD. Mark was also known to have ruled in Carhaix, in Cornouaille, in Brittany, as well as Carhays in Cornwall. We have already seen that many Celtic kings, even back to the time of Caesar, are noted to have ruled both in Britain and on the Continent. We have little factual knowledge of the Cornish Mark. In Brittany he was regarded as an unscrupulous tyrant. Urmonek, a monk of Landévennec, writing his *Life of St Pol de Léon*, about AD 880, is the person who identifies Mark as Cunomarus and says that he was a powerful king, under whose rule lived peoples who spoke four separate languages.

One motif that frequently occurs throughout the Celtic world is that of the magic cauldron, including the cauldron of plenty, which feeds everyone, and the cauldron of rebirth whereby the dead are put in and come out alive. Cauldrons can be found from the late Bronze Age period – vast cauldrons with a capacity of 60–70 litres. In May 1891, at Gundestrup, in north Jutland, a cauldron with a capacity of 130 litres was found in a peat bog. This silver dish had twelve rectangular plates, forming the inner and outer sides, and it is clear that it is of Celtic origin, although recently some academics outside the field of Celtic studies have disputed this by pointing out that it seems to have been manufactured in the Thracian area. These scholars did not, apparently, realise that Thrace had been settled by Celts by the fourth and third centuries BC. Kings of Thrace with Celtic names did not cease to rule until 192 BC.

The Celtic motifs are absolutely clear on the cauldron. We have the antler-headed god Cernunnos, with his neck ring, and a sequence of animal symbolism. One of the fascinating scenes on the cauldron is that in which a god accompanied by warriors holds a dead warrior over a cauldron while previously dead warriors march away. This is clearly the cauldron of rebirth.

Cauldrons have been found at Llyn Fawr in Mid-Glamorgan, dating from 600 BC, and at Llyn Cerrig in

Anglesey, dating from the second century BC and the first century AD. Cauldrons have been found throughout the Celtic world and back up the mythological traditions surviving in Irish and Welsh texts. They are found in both Hallstatt and La Tène graves, from Hochdorf to Duchov. In 1882 in Duchov, a town in Bohemia, which was the site of a spring sanctuary, a bronze cauldron was found containing some 2000 items of jewellery, fibulae, rings and other metal objects of the early La Tène period.

The Dagda had a magic cauldron that came from the fabulous city of Murias. It was so enormous, we are told, that the Formorii could make a porridge in it with goats, sheep, pigs and eighty measures each of milk, meal and fat. No one left the cauldron hungry. Cúchulainn and Cú Roi stole a magic cauldron that produced gold and silver from a castle. Midir the Proud, another of the gods, also had his magic cauldron.

In the Welsh tales, we hear that Matholwch of Ireland possessed a magic cauldron into which the dead were cast to appear the next morning whole and well except that they had lost their power of speech. We are told that the cauldron was originally the property of Bran Benedigeidfran (Bran the Blessed) who is perceived as an early god. He gave it to Matholwch but, after hostilities broke out, the cauldron had to be destroyed before Bran and his Britons could overcome Matholwch. The story recounts how the cauldron emerged from the Lake of the Cauldron on the back of a huge man accompanied by a huge woman. Were they deities whose role has been obscured?

Yet another magic cauldron appears in the tale of Culhwch's search for Olwen, for one of Culhwch's tasks is to obtain a magic cauldron which belongs to Diwrnach of Ireland and which is full of all the treasures of Ireland.

Our knowledge of Celtic mythology overall is greatly obscured by the Greek and Roman interpretations in the classical allusions. It has been argued that the Celtic peoples did not possess a uniform mythology but, instead, a plethora of different myths which are only comparable to a limited degree. As we have no systematic record before the insular Celts began to set down their stories at the start of the Christian era, it has also been argued that we have no means of forming a complete picture of pre-Christian mythology. However, knowledge in this field is still very fragmentary and new information is constantly coming through. The native sources are not yet exhausted and full comparisons with other Indo-European cultures have yet to be carefully made.

# 15

# EARLY CELTIC HISTORY

The Celts first emerged into recorded history in the sixth century BC. We learn of early trading contacts between the Phoenicians, the Greeks and the Etruscans. The earliest known point of contact seems to be the landing of Greek explorers and traders at the mouth of the Tartessus in the southern Iberian peninsula and the trading agreement reached between the merchant-traders from Phocis in Greece and the local Celtic king, Arganthonios. Herodotus says that he died in 564 BC, having lived for a long time.

Certainly during the sixth century BC, if not before, there was a lively trade established between the Phoenicians, the Greeks and the Etruscans and the Celts of the western Mediterranean. We know from tradition and from archaeological evidence, as well as from Greek accounts of the areas in which they were in contact with the Celts, that there had been a Celtic expansion from their original homelands for some centuries.

Massilia (Marseilles) had been established about 600 BC in the land of the Segobrigai – which seems to indicate 'exalted' (*brigia*) for 'daring of strength' (*sego*). Celtic tribes had already crossed into the Po valley and begun to settle but until the fifth century BC they were in conflict with the Etruscan empire for dominance in the area.

The Celtic tribes defeated the Etruscan armies near the River Ticino, a tributary of the Po, about 475 BC. Pliny, assumed to be quoting the Cisalpine Celt, Cornelius Nepos (*c.* 100–*c.* 25 BC), believed that the war against the Etruscan empire was conducted by a confederation of the Boii, Insubres and Senones, although it is arguable that the Senones were late-comers to the Italian peninsula. But certainly by the beginning of the fourth century BC most of the Etruscan ter-ritories north of the Apennines were in Celtic hands. Around 396 BC the Celts had inflicted a second major defeat – that is, the second worthy of record in Roman annals – on the Etruscan empire at the city of Melpum, which is thought to be Melzo, west of Milan.

In 390 BC the tribe called the Senones, led by Brennus, appeared outside the Etruscan city of Clusium, south of the Apennines. The Senones, an entire nation on the march, claimed that they wanted nothing more than to settle on Etruscan lands in peace for there was no other land to settle north of the mountains. The Etruscans, newly conquered by Rome, sent to Rome for ambassadors to help conduct the negotiations. The Roman ambassadors, patricians of the Fabii clan, proved partisan, ignored international law, and joined the Etruscans in doing battle with the Celts.

Brennus and his Senones were appalled at this breach of international law and sent a delegation to Rome demanding reparation. Rome showed her disdain for the Celts who then, ignoring the Etruscans, marched directly on Rome. On 18 July 390 BC, they fought a battle at the Allia, 20 kilometres north of Rome, against Rome's best legions and generals. The Romans were routed. By that evening the Celts were outside the city of Rome but did not enter until the next day. A rump of senators and military leaders shut themselves in the Capitol, the only part of the city never taken.

It was seven months before the Celts decided to withdraw from the city and only then after a payment of ransom by the Senate. Rome paid dearly for the arrogance of the Fabii. The price of the Celtic withdrawal was a fabulous 100 pounds' weight of gold. When the gold was being weighed, Sulpicius Lagus, the senior surviving Roman officer, objected to the fact that the Celts were using their own weights. Brennus then flung his sword on the scales and uttered the cry that became famous: 'Vae victis!' (Woe to the vanquished!) In other words, the conqueror dictates the terms.

Rome's defeat at the hands of the Senones always rankled with her historians and they frequently tried to rewrite history so as to extricate themselves from the shame of that defeat. From then on, Roman writers would paint the Celts as drunken, childlike barbarians, only one step removed from animals, and the Celtic peoples would suffer from the Roman prejudice as group by group they fell victim to the Roman empire.

But it took a while. In fact, it took two centuries for the Romans to conquer the Celts on the Italian peninsula. The Celtic victory over Rome caused the Celts to be welcome among the Latin city states, who still had not given up their freedom to Rome, and the Greek city states of southern Italy. Dionysius I of Syracuse recruited many Celtic warriors as mercenaries in his army. We learn that Celtic armies remained in the vicinity of Rome during the next fifty years.

Plutarch says a battle was fought at the River Anio in 377 or 374 BC, adding that the Romans 'mightily feared these barbarians who had conquered them in the first instance'. So great was the terror that there was a law stating that priests were exempt from military service 'except in the case of a Celtic war'. In 367 BC we hear of the Romans battling once more against a besieging Celtic army at the very gates of Rome.

It is at this time that we see the evidence of a Celtic alliance with the Greek city states of southern Italy. Dionysius of Syracuse had not only employed Celtic mercenaries in his army but had arranged for a contingent of 2000 Celtic mercenaries to serve his allies Sparta in their war against Thebes. The Celtic cavalry played a decisive role in the battle of Maninea in this war. This is the first time we find the Celts in Greece itself but, by this time, the Celtic tribes in their eastward movement along the Danube had begun to reach the Carpathians. At the same time, Pytheas of Massilia, the Greek explorer, had made contact with the insular Celts in Britain and Ireland. It was not until *c.* 300 BC that Eratosthenes of Cyrene correctly placed Ireland on the map of the world.

The Senones, who appear to be the only Celts who were enemies of Rome at this time, had settled in Picenum on the eastern seaboard of the Italian peninsula, from an area south of Ancona up to Rimini. Their main city seems to have been Senigallia, the place of the Senones Gauls. Again this may be seen as confirmation of their alliance with the Greeks for Ancona was a major trading colony of Syracuse.

During 361–360 BC a Celtic army was again in the vicinity of Rome and the Romans were still not able to defend themselves adequately. It would seem that the Celtic predilection for settling matters by means of single combat between champions or leaders was taking a toll on the Romans for in 340 BC the consul, Titus Manlius Imperiosus Torquatus, is said to have forbidden Roman commanders to engage in single-handed combat with the Celts. It was not until 349 BC that the first Roman victory over the Celts was achieved. In 344 BC the Romans finally concluded a treaty with the Celtic Senones. The Roman fear of Celtic invasion, however, remained intense for many years and rumours of Celtic attacks often caused armies to be formed and sent out. The real fear was replaced by a neurotic fear which was doubtless the basis of the Romans' subsequent racial antipathy to the Celts.

At this time the accounts show that whenever a Celtic army approached Rome, they would eventually withdraw to the south into Apulia, and not to the north. This supports the theory that they were in league with the Greek city states of southern Italy against the territorial ambitions of Rome. Even in 307 BC Agathocles of Syracuse was using Celtic mercenaries in his army against the imperial expansion of Carthage.

The Celtic eastward expansion along the Danube valley was now reaching towards the Black Sea. Celtic settlements were even found beyond the eastern shore around the Sea of Asov near the Crimea. Other settlements have been found in southern Poland, Russia and the Ukraine. In 335–334 BC Alexander of Macedonia met a number of Celtic chiefs on the banks of the Danube and apparently made an agreement with them so that they would not attack the northern frontiers of his empire while he set off to conquer the east.

It was not until after his death that the Celtic expansion began again and we hear that a Celtic leader named Molistomos caused a massive displacement of the Antariate, the largest group of the Illyrian (Bulgarian/Albanian) peoples, who were forced to flee before his advance. By 300 BC the Celts had settled in what is now Moravia and a few years later had conquered Thrace where they established a dynasty of Celtic kings, with Celtic names. The first of these was Cambaules.

In Italy, Rome's expansions now caused the Celts and Etruscans to form an alliance against Rome. A major war began and the Samnites also joined the alliance. There was a Celtic-Samnite victory over Rome at Camerium (Cameria), 140 kilometres north-east of Rome, in 298 BC. Lucius Scipio's defeat by the Senones was as shocking to the Romans as Allia. An entire legion was destroyed and the rest of the army fled. However, three years later the Romans turned the tables and won a victory over the Celts and Samnites at Sentium. The war continued and in 284 BC the Celts won another major victory when they defeated the praetor Lucius Caecilius at Arretium (Arezzo); the Roman commander was among the dead.

The following year, the Romans decided to concentrate all their forces against the Celtic Senones and entered their territory in Picenum. The Senones were defeated and the Roman commander Curius Dentatus burnt and pillaged his way through the countryside. Now the other Celtic tribes of the Po valley emerged by name into history and we find them as allies of the Etruscans against Rome. The Boii are identified as marching as far south as the Vadimo Lake, now Lago di Bassano, near the Tiber, 65 kilometres north of Rome. But here the Romans, under Publicius Cornelius Dolabella, annihilated the Etruscan half of the army before turning on the Celts as they were marching to the aid of their allies. The Celts were checked and withdrew but the next year they were at war again and this time were able to conclude a peace treaty with Rome.

Whatever their agreement with the Boii, Rome now took over all the Senones' territory up to Ariminum (Rimini) and began to clear the countryside of the Celtic inhabitants. To the Celts of northern Italy, the Roman 'ethnic cleansing' of the Senones and the building of Roman fortresses and colonies in the former independent countries of the Etruscans and Samnites was a warning. Rome might soon be marching across the Apennines and into Celtic territory.

When the Greek king, Pyrrhus of Epiros, landed in southern Italy, at the request of the Greek city states to protect them against Rome's imperial adventures, the Celts of the Po valley threw in their lot with him. The Celts knew Pyrrhus and he had employed Celts in his army in Greece. He had a high respect for their fighting qualities. Large contingents of Po valley Celts were in his armies when he defeated the Romans at Heraclea in 280 BC and at Asculum in 279 BC. They were still fighting for him when Rome secured a victory over him at

Beneventum, and ended his campaign. Pyrrhus returned to Greece taking a large number of Celtic warriors with him; Celts remained in the armies of Epiros and, indeed, of other Greek city states for many years afterwards.

Other tribes of the Celtic peoples were not so anxious to form alliances with the Greeks. These were the tribes of the eastward expansion. In 279 BC, a vast Celtic army, grouped into three divisions, had gathered on the northern borders of Macedonia. One division, under Bolgios, defeated the Macedonian army which had shortly before carved out Alexander's empire, and Ptolemy Ceraunos, the king of Macedonia, was slain. He had been one of Alexander's foremost generals. A second Celtic army, jointly commanded by Brennus and Acichorios, entered Greece, marched through Macedonia into Thessaly, and met and defeated an Athenian army commanded by Callippus, son of Moerocles, at the major battle of Thermopylae. The Celts swept through the mountain passes to Delphi and sacked the sanctuary. Greece was devastated by these Celtic victories and the Panathenaea (annual games) had to be cancelled for 278 BC.

Rumour has it that Brennus committed suicide, aghast at his sacrilege in sacking Delphi. It seems unlikely. We find that his army withdrew with the treasures of Delphi without suffering any military defeat from the southern Greeks.

The third Celtic army, commanded by Cerethrios, had occupied eastern Macedonia and there they were eventually defeated by the new king of Macedonia, Antigonatus Gonatas. While large sections of the Celtic invasion force withdrew back to the northern areas in what is now modern Bulgaria, Albania and Rumania, many others simply stayed in Macedonia posing a threat to the new king. Antigonatus Gonatas arranged that these Celts could be hired as mercenaries by the Greek kings. He himself recruited Celtic divisions into his own army. In 277/276 BC, a further 4000 of them went to Egypt to serve the pharaoh Ptolemy II. More importantly to the development of a Celtic state in Asia Minor, 20,000 Celts with their families, from the tribes of the Tolistoboii, Tectosages and Trocmi, led by their kings Leonnarios and Litarios, crossed into Asia Minor at the invitation of Nicomedes of Bithynia to serve him against Antiochus of Syria.

As for the Celts who went to Egypt, we find Celtic involvement in the affairs of Ptolemaic Egypt lasted until almost the beginning of the Christian era. In 217 BC 14,000 Celts constituted the major part of the army of the pharaoh Ptolemy IV at the battle of Raphia against Antiochus II of Syria. It was an Egyptian victory, thanks, so the account shows, to the Celtic cavalry. A Celtic cemetery has been found at Hadra, southeast of Alexandria. Not only tombstones but pottery bearing Celtic names have been found there. Famous Celtic graffiti have been found in the chapel of Horus, in the tomb of Seti I, at the great temple of Karnak. Egyptian coins with Celtic motifs on them were struck.

Forty years later we still find records of Celts serving in the pharaoh's armies and we also find that the famous Cleopatra (Cleopatra VII, 69–30 BC) had an élite bodyguard of 300 Celtic warriors. When Octavius Caesar (later Augustus) emerged victorious, he ordered this bodyguard to serve Herod the Great in Judea as a token of Roman gratitude and friendship to the king. When Herod the Great died in 4 BC his Celtic bodyguard attended the funeral obsequies. As twenty-five years had passed, these could hardly be the same soldiers who had served Cleopatra in the original bodyguard.

The Celts who had crossed into Asia Minor served Nicomedes well. Within one year of campaigning they had defeated the king of Bithynia's enemies and, after wandering Asia Minor for a while, they were allowed to settle the central plain of what is now Turkey but came to be called after them – Galatia. The settlement was made in tribal territories. The Tectosages made the town of Ancyra (Ankara) their capital.

The Tolistoboii renamed Gordium (where Alexander 'unravelled' the famous knot) as Vindia, while the Trocmi settled to the east of the River Halys. The Celts of Galatia established themselves as a state worthy of respect which the Greeks called 'the Commonwealth of Galatia'. Their independence and prestige were confirmed when the Galatians, in 261 BC, defeated the mighty Syrian army of Antiochus I at Ephesus and slew the king during the battle. The Celts of Galatia extended a sort of overlordship over surrounding Greek states such as Pergamum and it was not until Attalos I of Pergamum defeated the Celts at the headwaters of the Caioc in 241 BC that Pergamum was able to stop paying tribute to Galatia.

With Rome's emergence as an imperial power, having secured dominance in Italy from the Apennines to the south of the peninsula, their main trading and military rival appeared to be Carthage. It was inevitable that a conflict should arise between Rome and Carthage. In 263 BC the First Punic War, between the two rivals for dominance in the western Mediterranean, started and it is not surprising to find a force of 3000 Celts fighting for Carthage, commanded by one Antaros. Although the Celts fought as 'mercenaries', often the term is mistaken for they had their own agenda in fighting for powers which sought to curtail their arch-enemy – Rome. If the powers they were working for changed their allegiance then they withdrew their support. It mattered not about the financial rewards. They had turned down lucrative offers from Rome. The Celts of Italy knew who their main enemy was. In fact, Antaros withdrew his support from Carthage in 249 BC when an alliance did not suit his purpose.

The Celtic troops of Ptolemy II in 259 BC even attempted to take over Egypt but Ptolemy was able to put down their *coup d'état* and they were all driven to an island in the Nile where they were starved to death. Ptolemy struck some celebratory gold coins with Celtic motifs on them. It did not stop Ptolemy, however, from continuing to recruit other Celtic troops.

With Rome and Carthage at peace, Rome began to clear the remaining Senones of Picenum and turned her attention to the Celts of the Po valley. Meanwhile Carthage, unable to expand on the Italian peninsula, sent her armies to the Iberian peninsula and began to conquer and colonise among the Celtic tribes there. Timaeos, *c.* 260 BC, had been the first to use the term 'Celtiberians' to describe the Celts living in Iberia (Spain and Portugal).

The Celts of the Po valley, however, watched Roman expansion with alarm and turned to their cousins from north of the Alps to assist them. They appeared to believe that attack was the better part of defence. The Boii and the Insubres of the Po recruited the Gaesatae, professional warriors, who joined them and, together with the Taurini (of the Turin area), they crossed the Apennines before Rome could march her armies north. Aneroestes and Concolitanus commanded a Celtic army of some 50,000 infantry and 20,000 cavalry. Rome's resources totalled 700,000 infantry and 70,000 cavalry.

In 225 BC the Celtic army found itself in the vicinity of Clusium and facing a large Roman army. Better generalship won the day; Polybius tells us that 6000 Romans were slain and the rest put to flight. However, one victory did not win the war. Two consular armies were hastening towards the Celtic army, one from the north, having landed on the coast by ship, and one moving overland from the south. The Celtic army took its stand at Telamon, a town on the western seaboard of the Italian peninsula. The battle was one of the most spectacular in Celtic history and, alas for them, a major defeat for the Celts.

From 224 BC, for the first time, Rome began to conduct annual military campaigns across the Apennines into the Po valley. During the first campaigning season, both consuls, Quintus Fulvius and Titus Manlius, raided and devastated the territory of the Boii. In 223 BC, the consuls Gaius Flaminius and Publius Furius turned their attention to the south-east side of the country and the territory of the Insubres, whose capital was Milan. Major battles were fought during this campaign and the Roman armies returned victorious.

The next year, 222 BC, Rome prepared for yet another deadly campaign and this time the Celtic kings sent to the new consuls and asked for peace negotiations. Gnaeus Cornelius Scipio and Marcus Claudius Marcellus refused to discuss peace and made it clear that Rome's intention was a war of extermination. The Celts of the Po valley, unlike the Senones, or other tribes, were not a warlike people. Archaeological evidence shows they were pastoral and agricultural communities.

They asked for help from their Transalpine cousins again and this time 30,000 Gaesatae joined them to stop the Romans. It was now that a chieftain or king called Viridomarus (the name meaning 'Great Man') emerged as an astute military leader. The Romans had no easy victory. Before the campaign, Viridomarus had led a force of Insubres to Clastidium and laid siege to the Roman garrison in order to draw off the consular armies threatening the peaceful settlements of the Po valley. When Marcus Claudius Marcellus and his legions arrived, Viridomarus challenged him to a single combat to decide the issue. Marcellus, surprisingly, accepted and Viridomarus, hurling javelins from his chariot, approached the Roman consul. Marcellus managed to kill him and the Celtic army, not surprisingly, crumbled.

The Romans devastated the Po valley and, according to Polybius, 222 BC was seen as the end of the 'Celtic War' there. Certainly the Romans now began to set up permanent military garrisons in the Po valley and also to organise colonies to open up the territory for trade.

However, events among the Celts of the Iberian peninsula would play a further part in prolonging the conquest.

Carthage had succeeded in reducing much of the Celtic territory in what is now Spain and setting up a colony with New

Carthage (Cartagena) as their administrative capital. The territory did not fall easily to the Carthaginians. Hamilcar, the conqueror of these territories, was actually assassinated in 221 BC by a Celt. Then a new commander, Hannibal of Carthage, appeared. From childhood his enemy had been Rome and he began to court the Celts, pointing out that they shared the same enemy, and recruiting them into his army. He sent out embassies to the Celts of Gaul and told them his plan was to make war on Rome. The Celts, not only those of the Iberian peninsula but the Celts of southern Gaul, the Alpine valleys and the Po valley itself, threw their support behind the Carthaginian general.

Had it not been for the Celtic tribes of the Alpine region, Hannibal and his famous elephants would not have succeeded in passing into Italy at all. Indeed, Hannibal's army was over fifty per cent Celtic at the time he arrived in the Po valley. As soon as he arrived some 10,000 Celts of the Po valley joined him. They were to play a prominent part in his army during his campaigns in Italy from 218 BC through to 201 BC.

The Celts were used by Hannibal as the mainstay of his army in battle, occupying the central infantry positions at his famous victory at Cannae in 216 BC. In discussing Hannibal's campaign, most historians seem inclined to ignore the conflict between Rome and the Po valley Celts even though some of these battles were major disasters for Rome. For example, in 215 BC Lucius Postumius Albinus, the former consul, marched two legions and auxiliaries totalling 25,000 men into the territory of the Boii. At a place called Litana (Wide Hill) the Celts ambushed his army and completely destroyed it. Postumius was killed with his generals.

However, in spite of the long, arduous campaign, Hannibal never felt able to march on Rome and occupy it as the Celts had done 150 years earlier. Finally, Rome's victories in Iberia, where an army had been sent, pushed the Carthaginians out and Carthage summoned Hannibal back to help defend their city. Celts and Celtiberians went to defend Carthage. It was the Celtic formations which prevented the Roman victory at Utica in 203 BC from becoming a total rout of the Carthaginians. They also held the central battle lines at the last famous battle of Zama against Scipio. Ironically, at the same time the Po valley Celts had just defeated another Roman army.

With the destruction of the Carthaginian empire, nothing stood in Rome's way to distract them from concentrating all their energies on conquering the Celts of the Po valley. As well as that, Rome had taken over Carthage's role in Iberia as colonial conqueror. The Iberian Celtic tribes were also facing the Roman threat.

But if the Romans thought the conquest of the Celtic tribes in the north of Italy would be easy, they were in for a surprise. It took over a decade of fierce fighting to crush the resistance of the Celts along the River Po. The Boii seemed particularly resilient although in one battle alone, in 193 BC, they sustained, according to Livy, 14,000 dead, 1092 captured alive, with 721 horses, three chieftains and some 212 standards and 63 wagons. The Celts were not treated on honourable terms by the Romans when they surrendered. At best, they were sold into slavery. In 192 BC a Boii chieftain came to the consul Titus Quinctius Flaminius and surrendered himself, his wife and family. Flaminius had the chieftain and his family ritually slaughtered to provide entertainment for his boyfriend.

The end finally came in 191 BC and Cisalpine Gaul, the Po valley, became the first Celtic homeland to be conquered by Rome. Roman policy was now to drive out those Celtic tribes such as the Boii, Insubres, Taurini, Cenomani and others who had been fighting against Rome, while treaties of cooperation were sought from the Veneti and other tribes. A massive plan of colonisation began. The Celts were to be Romanised, new Roman towns would be built and the devastated countryside taken over to provide farm produce for Rome. It was a major step in Rome's imperial ambitions.

At the same time the Celts of Iberia were finding the war with Rome equally merciless. It had begun well enough with a Celtic victory over the general Aemilius Paullus. In 179 BC Tiberius Sempronius Gracchus switched policies, tried to agree treaties and encouraged Celtic enlistment into the Roman colonial army, giving chieftains positions of command. The treaties sought to alleviate the burden of taxes on the conquered people.

Many tribes held out against the *pax Romana*. In 152 BC a Roman army besieging the hill-fort of Numantia was driven off and almost destroyed by the Celts. Rome agreed terms with Numantia in 151 BC but the treaty was immediately broken when a new Roman commander, Galba, arrived. His activities in massacring the Celts and enslaving them even caused criticism in Rome from his former commander, Marcus Porcius Cato. In 148 BC the Celts took their revenge when the Roman governor and his army were defeated and a few years later a Roman consul and his army were forced to surrender. The leader of the Celtic resistance in both these victories was Viriathos. Rome's policy was, if you can't defeat your enemy in battle, employ an assassin. A Celtic traitor was bribed and Viriathos was murdered in his sleep. His loss was a severe blow to Celtic resistance to Rome in Iberia.

Yet the warfare continued. In 136 BC the Roman commander Mancinus, trying to reduce a Celtic hill-fort at Pallantia, had to retreat and the Celts turned the retreat into a spectacular rout in which some 20,000 Romans had to surrender.

In 134 BC Publius Cornelius Scipio, the adopted grandson of Scipio Africanus, was sent to Iberia. His job was to finally crush the Celts, and he chose to concentrate on Numantia, regarding it as the centre of Celtic resistance. Avaros was the leader at Numantia. Scipio brought his army up and laid siege to the great hill fortress city. Numantia slowly began to starve.

A Celtic chieftain named Rhetogenes was chosen, with a few comrades, to break out and seek reinforcements.

Rhetogenes' attempts to raise the siege failed. Some 400 of his men, taken prisoner, were paraded in front of the town and had their right hands cut off as a deterrent. Finally starvation and disease broke the spirit of the Celts. Altogether 8000 Celtic men, women and children had held out against Rome's 60,000 troops. They now surrendered and Numantia was put to the torch. Everyone was sold into slavery with the exception of fifty leaders who were sent to Rome to be ritually sacrificed in the ceremonial triumph.

Rome had scored another victory over the Celts although it could not be truly said that all the Celts of the Iberian peninsula had accepted the *pax Romana* until the mid-first century BC. From 81 to 73 BC, under the governorship of Sertorius, schools for the children of the Celtic kings and chieftains were established. Soon Latin was the language of the educated classes and the remnants of the old Celtic civilisation quickly disappeared.

The Celts of Galatia had been able to secure their independence for a time in spite of the antagonism of the surrounding Greek states. Attalos of Pergamum went so far as to recruit some European Celts, the Aegosages, into his army in 218 BC but these were promptly massacred by Prusias of Bithynia the following year. The Galatian rulers seemed to play politics to maintain their independence from the Greek kingdoms and were able, once again, to exert an overlordship over Pergamum and form an alliance with Antiochus III of Syria. This was their undoing for Rome declared war on Antiochus of Syria and, in 191 BC, the Celts formed the centre ranks of his ill-fated army at Magnesia.

Magnesia was a major Roman victory. The Romans were aided by Eumenes II of Pergamum. The victorious general was Lucius Cornelius Scipio whose brother had been the victor over Hannibal at Carthage. Hannibal had sought refuge with Antiochus III, one of the major political reasons for Rome declaring war on Antiochus. Rome demanded Hannibal be handed over, but he committed suicide soon afterwards.

Rome was now concerned to pacify and annex Asia Minor to its overlordship. They decided that the most dangerous people there were the Celts of Galatia and Gnaeus Manlius Volso was given command of a punitive expedition against Galatia in 189 BC.

Major Celtic defeats followed his invasion of their territory. The Tolistoboii and Trocmi were defeated at the battle of Mount Olympus near the city of Pessinus. Livy says this was won with a great slaughter of non-combatants, women and children and the elderly, before Volso marched on to defeat the Tectosages near Ancyra, at a hill called Magaba. Volso made Galatia a vassal territory of their allies, Pergamum. Livy was inclined to excuse the pitiless Roman crushing of the Galatians as an attempt to show the Galatians, once and for all, who was in charge.

A Celtic leader named Ortagion now emerged as a man of vision. He was a chieftain of the Tolistoboii and it seems that he was the first to unite the three Celtic peoples of Galatia under a central leadership in order to survive. Polybius was able to interview Ortagion's wife, Chiomara, when she was in Sardis.

While Asia Minor was nominally under Roman suzerainty, Rome did not interfere too much in the political developments there. The Galatian leaders, to keep some degree of independence, formed alliances, one with their former enemy Eumenes II in order to drive out Parnaces I of Pontus who attempted to exert his authority over Galatia.

An alliance with Prusias II of Bithynia then helped the Celts overthrow Pergamum's overlordship. An alliance with Rome against Cappadocia increased Galatian independence so that by 123 BC the Galatian state was independent and powerful

once again. However, a new threat came along in the person
of Mithridates V 'The Great' of Pontus who made Pontus into
a large empire encompassing the coastal regions of the Black
Sea, even to the north coast, including the Crimea and the
region around the mouth of the River Dniester.

In 88 BC he invited the sixty major Galatian chieftains to his
court to dine and discuss his intentions. It was part of Celtic
culture that no one would enter the feasting hall bearing arms
and Mithridates relied on this fact. As they started to eat, his
soldiers killed them. Only three chieftains had not attended
and Mithridates had sent assassins to deal with them. They
only managed to kill one. Out of those attending the feast, but
a single chieftain escaped – he was Deiotarus, son of
Dumnorix, of the Tolistoboii.

Deiotaros now led Galatian resistance against Mithridates
and, in 74 BC, he finally drove out Zeumachus, whom
Mithridates had made governor of Galatia. Mithridates had
made the mistake of declaring war on Rome and so Deiotaros
now emerged as undisputed king of Galatia. He was quick to
make treaties of friendship and alliance with Rome.
Mithridates was toppled and fled into exile where he ironically met his death at the hands of a Celt.

Deiotaros made friends with Pompey and Cicero, and even
entertained Julius Caesar at his hill-forts in Galatia. However,
he was subsequently tried *in absentia* in Rome where he was
charged with attempting to assassinate Caesar. It was a
trumped up charge and Cicero conducted his defence in 47 BC.
Deiotarus survived and died in old age. His son Deiotarus II
became king but ruled for only a few years. Amyntas became
the last independent king of Galatia for Rome had already
decided to take it over and administer it as a Roman province.

Rome had made some treaties with the Greek merchant
cities of the western Mediterranean, in particular with the
city of Massilia. Around 125 BC the Celtic Salyes had attacked
Massilia twice and Rome now intervened to protect the city.

But once in control of Massilia, and having defeated the Celtic Salyes and the Allobriges, Rome realised that her dominions could now extend across the southern territory of Gaul from the Alps to Massilia. In 118 BC Rome made a formal extension of this new province (Provence) as far west as Tolosa (Toulouse), the capital of the Tolostoboii of Gaul. Then the boundary was taken to Narbon. The new province was now called Gallia Narbonensis. Yet again, Rome had extended its empire at the cost of the lands of the Celts.

In what is now Rumania, the Celts and Dacians formed an alliance about 109 BC to stop Roman expansion in their territory. Around the same time, in Gallia Narbonensis, the Celts made a last-ditch attempt to throw out the Romans. Tribes called the Cimbri and Teutones (it is a subject of argument whether they were Celts or Germans, although their leaders bore Celtic names and their weapons and what is known about them identify them as distinctly Celtic) swept into the area and defeated a Roman army. Divicio, a Celtic chieftain of the Tugurni, defeated a second Roman army. A Roman garrison in Tolosa was besieged. More defeats of Roman forces followed, including the army of Caepio and of Manlius just north of Massilia. In 102 BC the army of Catalus was forced to fall back.

In spite of these reverses to their fortunes, the Romans reorganised their army, under the command of Caius Marius, and in 101 BC the Celts, some 120,000, were defeated in a battle at Vercellae.

It is now that we hear about the pressures on the Celts from the Germanic tribes to the north and the Slavic tribes to the east. Burebista of Dacia launched a war of annexation on the Celts in 60 BC and defeated the Boii of Bohemia, named after them. Some 32,000 Boii left Bohemia to join the Helvetii.

Against these pressures, the Helvetii, led by Orgetorix and his son-in-law, Dumnorix of the Aedui, formed a Celtic alliance with plans for a westward migration away from the incursions of the Germanic tribes and the Slavs. It was to be a mass migration. Apparently such Celtic migrations had been happening for a while as the Germanic and Slavic tribes pressed on the Celtic territories. Julius Caesar found documents in the Helvetian camp which were written in Greek characters and contained a register of all the people in this migratory alliance. The grand total was 368,000, of whom 92,000 were warriors. The Helvetii numbered 263,000, the Tulingi 36,000, the Latovici 14,000, the Rauraci 23,000 and the Boii 32,000.

The Celts were desperate to escape from the continuing raids on their homelands.

Rome had other ideas.

Julius Caesar had been given the governorship of Cisalpine Gaul. Chance gave him Transalpine Gaul (Narbonensis Gaul or Provence) because the governor died unexpectedly. Now news came of the proposed migrations of the Helvetii and allied tribes. Dumnorix had a pro-Roman brother, who was now ruler of the Aedui, and he was persuaded to seek a Roman alliance in case his territory was swamped by the migration. Thus Caesar was able to make this an excuse to intervene in the affairs of Gaul proper in 58 BC. The Helvetii tried to avoid confrontation with the Roman army led by Caesar but were forced into a battle and defeated at Bibracte. The vast majority were massacred. Only a third of the original band of emigrants were driven back into what is now Switzerland, still calling itself Helvetica.

Once with an army in Gaul, Caesar showed his true ambition, and Rome's too. He commenced the conquest of Gaul proper. Tribe by tribe, the Romans extended their power until they reached the Channel shore. The Romans also checked the incursions of the Germanic tribes, keeping them back on the eastern side of the Rhine.

In 55 BC Caesar even felt strong enough to make an exploratory expedition to Britain where he landed and defeated the Cantii confederation of tribes near Walmer or Deal, before being forced to return to Gaul by impending bad weather and unrest in the newly conquered territory. There were various uprisings which had to be put down. However, in 54 BC, Caesar made a second expedition to Britain and was able to march inland. The British tribes had given command to Cassivellaunus, and Caesar, fighting every foot of the way, was finally able to reach his capital at Wheathampstead, near St Albans, in Hertfordshire. A treaty was negotiated but bad weather made his withdrawal from Britain a necessity.

Once more he returned to Gaul to find that Celtic resistance there had grown stronger and unified behind a central leader. Indutiomarus of the Treveri appeared as the main leader, following the slaughter of Dumnorix of the Aedui while a hostage of Rome. It is certainly thanks to Indutiomarus that a Gaulish army was established with a central policy. However, the Gaulish leader was soon killed.

It is now that Vercingetorix of the Arverni is acknowledged commander-in-chief of the Celtic forces in Gaul, and he inflicted a severe defeat on Caesar at Gergovia. In 52 BC Caesar managed to besiege Vercingetorix at Alesia and finally the Gaulish king surrendered, to prevent his people starving as the Celts had starved at Numantia. He was taken to Rome in chains, imprisoned and, finally, in 46 BC was ritually slaughtered as part of the Roman triumphal celebrations.

However, Gaul was still uneasy under the *pax Romana*. Commius and the Atrebates of the Belgae decided to leave Gaul and settle among the Atrebates of southern Britain. Britain was able to maintain its independence. The Gaulish Celts continued to assert their independence in a series of insurrections. The Bellovaci rose in 46 BC, the Allobriges in 44 BC, the Aquitani and Morini in 33 BC. More insurrections occurred in 25/7 BC in south-west Gaul. Even into the first century of the Christian era there were uprisings to re-establish their independence from Rome. We find around AD 67 the

Druids of Gaul supporting a Gaulish uprising and, according to Tacitus, reminding their countrymen that their ancestors had once captured and occupied Rome itself.

With Cisalpine Gaul becoming officially part of the Roman state in 42 BC, Galatia became a Roman province, for Amyntas, who was killed in 25 BC, was the last king recognised by Rome. M. Lollius then became the first governor of the Galatian province. The Celts of Galatia became the first non-Jewish population to accept the new Christian religion: St Paul's famous epistle to the Galatians was written to this Celtic Christian community. Celtic was still spoken in Galatia, according to St Jerome, during the fourth century AD but over the following centuries it vanished, probably completely by the ninth century AD. Iberia had also been subdued and Latinised, although speakers of a Celtic language were resettled in the area of Galicia and Asturias in the fifth and sixth centuries AD. The Celtic world, which had once stretched from one end of Europe to the other, and beyond, was rapidly shrinking.

Only Britain and Ireland stood outside the Roman orbit at this time. Britain had recovered from the two brief campaigns fought by Caesar in 55 and 54 BC. With the southern British kings minting their own coins from the second century BC, and with a rich trade developing between their kingdoms and the Continent, it appears that Cassivellaunus and his descendants had also united the kingdoms under their overkingship. Cunobelinus, the Cymbeline of Shakespeare, became the best known of these monarchs, reigning from AD 10 to c. 40. As we have seen, Strabo was moved to write that Rome would accrue more financial reward by trading with Britain than attempting to conquer it.

The Roman emperors did not take his advice and under the emperor Claudius, in AD 43, a full-scale invasion, commanded by Aulus Plautius, took place. It took nine years to smash resistance in south-eastern Britain, ending with the capture of the over-king Caractacus, the son of Cunobelinus, and his family. Betrayed by Cartimandua, queen of the Brigantes, Caractacus was taken in chains to Rome and only his own eloquence saved him from a ritual execution. Britain, however, was never fully conquered. Rome never secured a foothold in the north and its rule elsewhere was tenuous. Its history over the next few centuries is marked by uprisings and finally, in AD 410, Zosimus reports that all Roman officials had been expelled from Britain and a native government re-established. Indeed, the old Celtic rulers, who had survived the three centuries of Roman rule, re-emerged, almost like the Indian princes who survived the two centuries of the British Raj in India. However, whereas in an independent India the old semi-independent principalities and kingdoms were taken over by the new state, it was the Celtic princes who were once more in charge of an independent Britain and with an over-king in control. We hear that around AD 425–450 the ruler of southern Britain was called Vortigern – the name means 'Overlord'. But the Celts of southern Britain were now faced by a new, even more remorseless enemy than Rome – the Anglo-Saxons, who eventually carved 'England' out of the former Celtic territory by forcing the indigenous population to migrate in large waves to such places as Brittany, Galicia and Asturias, and to Ireland. Those that did not migrate were simply massacred.

In Ireland, the Celts had survived unscathed by the threat of Roman empire, developing their native laws, literature and learning. Although Irish is the third literary language of Europe after Greek and Latin and we have texts surviving from the sixth century AD, recording earlier oral traditions, the history of Ireland prior to that date is obscure. Some historians do not believe that the Celts even arrived in Ireland until c. 200 BC, following the Roman conquest of the Iberian peninsula.

Ireland had become known to the Roman world by the first

century AD. Tacitus records: 'In soil and climate, and in the character and civilisations of its inhabitants, [it] is much like Britain; and its approaches and harbours have now become better known from the merchants who trade there . . .' Archaeology certainly provides evidence of trading links. From Tacitus also we hear of an Irish prince 'expelled from his home by rebellion', who arrived in Britain in c. AD 80 and whom Agricola considered using as a pretext for an invasion. However, he was too busily occupied trying to conquer northern Britain.

There was an Irish tradition, recounted in *Leabhar Gabhála* (*Book of Invasions*), that Míle Easpain (Soldier of Spain), the progenitor of the Gaels, led his people to Ireland from Spain. Archaeological evidence from the stone *chevaux-de-frise* fortifications at, among other places, Dún Aenghus, on the Aran Islands, is cited in evidence, for similar constructions are found in Spain and Portugal. However, Irish tradition and the Irish genealogies of kings, the king lists, put the date of the creation of the two major royal lines in Ireland to 1015 BC. These are the lines of Eremon and Eber, the sons of Golamh or Míle. This would place the arrival of Míle's sons in Ireland 700–800 years before a date archaeologists would be happy to accept.

Certainly the first known inhabitants of Ireland lived there in 6000 BC and the first farming communities were active in 3000 BC. Around 1500 BC Irish bronze and gold work was actually being exported to Europe. It may be possible that speakers of an Indo-European dialect had reached Ireland by this time. Is there, however, anything to suggest that a new group of people arrived in Ireland around 1015 BC which would give substance to the Irish literary tradition?

In fact, archaeologists have admitted to noticing 'a wind of change' in Ireland after 1200 BC. This 'change' was revealed in an important find from Bishopsland, Co. Kildare, where the equipment of a smith was unearthed. He had buried his anvil, vice, saw and other tools such as a socketed axe-head, chisel and palstave. These tools appear to be similar to Celtic developments in southern Germany. Similar finds were made in Lough Gur, Co. Limerick, and Annesborough, Co. Armagh. We also find Hallstatt-type swords in Ireland though these are not of sufficient number to indicate a large-scale invasion. But while it is in the archaeologist's nature to look for large-scale 'invasions', the less dramatic 'development' theories must also be considered: changes in society do not have to be brought about by invasions from outside cultures.

It is possible, therefore, that the first Celtic-speaking groups came to Ireland exactly when the Irish literary traditions say they did; small groups, perhaps, intermarrying with the previous Indo-European population and developing the Celtic language which was spoken throughout Ireland when the country emerged into recorded history. Ireland could still have been a haven for Continental Celts fleeing from the Roman conquests towards the end of the first century BC, which would have reinforced this culture.

Cecile O'Rahilly, in *Ireland and Wales: Their Historical and Literary Relations*, demonstrated the evidence of a continuing movement of small population groups between Ireland and Britain from the prehistoric period through to medieval times. She shows that groups of British Celts fled both Roman and Anglo-Saxon conquests and settled in Ireland.

The La Tène culture had reached Ireland by the third and second centuries BC, although more examples have been found in the northern half of the country. The surviving archaeological material really gives us no reliable evidence of any large-scale Celtic migrations. The fact is that Ireland was Celtic-speaking from earliest references, such as Avienus' *Ora Maritima*. Though surviving from the fourth century AD, this is known to contain material based on earlier Greek exploratory voyages of the fifth century BC. Strabo speaks of Ireland in his *Geography*.

It is at this point, the start of the Christian era, that we may leave the world of the ancient Celts.

Today, the Celtic world has indeed dwindled to the sixteen millions dwelling on the north-west periphery of Europe, of which only two-and-a-half millions still speak a Celtic language. These are the lineal descendants of the once extensive civilisation of the ancient Celts, the inheritors of 3000 years of a unique and rich cultural continuum.

# SUGGESTIONS FOR FURTHER READING

ARMIT, IAN. *Celtic Scotland*, B.T. Batsford, London, 1997.

AUDOUZE, FRANÇOISE, and BÜCHSENSCHÜTZ. *Towns, Villages and Countryside of Celtic Europe*, B.T. Batsford, 1992.

BRUNEAUX, JEAN LOUIS. *The Celtic Gauls: Gods, Rites and Sanctuaries*, Seaby, London, 1988.

CHADWICK, NORA K. *The Druids*, University of Wales Press, Cardiff, 1966.

CHADWICK, NORA K. *The Celts*, Pelican Books, London, 1970.

CLANDERMOND, COUNT OF. *Links in a Golden Chain: A Collection of Essays on the History of the Niadh Nask or The Military Order of the Golden Chain*, Royal Eóghanacht Society, Clonmel, Co. Tipperary, 1998.

CUNLIFFE, BARRY. *The Celtic World*, new ed., Constable, London, 1992.

CUNLIFFE, BARRY. *The Ancient Celts*, Oxford University Press, Oxford, 1997.

CURCHIN, LEONARD A. *Roman Spain: Conquest and Assimilation*, Routledge, London, 1991.

DILLON, MYLES, and CHADWICK, NORA. *The Celtic Realms*, Weidenfeld and Nicolson, London, 1967.

DILLON, MYLES. *Celts and Aryans: Survivals of Indo-European Speech and Society*, Indian Institute of Advanced Study, Simla, Rashtrapati Nivas, Simla, 1975.

ELLIS, PETER BERRESFORD. *Celtic Inheritance* (first published, 1985), new ed., Constable, London, 1992.

ELLIS, PETER BERRESFORD. *Dictionary of Celtic Mythology*, Constable, London, 1992.

ELLIS, PETER BERRESFORD. *The Celtic Empire*, Constable, London, 1990.

ELLIS, PETER BERRESFORD. *A Guide to Early Celtic Remains in Britain*, Constable, London, 1991.

ELLIS, PETER BERRESFORD. *The Druids*, Constable, London, 1994.

ELLIS, PETER BERRESFORD. *Celtic Women*, Constable, London, 1995.

ELLIS, PETER BERRESFORD. *Celt and Greek, Celts in the Hellenic World*, Constable, London, 1997.

ELLIS PETER BERRESFORD. *Celt and Roman, The Celts of Italy*, Constable, London, 1998.

FILIP, JAN. *Celtic Civilization and its Heritage*, Publishing House of the Czechoslovak Academy of Sciences, Prague, 1962.

GREEN, MIRANDA. *The Gods of the Celts*, Alan Sutton, Gloucester, 1986.

GREEN, MIRANDA. *Symbol and Image in Celtic Religious Art*, Routledge, London, 1989.

GREEN, MIRANDA. *Animals in Celtic Life and Myth*, Routledge, London, 1992.

GREEN, MIRANDA. *Dictionary of Celtic Myth and Legend*, Thames and Hudson, London, 1992.

GREEN, MIRANDA. *The Celtic World*, Routledge, London, 1995.

GREEN, MIRANDA. *Celtic Goddesses*, British Museum Press, London, 1995.

GREEN, MIRANDA. *Celtic Art*, Everyman Art Library, Weidenfeld and Nicolson, London, 1996.

GREEN, MIRANDA. *Exploring the World of the Druids*, Thames and Hudson, London, 1997.

HARBISON, PETER. *Pre-Christian Ireland: From the First Settlers to the Early Celts*, Thames and Hudson, London, 1988.

HUBERT, HENRI. *The Rise of the Celts*, new ed., Constable, London, 1987.

HUBERT, HENRI. *The Greatness and Decline of the Celts*, new ed., Constable, London, 1987.

JAMES, SIMON. *Exploring the World of the Celts*, Thames and Hudson, London, 1993.

LAING, LLOYD. *Celtic Britain*, Routledge and Kegan Paul, London, 1979.

LAING, LLOYD and JENNIFER. *Celtic Britain and Ireland: The Myth of the Dark Ages*, Irish Academic Press, Dublin, 1990.

LEHANE, BRENDAN. *Early Celtic Christianity*, new ed., Constable, London, 1994.

MACCANA, PROINSIAS. *Celtic Mythology*, Hamlyn, London, 1970.

MACCULLOCH, J.A. *Celtic Mythology*, reprint, Constable, London, 1992.

MACCULLOCH, J.A. *The Religion of the Ancient Celts*, reprint, Constable, London, 1991.

MACKILLOP, JAMES. *Dictionary of Celtic Mythology*, Oxford Universtiy Press, Oxford, 1998.

MAIER, BERNHARD (trs Cyril Edwards). *Dictionary of Celtic Religion and Culture*, The Boydell Press, Suffolk, 1997.

MARKLE, JAN. *Women of the Celts*, Cremonesi, London, 1975.

MEGAW, RUTH and VINCENT. *Celtic Art: from its Beginnings to the Book of Kells*, Thames and Hudson, London, 1989.

MOSCATI, SABATINO and OTHERS. *I Celti*, Bompiano, Milano, 1991. English trs. *The Celts*, Thames and Hudson, London, 1991.

NASH, DAPHNE. *Coinage in the Celtic World*, Seaby, London, 1987.

O'RAHILLY, CECILE. *Ireland and Wales: Their Historical and Literary Relations*, Longman, Green and Co., London, 1924.

O'RAHILLY, THOMAS F. *Early Irish History and Mythology*, Dublin Institute for Advanced Studies, Dublin, 1946, new ed. 1984.

PIGGOTT, STUART. *The Druids*, Thames and Hudson, London, 1968.

PLEINER, RADOMIR (and contributions by B.G. Scott). *The Celtic Sword*, Clarendon Press, Oxford, 1993.

POWELL, T.G.E. *The Celts*, new ed., Thames and Hudson, London, 1980.

RAFTERY, BARRY. *Pagan Celtic Ireland: The Enigma of the Irish Iron Age*, Thames and Hudson, London, 1994.

RAFTERY, JOSEPH, ed. *The Celts*, The Mercier Press, Cork, 1964.

RANKIN, H.D. *Celts and the Classical World*, Croom Helm, London, 1987.

REES, ALWYN and BRINLEY. *Celtic Heritage*, Thames and Hudson, London, 1961.

RITCHIE, W.F. and J.N.G. *Celtic Warriors*, Shire Archaeology, Aylesbury, Bucks, 1985.

ROLLESTON, T.W. *Myths and Legends of the Race*, new ed., Constable, 1985.

ROSS, ANNE, *The Pagan Celts*, new ed., B.T. Batsford, London, 1980.

ROSS, ANNE. *Pagan Celtic Britain*, revised ed., Constable, London, 1992.

SJOESTEDT, MARI-LOUISE. *Gods and Heroes of the Celts* (trs Myles Dillon), Methuen, London, 1949; new ed., Four Courts Press, Dublin, 1994.

SQUIRE, CHARLES. *Celtic Myth and Legend*, new ed., Newcastle Publishing Co. Inc, USA, 1975.

STARY, P.F. 'Foreign Elements in Etruscan Arms and Armour: 8th to 3rd Centuries BC', *Proceedings of the Prehistory Society*, Vol. 45, December 1979.

STEAD, I.M. *Celtic Art*, British Museum Publications, London, 1985.

THOMAS, CHARLES. *Celtic Britain*, Thames and Hudson, London, 1986.

# INDEX

Acichorios 113, 203
Aedh Ruadh 34, 90
Aedo Sláine 31
Aedui 31, 32, 42, 53, 120, 132, 151, 152, 214, 215, 216
Aegosages 211
Aethicus of Istra 23
Agricola 44, 135, 219
Agron, king 82, 83
Aibhistín 121
Ailill 34, 90
Airmid 109, 110
Alesia 42, 153, 216
Alexander the Great 123, 201, 203
Alexandrian school 48, 56, 57, 170
Allobriges 214, 216
Ambicatus, king 41, 191
Ammianus Marcellinus (c. AD 330–95) 50, 82
Amyntas, king 217
Aneirin 192
Aneroestes 31, 41, 206
Anglo-Saxons 94, 100, 169, 191, 192, 218, 220
animals, domesticated 102, 103, 104
Antaros 105
Anthedius 120

Antiochus of Syria 113, 204, 205, 211
Antonius, king 94
Anu 7, 162, 163
Appian (Appianos of Alexandria) 3, 72
Aquitani 82, 216
Arabs 121, 122
Aran Islands 219
Arborius, Caecilius Argicius 120
Arganthonius, king 1, 41, 107
Argentocoxos 92
aristocracy 32, 35, 45, 46, 63
Aristotle 57, 116
armour 66
Arrian (c. AD 85–90) 70
Arthur, king 93, 94, 191, 192, 193
Arthurian sagas 186
Arverni 36, 131, 153, 216
Asia minor 13, 15, 204, 212
Asparn open air museum 150
astrology 115–123 passim
Atrebates 31, 216
Ausonius 120, 173
Austria 11, 144, 150
Avaros, king 42
Avienus 220

Babylonia 116, 119, 120, 123
*Banshenchas* 26, 34, 94
baths 108, 109
Belenus 42, 43, 109
Belgae 12, 13, 31, 132, 161, 216
Belisma 20
Bellovaci 216
Bellovesus 41
Bericus, king 43
Béroul 193
Bibracte (Mont Beuvray) 151, 152, 153, 215
Bíle 7, 162, 169, 173, 185
birds 176
Bithynia 204, 211, 212
Bituitus, king 131
Bituriges 41, 75
*Black Book of Carmarthen* 24
Black Sea 5, 13, 201, 213
Blathmac 31
Boduognatus 78
Bohemia *see also* Boii 13, 109, 195, 214
Boii 13, 73, 151, 167, 173, 198, 202, 206, 208, 209, 214, 215
*Book of Invasions* 219
*Book of Leinster* 24, 74, 174
*Book of the Dun Cow* 24
Boru, Brian 45
Botorrita, Spain 20
Boudicca (Boadicea) 33, 44, 77, 82, 86, 87, 88, 147
boundary stones 103
Bran 169, 186, 187, 195
Brehon Laws 6, 24, 25, 26, 32, 33, 34, 90, 103, 112, 113, 130, 135, 157, 174
Brendan of Clonfert, Saint 135
Brennus 42, 62, 160, 161, 198, 199, 203
Breton language 24, 185, 193
bridges 130, 131
Brigantes 12, 29, 44, 84, 85, 166, 218
Brigantia 166
Brigit (goddess) 29, 166
Brigit, (saint) 90, 142, 166
Britain 12, 13, 40, 42, 44, 48, 52, 55, 58, 68, 76, 77, 81, 85, 88, 93, 94, 100, 101, 102, 107, 108, 121, 127, 132, 133, 134, 135, 140, 144, 145, 146, 147, 150, 154, 161, 165, 169, 182, 186, 190, 194, 215, 216, 217, 218, 219, 200
  coinage 140
  houses 103, 104
  kings of 42–5
  mythology 186–190
Brittany 31, 45, 109, 138, 190, 194, 218
brochs 155, 156
Bronze Age 10, 34, 39, 97, 126, 194
Bu round house 155
bull rituals 30, 102
burials *see* graves
Butser Celtic farm, Hampshire 101, 102, 150

Cabillonum 132
Caesar, Julius 2, 8, 12, 14, 17, 18, 24, 31, 32, 42, 43, 48, 49, 50, 51, 52, 53, 59, 68, 69, 76, 77, 78, 91, 97, 102, 103, 115, 119, 127, 128, 131, 132, 133, 140, 151, 153, 154, 160, 164, 173, 177, 180, 187, 190, 194, 213, 215, 216, 217
calendar 116, 117, 118, 199
Calgacos, king 94
Cambaules, king 201
Camma 84
Camonica rock carvings 98, 161
Camulos 165
Cantii 42, 94, 216
Caractacus (Caradog) 43, 85, 218
Carnutes 51
Carthage 11, 13, 136, 201, 205, 206, 208, 209, 211
Cartimandua, queen 33, 43, 44, 77, 82, 84, 85, 218
Cassivelaunus, king 42, 127, 216, 217
cattle 102, 128, 134, 141
Catuvellauni 87
Catuvolcus, king 77
cauldrons 194, 195
  *see also* Gundestrup Cauldron
cavalry 67, 68, 69, 70, 71, 127, 128, 200, 204, 206

Cellach 31
Celtchair 3
Celtillus, king 3, 42
Celts
  communication between 136
  hospitality of 176
  migrations 1, 10, 13, 14,
    198–202, 214, 215
  morality of 174, 175
  name, origin of 1, 2, 3
  origins of 1–15 passim, 162, 163,
    187
  Roman view of 14, 15, 17, 26, 50,
    51, 63, 64, 91, 92, 160, 167,
    195, 199
  royal succession 32, 34
  society and economy 12, 24, 47,
    48, 76, 97, 114, 143
Cennfaelad 106
Cenomani 188, 209
Cerethrios 203
Cerne Abbas Giant 162
Cerunnos 9, 97, 160, 161, 162, 163,
  194
chariot graves 35, 36, 37, 40, 81
chariots 11, 12, 67, 68, 69, 70, 126,
  127, 128, 129, 130, 131, 132
Charmis 112
Children of Danu 38, 109, 162, 180
Chiltern Open Air Museum 150
Chiomara 83, 84, 212
Christianity 22, 23, 55, 57, 58, 90,
  91, 92, 93, 94, 95, 105, 108,
  111, 112, 120, 121, 122, 134,
  135, 140, 142, 145, 159, 163,
  170, 173, 175, 178, 179, 180,
  192, 196, 204, 216, 217, 220
Chrysostom, Dion 56
Chysauster, Cornwall 155
Ciaran 104
Cicero, Marcus Tullius (106–43 BC)
  53, 177, 213
Cimbaeth 90
Cimbri 214
Cingetorix, king 42
Clement of Alexandria
  (AD 150–211/216) 56, 57
Clickhimin broch 155
clothing 71–2, 147
Clusium 62, 63, 83, 198, 206

Cogidubnus, king 75
coins 12, 13, 21, 43, 139, 140, 141,
  142, 151, 161, 163, 204, 205,
  217
Colaeus 1
Colchester 44, 87, 165
Coligny Calendar 19, 25, 116, 117,
  118, 119
colleges 52, 63
Commius, king 31, 216
Conall Cáel 31
Conchobhar MacNessa 108
Concolitanus 31, 41, 206
Connacht 28, 34, 40, 74, 181
Coritani 87
Corlea roadway 128, 129
Cormac Mac Art 100, 183
Cormac's Glossary 103, 107, 108,
  130, 142
Cornwall 22, 30, 44, 101, 135, 145,
  154, 185, 193, 194
  language 184
Crannogs 156, 157
Credhne 143, 163
Crinias 112
crops 98
Cúchulainn 169, 170, 172, 180, 181,
  182, 188, 195
Culhwch 21, 144, 186, 195
Cunobelinus (Cymbeline) 43, 134,
  140, 168, 217, 218
Cunomarus 193, 194
Cynesii 9
Cystennin, king 94

Dacians 214
Dagda, the 161, 162, 165, 166, 195
Danebury fort, Hampshire 152
Danu 7, 144, 162, 166, 173, 185,
  187
Danube, river 7, 9, 13, 39, 82, 132,
  151, 200, 201
Degad 74
Deiotarus 43, 213
Delphi 41, 160, 161, 203
Demetus, king 94
Desborough mirror 139, 145
Dian Cécht 109, 110
Diarmuid Mac Murrough 76
Diciul 121, 135

Dillon, Professor Myles   5, 174, 184
Dinas, Emrys   94
Dio Cassius (AD 150–235)   88, 89,
    91, 92, 109
Diodorus Sicilus   3, 49, 50, 51, 65,
    66, 68, 71, 77, 79, 82, 125, 160,
    170, 176
Dionysius of Halicarnassus   3, 72
Dis-Pater   8, 187
Dithorba   90
Diviciacus, king   31, 42, 53
Divicio   214
divinations   53, 176
Domnall   31
Donal IX MacCarthy Mór   45, 74
Dream of Rhonabwy, The   186, 189
Druids   2, 3, 6, 8, 17, 23, 26, 27, 28,
    30, 47–59 passim, 110, 111,
    115, 119, 120, 163, 173, 176,
    187, 217
  females   49, 58, 59
  functions of   48–57 passim, 173,
    176
  as healers   110
  and oak trees   53, 54
  origin of name of   4
  Romans and   56, 176
Dumnorix   43, 213, 214, 215, 216
Dun Aenghus   157, 219
Dun Twelve broch   155

Eber   24, 219
Eburones   31, 77
Egypt   13, 121, 181, 203, 204, 205
Elen Luyddog   93, 94
Emain Macha   111
Emrys (Ambrosius)   94
enamelling   144, 145
England   10, 25, 44, 130, 156, 162,
    218
Entremont   100, 150, 168
Eóghanacht dynasty   46, 74, 160,
    163
Ephoros of Cyme   14
Epona   19, 20, 31, 69
Eratosthenes of Cyrene   200
Eremon   29, 46, 219
Etruscans   13, 18, 19, 35, 62, 65,
    100, 139, 176, 197, 198, 200,
    202

Fabii brothers   62, 63, 83, 198,
    199
farm buildings   103, 150, 151
Fastidius, bishop   175
Favorinus   120
Fenechus, laws of the   6, 32
Fenian Cycle   183, 192
Fergus   31
Fianna   74, 183, 192
Fidelmid, Brother   121
Fingin   108
Fionn Mac Cumhail   38, 74, 165,
    183, 185, 192, 193
Firbolg   180, 181
Fomorii   109, 181, 185, 189, 195
forts see towns
France   11, 13, 34, 35, 36, 45, 51, 64,
    145, 153, 163, 164, 168, 191
  See also Gaul

Gael, the   29, 180, 219
Gaesatae   72, 206, 207
Galatea   3
Galatia   13, 21, 32, 43, 56, 84, 136,
    204, 205, 211, 213, 217
Gamanrad   74
Ganna   89
Gaul   3, 10, 12, 19, 21, 31, 48, 51,
    53, 55, 58, 74, 76, 83, 88, 89,
    93, 99, 100, 101, 103, 108, 131,
    134, 136, 146, 151, 154, 173,
    182, 187, 208, 214, 215, 216,
    217
Gauls   1, 3, 13, 17, 18, 42, 50, 91,
    120, 126, 133, 141, 164, 170,
    200
geese   190, 191
Geoffrey of Monmouth   192
Gergovia   153, 216
Germanic language   28
Germanic tribes   15, 154, 214, 215
Germany   9, 10, 32, 35, 109, 117,
    127, 144, 147, 153, 163, 200
Gildas (AD 500–700)   192
Giolla Iosa Mór Mac Firbis   23
Giraldus Cambrensis   30
Glanum
glass   144, 145
goddesses   21, 28, 35, 107, 160–78
    passim, 181, 188, 190

gods   8, 9, 28, 51, 116, 141, 144,
    160–78 *passim*, 181, 188, 190,
    192, 194
Gofannon   143, 144
Goibhniu   143, 163
Gospels, illuminated   24
Graggaunowen   153
Grannus   109
graves   11, 27, 171, 219
    princely   34, 35, 36, 37, 38, 39, 40
    warrior surgeon's   106
    *see also* chariot graves; warrior
        graves
Greece   1, 11, 12, 35, 29, 81, 116,
    119, 123, 200, 203
    alphabet   3, 17, 18, 19, 21, 215
Greek mythology   3, 8, 143, 162,
    163, 164, 165
Greeks   1, 3, 14, 32, 35, 36, 41, 47,
    53, 56, 63, 66, 71, 82, 91, 100,
    108, 135, 137, 139, 140, 142,
    149, 160, 163, 171, 173, 176,
    178, 187, 197, 200, 202, 205,
    211, 220
Gundestrup Cauldron   30, 52, 79,
    141, 161, 194

Hallstat culture   10, 11, 27, 34, 35,
    36, 38, 39, 40, 81, 97, 125, 138,
    139, 146, 147, 149, 156, 195,
    200
Hannibal   81, 136, 177, 208, 211,
    212
Hasholme, Yorkshire   194
heads   140, 141, 142, 167, 168, 169,
    170
Hecataeus of Miletus (*c.* 500–476 BC)
    9
Heidengraben   153
helmets   19, 64, 65, 145
Helvetii   12, 153, 154, 214, 215
Heracles (Hercules)   3, 162, 165
Herodotus of Halicarnassus
    (*c.* 490–425 BC)   1, 9, 56, 197
Heuneberg   39, 138, 150
Hilary, bishop of Poitiers
    (*c.* AD 170–236)   58, 164
Hinduism *see* Vedas
Hippolytus   57, 116, 120
history   23, 197–221 *passim*

Hittites   117, 143
Hochdorf grave   195
Hohenasperg   39, 138
Hohmichele   39
horses   30, 70, 103, 104, 132, 141
hospitals   111, 112, 113
houses   150, 151, 152, 154, 156
Hubert, Henri   2, 9, 10, 188, 191
human sacrifice   176, 177, 178
hunting   103
Hy-Breasail   172
Hywel Dda   25, 90

Iberian peninsula   12, 21, 41, 42,
    131, 132, 135, 136, 138, 197,
    206, 207, 208, 209, 210, 211,
    217, 218
Iceni   77, 86
Illyria   13, m82, 201
India *see also* Vedas   75, 111, 122,
    162, 170, 218
Indo-Europeans   1, 3, 4, 5, 6, 18, 27,
    28, 30, 32, 48, 64, 74, 77, 100,
    107, 111, 117, 118, 119, 120,
    123, 143, 149, 160, 161, 163,
    165, 169, 170, 171, 174, 177,
    184, 196, 219, 220
Indutiomarus   216
inscriptions   17, 21, 163, 164, 165
Insubres   22, 73, 198, 206, 207, 109
Ireland   12, 13, 23, 26, 32, 46, 48,
    52, 55, 58, 76, 85, 89, 100, 101,
    103, 107, 111, 112, 122, 128,
    132, 133, 134, 135, 140, 142,
    143, 145, 150, 156, 163, 164,
    165, 166, 183, 190, 200, 217,
    218, 219, 200
    castes   27, 28
    coinage   140, 141, 142
    cosmology   120, 121, 122
    Druids   48, 50, 55, 58
    genealogies   26, 34, 41, 45, 46,
        219
    graves   40
    houses   103, 151, 156, 157
    kings   8, 25, 26, 28, 29, 30, 31,
        32, 38, 40, 41, 45, 90, 102, 130,
        141, 157, 161, 182, 219
    literature   22, 23, 24, 25, 95, 102,
        174, 218, 219, 220

medicine 111, 112
roads 129, 130
sea trade 135, 136
women in 90, 92
Irish language 1, 5, 6, 8, 32, 48, 66, 82, 92, 100, 102, 112, 118, 119, 123, 130, 135, 164, 165, 171, 174, 218
Irish mythology 3, 7, 8, 23, 69, 89, 90, 102, 103, 109, 161, 162, 169, 172, 173, 180–96 passim
iron 11, 12, 34, 99, 134, 142, 145, 146
irrigation 12, 104
Isle of Man 23, 94, 185
Italy 12. 64, 101, 122, 126, 137, 199, 200, 201, 202, 205, 208, 209

jewellery 138, 139, 144, 152
Julia Augusta, empress 91

Keltoi 123
Keltos, king 3

La Graufesneque graffiti 19, 21
La Tène culture 10, 11, 12, 13, 35, 39, 40, 65, 67, 68, 81, 139, 146, 150, 151, 154, 195, 200
Laertius, Diogenes 47, 49, 56, 57, 174
Lampsacos 36
languages 1–8 passim, 12, 17, 18, 19, 24, 27, 28, 30, 70, 71, 98, 124, 125, 130, 131, 171, 172, 214–19 passim
Laoghaire of Tara, king 25
Lapis Niger 21
Latin language 1, 4, 5, 18, 19, 20, 21, 23, 28, 52, 65, 72, 74, 100, 120, 125, 131, 132, 135, 141, 142, 150, 165, 181, 187, 193, 211, 217, 218
Latovici 215
laws 6, 24, 25, 31, 59, 76, 86, 91, 92, 93, 142, 157, 176, 199, 218
learning 23, 218
leather 147
lenus 109
Leo, king of the Cantii 94

L'Hospitalet-du-Larzac 21
literature 26
Livy 61, 62, 68, 71, 75, 79, 167, 177, 187, 188, 189, 190, 191, 211
Lleu Llaw Gyffes 8, 164, 185
Loeghaire, king 38
London 10, 43, 87, 131, 145, 169
Lucan 54, 172
Luchta 143, 163
Lugaid Riab nDerg 46
Lugh Lamhfhada 8, 28, 164, 181, 185
Lugus 164, 165
Lusitani 42

Mabinogion 185, 186
Macedonia 201, 203
Macha (goddess) 164, 182
Macha of the Red Hair 34, 89, 90, 111
Macsen Wledig 93, 94, 186
Máele Cobo 31
Magnesia, battle of 201
Magnus Maximus see Macsen Wledig
Maiden Castle, Dorset 152
Manching 151, 153
Mandubracius 76
manuring 104
Maol Callum (Malcolm) 76
Maponus 21
Mark of Cornwall, king 31, 193
Martial 67, 131
Martin of Tours 93
Massilia (Marseilles) 35, 136, 197, 213, 214
Matholwch of Ireland 186, 195
Medb, queen of Connacht 29, 30, 34, 38, 90, 181, 182
Medb Lethderg 29
medicine
  books 108
  and healing 60, 61, 108, 109
  herbal 110, 111
  laws and 112, 113
  schools 106, 112
  surgical 105, 106, 100, 111, 112, 113
  system of 112, 113, 114
Mediterranean world 12, 35, 36, 64, 134, 139, 203, 205, 213

Megaliths 150
Mela, Pomponius 116, 172
Mercenaries 15, 71, 82, 140, 199, 200, 203, 206
metals 11, 12, 139, 141, 143, 146
Miach 110
Mile Espain (Milesius) 29, 46, 181, 219
mirrors 145
mistletoe 53, 54, 111
Mithridates V, 'The Great' 213
Monte Bibele 151
Morann mac Cairbre 174
Moravia 112, 153, 201
Morini 216
Mousa Broch 155
Muirchertaig 31
Munster 23, 45, 46, 74, 104, 163
mythology 6, 7, 8, 23, 30, 38, 72, 102, 159, 160, 164, 165, 166, 179–96 passim,
   creation myths 3, 7, 181
   definition of 180
   sources of 183, 187–91 passim
   see also religion

Namnetes 89, 135
Nasc Niadh 74
Nautae Parisiaci 161
Negau, Lower Syria 19
Nemain 164
Nennius 94
Nepos, Cornelius 191, 197
Nervii 78
Niall Noíghiallach (Niall of the Nine Hostages) 46, 182, 183
Nuada 109, 164, 185
Numantia 41, 152, 210, 211, 216
numbers 37

oak trees 54, 55
Obermenzing 106
O'Brien family 45
Oenghus Olmuchada of the Long Hand 28
Ogam script 23, 24, 165
Ogma 22, 165
O'Lees, Book of 112
Ollamhs 25, 26, 157
Olwen 21, 144, 186, 195

Onomaris 33, 82
oral tradition 21, 22, 23, 24, 180, 188, 218
Orgetorix 214
Ortagion 83, 84, 212
Ovid 3, 132
Ovingdean skull 106
Owain ab Urien 94, 186, 187, 190

Parisii 36, 82, 128
Patrick, Saint 23, 25, 38, 158, 180
Pausanias 61, 70
Pelagius (c. AD 354–420) 59, 175, 176
Pergamum 205, 211, 212
philosophy 22, 53–9 passim, 174, 175
Philostratus of Tyana 171
Picts 33, 134
Piggott, Professor Stuart 56, 130, 131
pigs 16, 102, 103, 195
place names 10, 165
Plebig 94
Pliny the Elder 48, 53, 54, 67, 99, 102, 112, 117, 119, 120, 197
plough 97, 98
Plutarch 62, 63, 66, 81, 84, 119, 199
Po valley 12, 13, 22, 81, 99, 100, 103, 132, 137, 139, 151, 198, 201, 206, 207, 208, 209
poetry 22, 107
Polybius 66, 73, 83, 137, 138, 206, 212
Pompeius, Trogus (27 BC-AD 14) 191
Portugal 13, 46, 206
Poseidonius (c. 135–50 BC) 49, 176, 177, 178
pottery 19, 145, 146, 151, 204
property 91
Pythagoras 57, 116, 170
Pythias of Massilia 200

Rauraci 215
ravens 189, 190
Rawlinson Manuscript B502 24, 183, 184
Red Branch 74, 181, 182, 198, 192
Red Hand 28
Regni 75

religion 1, 51, 52, 53, 59, 159–78 passim
Remi 141, 163
'Rheinheim princess' grave 36, 81
'Rhenus' 10, 41
Rhetogenes, king 42, 211
Rhine, river 9, 41, 132, 215
Rhône, river 9, 35, 131
Ríglach 75
ring forts 154, 156
rivers 9, 10, 35, 107, 132, 169
roads 11, 12, 125–36 passim
Rodenbach 39
Rom (Deux-Sèvres) 19
Romans 3, 11, 13, 14, 21, 22, 31, 41, 42, 43, 44, 47, 49, 55, 62, 64, 65, 67, 68, 71, 72, 75, 77, 78, 82, 84, 86, 88, 91, 97, 98, 100, 107, 120, 121, 125, 129, 131, 132, 133, 134, 136, 137, 140, 146, 154, 155, 167, 168, 173, 176, 177, 178, 187, 188, 189, 198, 219
Rome 11, 12, 13, 15, 19, 22, 31, 32, 41, 42, 43, 44, 50, 55, 59, 62, 63, 69, 72, 81, 83, 85, 86, 92, 93, 102, 111, 119, 126, 131, 134, 136, 137, 139, 147, 149, 151, 152, 165, 188, 190, 191, 198–221 passim
Roquepertuse 190
Rumania 214

saddles 71
St Orland's stone 134
salt 12, 100, 101
Saluvii 100, 168
Salyes 213, 214
Samhain 143, 173
Samnites 201, 202
Sanskrit 2, 4, 5, 6, 19, 28, 48, 64, 74, 123, 166
Scipio 152, 201, 206, 208, 210
Scordisci 82
Scotland 30, 33, 76, 135, 155, 164, 165, 166, 181, 185
sea transport 131–35
Second Punic War 136
Segobrigia 197
Segovesus 41

Seine, river 33, 51, 107, 132, 166
Senchus na Relec 41
Senigallia 200
Senones 12, 13, 41, 62, 63, 89, 167, 198, 199, 200, 201, 206, 207
Sentium, battle of (295 BC) 67, 75, 201
Sequana 35, 107
Setanti 85
Sevira 94
shields 65, 66, 75
ships 132, 133, 135
silver 1, 12, 134, 140, 142
Slavs 14, 153, 214, 215
smith gods 143, 144
solar symbol 8, 127, 142
Soton of Alexandria (c. 200–170 BC) 48, 49, 56
soul, immortality of 51, 52, 53, 171–82 passim, 184
Spain 1, 13, 20, 46, 152, 191, 206, 207, 219
Staigue fort, Kerry 157
Staré Hradisko 153
Stary, Dr P F 64, 65
Strabo 14, 48, 49, 50, 51, 61, 69, 89, 125, 133, 134, 167, 176, 217, 220
Sucellus 144
Suessiones 31, 43
Sulis 108
Sumerian language 124
swastika 142, 166
Switzerland 9, 10, 11, 121, 215
swords 66, 67, 143
symbolism 7, 8, 28, 141, 142, 160
Syracuse 199
Syria 13, 204, 211

Tacitus 33, 44, 55, 84, 85, 86, 88, 135, 176, 217, 219
Taín Bó Cuailgne 183
Taliesin 186, 187
Tartessus, river 1, 9, 197,
Taurini 206, 209
Tectosages 204, 212
Telamon, battle of (222 BC) 21, 41, 68, 72, 73, 206
Teuta, queen 82, 83
Teutones 214

Theodosius, emperor 93, 94, 182
Thermopylae, battle of (279 BC) 70, 203
Thrace 13, 194, 201
Tighernach 90
Timaeus 56
Timagenes 49, 50
Tolistoboii 83, 204, 205, 212, 213, 214
Tolosa (Toulouse) 214
'Toutiorix' 82
towns 150, 151, 152, 153, 154, 209
trade 1, 12, 36, 42, 102, 131–35, 197
transport 12, 97, 125–37 passim
Treveri 109, 216
Triads 57, 163
Trinovantes 76, 87, 165
Tristan and Iseult 193
Trocmi 204, 205, 212
Tuam Brecain school 106
Tuatha de Danaan see Children of Danu
Tugurni 214
Tulingi 215
Tumulus culture (c. 1550–1250 BC) 10
Tungri 89

Uffington White Horse 193
Ui Néill dynasty 28, 46, 182
Ulster 28, 45, 46, 74, 181, 182
Urnfield culture (c. 1200 BC) 10, 11, 27

Vedas 5, 6, 7, 8, 19, 25, 27, 30, 31, 55, 56, 75, 92, 107, 117, 119, 120, 121, 123, 160, 161, 162, 163, 164, 166, 174, 184, 187
Veleda 89
Veneti 74, 133, 134, 188, 209
Venutius 44, 85
Vercellae, battle of (101 BC) 214
Vercingetorix, king 2, 42, 141, 153, 177, 216
Verulamium (St Albans) 45, 88
Vindelici 151
Vindonnus 109

Virgil 3, 15, 132
Viriathos 210
Viridomarus 41, 217
Virithos, king 41, 42
Vix 'princess of' 53, 56, 81
Vocontii 88
Volcae 81
Vopiscus, Flavius 66, 89 120
Vortigern, king 94, 218
votive offerings 12, 21, 107, 166, 167

wagon burials 35, 36, 37, 39
wagons 11, 98, 99, 102, 125, 126, 129, 131, 132, 137
Wales 23, 25, 45, 82, 88, 129, 135, 143, 156, 172, 187, 192
  law 25, 91, 92, 93, 94
  literature 24, 172, 173
  see also Welsh language; Welsh mythology
warfare 62, 87–90
warrior graves 34, 38, 64, 105
warriors 61–79 passim
  elite 72, 73, 74
  naked 72
  and single combat 76, 77, 200
  and suicide 77
water mill 100, 101
weapons 34, 61, 64, 65, 127, 138, 143
Welsh language 1, 7, 24, 29, 48, 66, 100, 102, 118, 121, 185, 192
Welsh mythology 8, 103, 144, 162, 154, 169, 185, 186, 193
wheel 126, 127, 143
women 81–95 passim
  education 91, 92
  equality 90–2
  genealogies 24, 34, 95
  graves of 36, 81, 82
  priestesses 89
  and royal succession 33, 34, 95
  in war 77
wood 129, 146, 147, 150, 154

Zalmoxis 57
Závist 153, 154

# THE LETTERS OF
# PAUL